MW01281998

The Book of Tom

A Journey to Authenticity

An Autobiography by Tom Schellenbach

FIRST EDITION
Published by Nabu Scholar
www.nabuscholar.com
ISBN-13: 978-1724623874
ISBN-10: 1724623877

CONTENTS

FOREWORD

Have you ever experienced meeting someone for the first time and feeling an instant familiarity as though your first hello is like picking up mid-conversation, or, more accurately, mid-friendship? That was my experience when I met Tom. I think I have finally figured out why. Tom is an observer. When I talk with him he gives our conversation his full attention, not in the way most people do when they appear to be listening but they are actually focused on their own thoughts as they formulate their response. The difference, I realized, is that Tom doesn't listen to judge. He listens to understand.

Though our conversations have flowed over the years, Tom has rarely talked about his past beyond sharing the odd, interesting anecdote from various periods of his life. I remember when he told the story of being a young teenager traveling home to visit his family during a holiday break from the seminary. When he arrived, he discovered his family had moved to another house in town. I was incredulous. "How could that happen without you knowing?" I asked, imagining his confusion as he stood alone on the sidewalk, his suitcase resting at his feet, finding the home empty. Tom shrugged and explained that as soon as his parents realized their mistake, they rushed across town to pick him up, and his mother profusely apologized. She had been so busy tending to his many brothers and sisters that it had simply slipped her mind to tell him about the move. Tom found this a perfectly reasonable explanation. See what I mean? He was content to understand the situation from his mother's perspective. No judgment.

Because Tom is so private, it is no small event that he has written his memoir. His entry into the seminary as an adolescent dictated the trajectory of his life into early middle age. However, from virtually the beginning, his optimism and faith in others and in institutions would be challenged. But Tom persisted. He continued to try to work within the structure of the Church to build a life of service. This determination was eventually rewarded with the opportunity to live and serve in the Navajo community in Chinle, Arizona. This experience was and continues to be one of the most influential and fulfilling experiences of his life. But his growing disillusionment with the church made him restless even as he redoubled his efforts to commit his life to service.

It took an extended period of reflection and personal struggle before Tom realized that his faith is not something to project onto other people or institutions to uphold. Faith is something that must be rooted in oneself. This realization set Tom on his most difficult and ultimately rewarding journey--to live his life of faith rooted in authenticity.

I was struck by how Tom's life experiences parallel that of the archetypal *Hero's Journey* identified by Joseph Campbell, the point of which was best summed up by Glinda the Good Witch when she said to Dorothy in *The Wizard of Oz*: "You always had it my dear. You could always go home." And that, after years of struggle, is what Tom did. He is no longer that young man standing outside of an empty home where he no longer belonged. Instead he dared to create a full life and a full home for his authentic self. In this book he shares the challenges he has overcome to achieve that with the hope that we, too, have found--or will dare to find--our authentic home as well.

- Christina Young, July 2018

PREFACE

No doubt many of you, like me, have been encouraged to write down your life experiences and have been told "You ought to write a book." For most of 45 years I have been jotting down notes and stories and journal entries with the intention of doing just that someday. My one expandable file titled "Book of Tom" grew to four very expanded files and four journal volumes with the expectation that "someday" I would put it all together.

My original intention was to one day organize the material for me to reflect on, not with the intention that others would read it. I would do it to remember experiences both small and large, some life-enhancing, some totally life-changing, in order to more deeply examine the painful or joyful feelings that anchored those memories.

I was in college in my early 20s studying modern philosophy towards a B.A. degree in Philosophy, when I was introduced to the work of the German philosopher, Martin Heidegger. His work emphasized the importance of authenticity in human existence, the limited time and being we are given, and the closing down of our various possibilities for being through time. It really spoke deeply to me. "We have this one life," he seemed to be saying to me. "Shouldn't we dare to make it a priority to know and be our authentic selves before it all ends?"

Arriving at this vantage point with a wealth of hindsight, I decided to take up Heidegger's dare. In these pages I have put into narrative form my best understanding of me and my experiences of my life so far. But, rather than keep the story of my life private as I had long assumed I would, I have chosen to be braver than the constant drumbeat of my anxiety typically allows, and share my experiences, memories, fears, aspirations, disappointments and insights openly with the hope that it inspires others to honestly reckon with and embrace the truth of their own authentic selves.

In this book I feel I have done that. What I have expressed took courage to write -- some of it raw, some of it brave, some of it light-hearted and funny, some of it deeply spiritual, some of it deeply disturbing, perhaps scandalous to some -- all of it me, very me.

In writing this memoir, I was fortunate to have not only my years of journals and notes to refer to, but also to have been connected with Duncan Blount, the owner of Nabu Scholar LLC, who professionally directed and coordinated my efforts, and whose team assisted tremendously in editing and transcribing. Otherwise, I would not have known where to go with all my thoughts or how to put them in book form.

How Roy Ricci of Ricci Photography LLC ever found time to scan photos, tweak each one for the best printable quality, arrange a photo shoot, and make it all easily accessible for me is beyond my comprehension. Surely his high energy, zest for life, multi-tasking experience, and our warm friendship graciously opened his busy schedule for the very grateful me.

I would also like to thank my early readers who added valuable insights that helped sharpen my early drafts. I especially thank Tina Young, a consummate professional and friend who understands the inner me. Her suggestions helped me clarify the chronology of events, and her questions sent me back to revisit pivotal events, requiring me to dig a little deeper, and realize I may have unconsciously minimized some events that where in fact far more influential in shaping my life.

The Franciscan Friars of the Province of St. John the Baptist in Cincinnati, Ohio played a huge role in the most critical developmental years of my life. They guided me and taught me in deep spirituality and meditation. They provided a stellar education. They emphasized the need to meld the sacred with the secular, and to advocate for peace and justice for all. They instilled in me the importance of empathy to actively care for others, the ability to think for myself, as well as the impetus to seek to be my own best self. I cannot thank them enough.

Naturally, my Dad and especially my Mom nurtured my early years as I learned my place in our much broader family of fifteen. They instilled in me the importance--in fact the necessity--of doing things on my own and to be independent, to be considerate toward others, the power of love and friendship, the ethics of right and wrong, to make space for others in my life, and so very much more. Who they were for me has helped me in my quest to be who I am. Of course, my twelve brothers and sisters helped to hone those skills. To each other we were and continue to be like rocks in some mighty family stream. In our years of sibling interaction we have had our corners and sharp edges worn down and smoothed and polished into companionable ease, more or less. Though our personalities and outlooks differ, I respect each of them as they express their own authentic selves.

My deepest gratitude goes to Joe Perea, my friend, my partner, my love for 35 years, and my husband. We have shared the journey of the most and best years of our lives together. It is Joe who welcomed me into his love and into the most authentic version of my loving self. Without him and his children Joe and Margaret, I may have missed out on the joys of being a father and grandfather. His patience and acceptance of me this past year that I have been so absorbed in feeling and writing, mostly 4-6 hours a day, is indicative of the kind man that he is.

My hope is that the readers of this book will allow these words to echo deep into the crevices of their own beings, and see that no matter what our different life paths may be, we are not all that different from each other as we each struggle to come to grips with our own being and perhaps "climb out of the pit of inauthenticity."

-- Tom Schellenbach

*"If we notice our conformity, inauthenticity, and lostness, and confront these,
perhaps we have the possibility of emerging and creating lives that we clearly own.
However, in addition to being products of human culture,
we are also our own powerful and pervasive internal threat-to-being.
In the light (or in the shadow) of this constant internal threat-to-being,
we are empowered to choose our Authentic projects-of-being
-- those basic endeavors that correlate best with our own ontological anxiety
-- our own being-towards-death.
Returning to this deepest truth of our being can bring us back to ourselves.
On this foundation, we can begin to construct our Authentic Existence.
Our Existential Predicament (loneliness, depression, anxiety, and death)
-- perceived, perhaps, as ontological anxiety --
is the rope by which we can climb out of the pit of inauthenticity;
it is the handle by which we can grip our own beings."*

-- James Leonard Park, Martin Heidegger's Vision of Becoming More Authentic

SECTION ONE

TRUE MEMOIRS OF MY YOUTH, FAMILY, SEMINARY, THE CATHOLIC CHURCH, PRIESTHOOD ON THE NAVAJO RESERVATION, BEING GAY, AND MY STRUGGLE TO FIND AND ACCEPT MY AUTHENTIC SELF

Chapter One
The Early Years

"He was so impatient—he will either be a great saint or a great sinner," the nun told Mom as I was born kicking and screaming on the gurney in the hallway halfway to the delivery room: ten fingers, ten toes, a Valentine's Day baby, Thomas Anthony Schellenbach, blond hair, deep blue eyes, the fifth child of Doris and Louis Schellenbach. Mom had very little warning, so she had to call her father to get her to the hospital as Dad was working. Mom remembers me as a very quiet baby who used to climb over the crib and flop into bed with her and Dad; never wanting to be left alone, but who used to play by himself all the time.

"You come from good stock. Stand up straight. Don't slouch. Suck your gut in. Chest out. Always be proud of who you are." These were Mom's instructions to us from a very early age, and the instructions to her from her parents and grandparents who, I am sure, received them from their parents and grandparents. Strong German stock, as she was the great-granddaughter of Anna Maria Von Mitbar née Westbrock Lemkuhle and Teodor Bergedick, both having emigrated in the 1830s and 1850s from Germany. My friends in Germany say I am a Blaublut – a blueblood – a "Von" -- descended from royalty whose family must have had a castle at one time and maybe still does. Dad's side of the family came over from the Saarland Alsace-Lorraine area of Germany at about the same time to escape the political and economic turmoil.

"Don't ever mix the blood." Great-grandma would pass this advice down to her family, and they to their families, and then to our family. A story goes that her son married an Irish woman, and Great-grandma disowned him and never spoke to him again. Having recently gotten my DNA tested and reported, I am 99% Northern European German and Eastern French, including 2.9% Neanderthal (for strength and durability...). So, as far back as I can trace my genealogy on both sides for hundreds and hundreds of years, "Don't ever mix the blood" must have been the only marital prerequisite. And of course - that they be Catholic.

This heritage also included an unspoken call to be someone, to always be contributing to the good of the family and the good of society so we and others could thrive. "Be proud of who you are", make Mom and Dad proud of who you are, make the family proud of who you will become. I felt I always had to be busy doing something for the family's betterment, for the Catholic Church, for friends and the neighbors, even for those who had less than the very little we had. Mom and Dad were great examples of this. If you were in need, Dad would do anything for you. If you were poor, or hungry, or lonely, or just needed someone to talk to, Mom was there. I learned by watching them. As a child I would spend hours in the afternoons talking to, and listening to, and watching Mom do the ironing. There was always a very deep psychic connection between Mom and me.

There were always babies at our house due to Mom and Dad having 13 children, no twins, seven boys and six girls, all within the span of 20 years! First to last there were two boys, two girls, me, two girls, two boys, two girls, two boys -- named Daniel, James, Ann, Carol, Thomas, Mary Clare, Linda, Edward, Alan, Paula, Julie, Philip, and Theodore. When Mom was pregnant, the boys would fight the girls, and vice versa, hoping for another girl or boy to keep their count on top. Mom said every time she gave birth, Dad would bring her one red rose in the hospital, and it seemed like we would get a new dog. In fact, we used to tell people that Mom and Dad went to the hospital to get a new dog for us.

I learned very early that the babies came first—this one needed fed, that one needed the diaper changed, another needed to be held and cuddled or rocked to sleep. I feel I grew up attention deprived, affection deprived, affirmation deprived (there just wasn't enough to go all around), and that my needs had to wait my turn, if it ever came, or I had to do it myself -- to become independent. And also, even then, I learned to serve others and give of myself for the good of the family. But, that too was a ploy for attention.

There was one incident in particular when I was very young and could not find my shoes. I yelled out the window to Mom directly below in the kitchen with the back door open, "Mom I can't find my shoes!" No answer. I yelled again louder, "I can't find my shoes!!" No answer. And a third time with no response. I cried because Mom would not come upstairs and help me find my shoes. After looking and looking I found my shoes, put them on, and angrily went downstairs to the kitchen to confront Mom who softly asked, "Did you find your shoes?"

"Yes I did." "See, I knew you could do that on your own." From then on I tried to do everything on my own and not ask for help.

Middle Boy

> *Caught in the crevice,*
> *Not knowing who his friends are,*
> *Alone much of the time inside,*
> *Riding his bicycle*
> *Searching for friends,*
> *Straining the sides of rejection from caving in.* -- Tom

Food was not plentiful, and it wasn't "the best", but it was good down home simple cooking. Nowadays I call it "comfort food" when I try to imitate those meals. I don't remember going to bed hungry. There were lots of beans, potatoes, pasta, oatmeal, and any ground meat was extended into meatloaf, goetta, or meatballs. To this day, I find it very hard to eat any kind of beans or potatoes. If we had chicken for supper, Dad would always eat the wings and the backs -- not much meat on them, but he said he liked them. Even then, I thought he just saved the better pieces for us. Sometimes the Sisters of the Poor would call to let Mom know they got in a donation of bread, and Mom should send us down to pick some up. Mom's pride did not like to accept handouts, she thought others needed them more than we did, and most of the time she would not send us. So, a few of us kids, unbeknownst to Mom, would show up at the convent door and stuff ourselves with sweet rolls and milk as we sat on the curb out front.

Deep into her years, Mom would preserve whatever she could: bushels of tomatoes, green beans, peaches, and jellies and jams produced hundreds of quarts on the shelves in the basement. She tried to make her own sauerkraut once, fermenting it in an old crock in the basement, but it was stinking so badly that Dad made her throw it out. Nothing went to waste (except that sauerkraut). "Waste not. Want not." I am still that way preserving apricots, plums, black currants, and peaches into jams, tomatoes into soup and freezing it, and corn into everything. Sauerkraut comes from a can.

As we got older, we could help with the chores -- cleaning the house and small yard, doing laundry, ironing and cooking. The older ones each had a day when we would cook, set the table, wash all the dishes, and clean up the kitchen. My day was Wednesday, and most times the menu was spaghetti and meatballs. I would have to set the table, cook, clean up the table after, wash all the pots and pans and dishes, and sweep the floor. I remember being up until 10:00pm some Wednesdays washing dishes and cleaning up the kitchen. As I got older I could pay a willing younger brother or sister to do the clean-up.

One Thanksgiving there was no money for a turkey, so Dad went by himself to the Church bazaar and took a ten-cent chance to win a turkey. Perhaps those who ran the bazaar rigged the raffle, but Dad actually won a live white turkey. He was so proud when, with a lot of effort, he carried that thing home, and all the kids went wild with excitement wanting to keep it for a pet. Neither Dad nor Mom knew anything about killing or preparing the bird, so he tied it to the backyard clothesline by its neck and began hacking at the neck with a dull butcher knife. There was a lot of wing-flapping and blood spewing everywhere until the bird fell to the bare ground running around the yard and flapping and spewing blood with its half-hacked neck hanging and swinging and us kids with sheer delight running all over trying to catch it. When we did, we seemed like caveman's kids catching the beast as there was turkey blood all over us and the bird was red. Dad finished off the lifeless thing by cutting the skin that held the neck and head, as Mom boiled water to pour over the carcass in the large galvanized tub so all of us could join in the feather-plucking. Reality soon set in with the awful smell of dirty, hot, bloodied feathers and the cutting and ripping out of the insides. Mom prepared it as best she could without stuffing it, but we didn't feel much like eating our short-lived would-be pet, but then again, it tasted good and we were hungry.

I learned a lot from that experience about improvising and became a pretty decent cook (although my brothers and sisters would dispute that claim), and I would sometimes cook sauerkraut and spareribs for an old man down the street. Cooking and baking are still one of my favorite pastimes. Mom used to wake me up about 6am on Thanksgiving Day to help her slice and dice the onions and celery and bread for the raisin dressing used to stuff the turkey. Thanksgiving dinner with all the fixings was my all-time favorite meal back then, and now it is my favorite meal to cook all year.

I also took care of the yard work: raking, trimming, digging, planting flowers, watering. I really enjoyed it then, and it is a great joy in my life now. Speaking of yard work, some of the neighbors would have me do work in their yards. The pay was ten cents an hour. I also shoveled snow twice a day sometimes in the winter all through the neighborhood for ten cents an hour. We had a lot of snow back then in southwestern Ohio.

The Pater's House

These neighbors, in particular, would have a great influence on my life – Mrs. Pater and Doctor Pater. They lived directly behind our house across the alley in a large three-story, 18 room, red brick, Italianate Queen Anne Victorian home on Dayton Street. Doc Pater was a bit of a recluse, but Mrs. Pater was outgoing, vivacious, and colorful, and wanted their large yard looking lovely all the time with flowers, overgrown bushes, trees and boxwoods. They were childless, and she loved kids, and took a special shining to me. She called me "Master Thomas." He called me "The Kid." One time they even approached Mom and Dad about adopting me. Of course Mom and Dad said no, but in effect she did anyway. She and Doc would take me (and sometimes my younger brother, Ed) to their farm where there were cattle, trees, the musty odors of raw nature, dirt roads, cow patties everywhere, and flies everywhere. We would swim in the summer-warmed, spring-fed lake and enjoy a big picnic lunch. Doc would teach me how to swim better (I hated the freezing cold swim lessons Mom forced us to take at the city pool), and to be afraid of the bulls but not the cows, and Mrs. Pater would sit under the porch cover of the small cabin chatting with some friends who showed up to visit. That's where I learned how to play Canasta and Hearts. It was a big break from my family life at home.

From October through March of each year, the Paters snow-birded to their home in Hialeah, Florida about a mile from the famed Hialeah Racetrack. Doc would spend most of his days "working" at the racetrack where, he said, he made most of his money. While they were gone, Mrs. Pater would entrust her ten-plus outdoor cats to me. I had to feed them twice a day with canned cat food and warmed diluted evaporated milk. They gave me a key to their huge house to get cat food and to check on the house for leaks, broken windows, break-ins, or whatever. "Don't bring anyone else into the house" was their only stipulation. Wow! Was I in heaven! It was my castle. It was my quiet space. It was my place!

The house had a library with a large fireplace that smelled of old smoke, and bookshelves filled with old books lining the walls. The front foyer walls had Italian hand-painted pastoral scenes above the dark wainscoting to the ceiling. The European scenes were quite dirty and could have used a good cleaning, but were still clear enough to pull me into them. For hours I would stand in front of them and try to imagine myself taking part in the action in the scenes. A music room with golden violins painted on the ceiling around the crystal chandelier, and upholstered benches built into the walls with secret places under the seats, and another large fireplace. The formal dining room contained a huge crystal chandelier hanging over the twenty-seat Jacobean oak table, and another huge fireplace brought from Italy with an intricately hand-carved high relief walnut mantle with birds and flowers and vines and two four foot tall very muscular bearded men in black walnut holding up each end, and a secret passage for the servants to bring the meals in directly from the kitchen. One half story down was the game room with a billiard table and an octagonal game table with a green felt top, and a small fireplace. The kitchen with white and black tiles on the floor and walls to the ceiling seemed rather small in proportion to the rest of the house. It also had a cook's apartment behind it. The pantry with light green cabinets floor to ceiling along one wall in the walkway was hiding a secret stairwell to the third floor where the servants would have lived. There were beautiful, many-colored hardwood parquet floors throughout the first floor.

One half story up the red carpeted grand staircase was the large ballroom with a large crystal chandelier from the high ceiling halfway to the floor, and a black baby grand piano, and from the built-in red cushioned seating all across the bowed north wall all the way to the ceiling was an indescribable stained glass window in golds and blues and greens and pinks and more colors than I can remember. I could imagine the evening parties, the dances, the waltzes, and the music from the small orchestra on the balcony on the south wall. The only music now was silence. This led up the other half of the grand staircase to the second floor where there were five large bedrooms, each with their own large fireplace and beds with tall Victorian headboards and heavy ample curtains to keep the cold out from the loose-fitting windows. It was said that when President McKinley visited Hamilton, he would stay in the front master bedroom. The large bathroom had white and black tiles on the floor and halfway up the walls. There was a pedestal sink and a big, white, claw-footed tub with gold colored faucets and spout. In the rear of the house were Doc's office and laboratory with glass front cabinets floor to ceiling containing medical books and innumerable jars and flasks, some with old medicines and some with specimens preserved in some kind of liquid, and a real human skull that smelled like year old chicken bones left out in the summer sun. Perhaps these rooms sparked an early interest in my wanting to become a doctor and surgeon, but I knew I could never afford it, and it never happened.

The third floor could only be accessed by a servant's stairway at the back of the house that went from the basement all the way up. There were three bedrooms with large cedar-lined closets and a big open space used now for storage of antique furniture and many boxes filled with Christmas decorations, items for parties, and personal things.

The whole house and every room was filled with wonderful antiques, old pictures, oriental rugs, silver sets on the side tables, chairs with carvings, large red leather club chairs, and more and more, mostly Victorian, some other eras, but nothing new. One item I remember very clearly was a six-foot palm tree lamp with a curved bright brass trunk and colored crystals making up and hanging from the palm fronds, and a multi-colored parrot perched on top. The magic happened when the lights were turned on and the tree was shaken -- sending crystal sparkles all over the ceiling and walls!

There were spirits attached to that house. I would feel their presence, or a cold air draft, rocking chairs moving, and catch movement off the side of my eye. At night, from the back window of our house I would see globes of light moving up and down the rear servants' stairwell. Thinking there might be intruders, the next day I dusted each of the stairs with flour. When I saw the lights again, the next day I went to investigate, but there were no footprints at all. Oddly, nothing of this made me afraid or wary of going in or walking around inside the house. In fact, I kind of felt one with them and considered them my friends, and that we both belonged there. Throughout life, I have been able to perceive spirits and the dead, seeing things others don't, feeling things others don't, hearing things others don't, dreaming of future incidents, premonitions, knowing health concerns of others, having foresight and clairvoyance, telepathically finding lost items for people. It was like I access a different realm, a different level of reality – there but only few can perceive. It isn't a matter of believing whether they exist, but being receptive to the reality that they do exist. It was and is a gift with which I have to be very careful.

When I was twenty-one, some years after Doc had died, Mrs. Pater told me that if I had chosen a different life and gotten married and had children she would have given the whole house and contents to me, but she knew as a Franciscan I couldn't own anything. Instead, she gave it to the Franciscan Sisters of the Poor to be used as an orphanage. They never did, and they sold it on the market. I was totally heartbroken.

Our House

In contrast, our house, which was Dad's boyhood home, and which Dad bought from his father for way too much money, was kind of small with three bedrooms upstairs and a bathroom. The front bedroom was Mom and Dad's and whichever baby was in season that year in the crib. The middle bedroom slept eight in two full size beds, two bunk beds, and a single bed, and a large dresser. The back bedroom was for the two older brothers, and contained a closet, their dresser, another dresser, and a curtain covering the door. We weren't supposed to go in there except to get our clothes from the dresser or closet and then run back out. Sometimes on Saturday afternoons, I was allowed to go in and watch my brothers spit-shine and burnish their black leather shoes before they went on dates. Everything had to be ready and perfect after their bath: clothes cleaned and ironed, shoes shining, hair slicked down, and lots of aftershave that they thought smelled pretty swell.

Downstairs was a front living room with an old sofa which was Dad's when he wanted to rest and which let off "smoke dust" when you slapped it real hard, a big chair which was Mom's when she had time to sit down and have us climb up behind her shoulders to take turns combing her hair, and a television set which we watched from the floor. The middle room was a dining room which we didn't use as a dining room except for very special celebrations when Mom would pull out the special china and silverware. There were two side cabinets, one of which became the changing station for the babies, and there was a bassinet and a playpen, and lacey curtains on the windows. That room was used for the ironing board as needed, the old foot-pedaled Singer sewing machine, the record player which scratched every one of the blue Reader's Digest album's twelve records of great classical music and show tunes – every note of which my ears devoured as often as they could – and a large dining table with chairs in the middle of the room under which I would hide and peer out through the lacey table cloth hanging over the edge. Off the dining room was a smallish play room containing some toys and other things to occupy our time. When they got older and needed their own room, this room became my two older sisters' room, thereby cutting out a big chunk of our play space.

Through the south wall of the dining room was a doorway that led to what always seemed to be the cramped kitchen with a large oilcloth-covered table and benches and chairs to seat us all, and the sink with white metal cabinets below and above, the door into the large pantry containing cases of canned goods, hooks for coats and work clothes, boots on the floor, shelves to the ceiling with kitchen pots and pans and things, and also a floor trap door to the basement. The tired white enameled stove and oven combination had a white metal cabinet next to it, then the always-used and indestructible high chair, a hard-to-keep-full refrigerator, a freezer stuffed with ten-for-a-dollar loaves of bread from Kroger, and the constantly opened and closed door to the back yard. Somehow, I remember a water pump to the right of the sink tapping into and bringing up water from the cistern below. The cistern was later filled in, and bags of lime were poured into it to control the water-bug roaches; it was sealed and the pump was removed. Mom always insisted that the kitchen be kept clean at all times, and somehow it was.

The trapdoor in the pantry was part of the floor until it was lifted with as much strength as one could muster. Only the older siblings were strong enough. I don't even know how Mom could do it; or, especially, how Dad could lift it since he was thin and not muscular. But, it did get opened and led by very steep worn wooden steps down to the unfinished half basement with the gray limestone walls as a foundation for the house. Dad told us that his mother died at the bottom of those steps, and that he found her there when he was seventeen in 1936 and had come back to the house after high school that day. Very sad. I can't even imagine how Dad felt when he found her, or what it was like to live without her, but I never felt Grandma's spirit there or anywhere in the house. The old ringer washer was there and clotheslines strung up about a foot apart for drying clothes when they couldn't be hung outside. The huge, round, coal-burning furnace dominated a large area, as did the coal bins which we had to access for the coal to keep the furnace stoked in the winter. Later, the old furnace was removed and a smaller, new, gas-fired furnace was installed. There was no more shoveling coal and dust and ashes and cinders, and we were cleaner and the house was cleaner.

Outside, the house still smelled like acrid coal smoke from everyone else's coal furnaces, and from the coal-fired locomotives on the train tracks a block away billowing their smoke down our street right at us when the wind blew right, until they were changed to sleek diesel locomotives. A new washer along with a dryer replaced the old ones in our basement, but the clotheslines stayed. The coal bins were dismantled and removed, the stone walls and floor somehow cleaned, and a donated ping-pong table installed, which soon became quite a hit with us and the neighborhood kids. My older brother Jim had a "thing" with knives (still does), but whenever Dad found any of them he would shove them up behind the stone wall into the empty space under the kitchen. What a treasure trove is to be found when the house is torn down! They are also sure to find a number of paddles which we liberally threw behind that same wall.

My Falling Accident

I want to mention an accident Mom told to me about that happened when I was younger than two years old. As I pulled over the pot of tomato soup on the stove I leaned over my highchair tray to see what happened and fell out of the highchair landing on top of a white bowl that had shattered on the floor. My forehead was split from the left side above my eyebrow to the lower edge of my right eyebrow. After Mom's frantic rush to the emergency room I ended up with eighteen stitches, and my brother Jim remembers that I just would not stop crying all the time. Mom said that, at the same time, I got chicken pox and measles and licked the <u>Drano</u> spoon under the sink. Of course, the residual drain chemical caused painful blisters inside my mouth, on my tongue and lips. I couldn't believe it later when she actually told me that I was such a mess at the time, she didn't know what she could do to make it any better, and that she considered wrapping me up in newspaper and putting me in the trash. Certainly she wouldn't have, and obviously she didn't, but it really hurt me when she told that to me. Not knowing just what, but it seemed to verify how I felt about myself and what my place in the family was.

Through the years I would develop small boils on the sizeable forehead scar, and eventually a small piece of white glass would work its way through. Some kids my age made cruel jokes and said I looked like Frankenstein. Later in life a doctor asked me if I had fallen when I was an infant because I had a misaligned right collarbone that had broken in half and knitted back together on its own at a very early age. He also raised the question as to whether I might have had a concussion at the time. I wondered after that if it might help explain my difficulty learning in school, especially in high school and college. It seemed that I struggled and had to study so much harder than the other students. They would be out having fun while I was by myself trying to absorb and remember the studies. Also, noise of any kind, bright lights, and large groups of people bothered me. Living in a large family in a small house downtown didn't help either. The damp cold basement next to the furnace was my study place. When I was twenty-eight, I started having seizures which gradually decreased and ceased ten years later, and I was told I had irregular brain wave activity. I'm just wondering.

Christmas

Gradually, Christmases got to be something I did not look forward to and still don't. St. Nicholas Day, December 6th, was better. We would hang our Great-Aunts' old long brown stockings on the non-functional and sealed fireplace in the living room, and in the morning each one of them would have lots of candy, nuts, apples, and oranges. Then "The Curtain", the dreaded curtain, actually a bed sheet, would be tacked all around the doorway into the front living room, covering it completely. It would easily cut off one third of our play space and living space and access to the television. Explanation: a giving up of something to prepare for the birth of Jesus; and to give Santa Claus a place to store gifts and set up decorations; and it was a "German thing" during Advent. If we tried to peek inside, we risked having our nose cut off.

On Christmas Eve, after a light supper and taking our baths, from youngest to oldest, we were allowed inside the curtain one by one, and we would see the lights and the Christmas tree and the train going through the tunnel in the tree stand, and Mom and Dad had a great time spending special moments giving us our presents that Santa Claus had left for us. The little ones got at least one toy or doll and the school aged ones usually got clothes, underwear, or socks (other clothes and shoes were handed down when the older siblings outgrew them). Rarely ever getting what I had hoped for, it was difficult for me to be happy or grateful, but by then I knew how poor we were. In fact, one Christmas there was no Christmas tree on Christmas Eve. Christmas morning, a few of us scoured the neighborhood alleyways and beyond looking for a tree hopefully discarded by some family leaving on vacation. We found one that still had green needles and tinsel on it and dragged it home and set it up.

One memorable gift to me about the age of seven, one I had actually requested, was a vinyl plastic "priest kit" chasuble and stole to pretend having Mass, although I was so serious about it that it wasn't pretending. Mom made me a white tunic (an alb) to wear with the kit. My poor sisters and brothers and some of the neighbors were bribed into attending the "service" so they could get a Necco holy-candy wafer for the Communion host. The problem was that I ran of the chocolate ones fast. I said "Mass" for a few years until I outgrew the set, and grew more into the Church.

"I miss my Dad"

I'm not sure of how long it was, but I am sure of the details and memories and feelings, and that Dad was gone for perhaps the three years between when I was three and six. It seemed he was sick most of his life and all of our lives. But, during this time he had a severe and complete mental breakdown at about age 34, for which he was hospitalized and away from the family, and took strong medication for the rest of his life. His recovery was long and difficult on him, on Mom, and on us. Initially, he was in and out of deep depression and paranoia -- staying home from work, not eating, and staying in their bedroom with the shades drawn. Then he was at the local hospital for psychiatric evaluation before he was transferred and admitted to a mental hospital in downtown Cincinnati. From there he was admitted long term to another mental hospital on the outskirts of Cincinnati. Mom visited every chance she was allowed to visit, loading us all in the station wagon for the three-quarter-hour trip down there. We were never allowed to go in with Mom to see Dad. Everytime, summer or winter, we had to stay in the car until she returned trying to hold back her tears. Mom didn't understand what was going on with him, and all her days she blamed herself for signing him into those institutions. She was trying to do what was best for him, hoping and praying that he would get better. His doctor told her not to expect her husband, in the mental state that he was in, to ever be released. The treatments of drugs, electric shocks and group sessions were just not working for him.

All her life she tried to keep this part of his life and her life and our lives a secret. She tried to protect him and us from others' judgements. Particularly, she was worried that no one would want to marry her children if they knew this about our father. Money became even more scarce, and there were no government social programs in those days, not that Mom would accept "charity" anyhow.

Dad's uncle, Carl, would come over and visit with us as he smoked his fat cigar, and he would always have chocolate candy bars in his jacket pockets, usually Milky Way and Three Musketeers. After we said hello to him and gave him a hug we were allowed to reach into his pocket and retrieve our surprise candy treat. As soon as he left, we would pound on the old couch and watch the cigar smoke-dust waft about in the light. Anyhow, Mom and Uncle Carl would spend some time talking together after we were dismissed to the back yard or the other room. Mom didn't share the conversations with us, but it seems he told her that she and Dad were to be the only heirs of his estate as specified in his new will. Not very long after that he passed away kind of suddenly.

Mom spoke with his lawyer and told him what Uncle Carl had said, but she was told that she and Dad were not mentioned in the will he had on file. I am sure Mom was counting on the estate to keep the family going. She was worried. That night she had a dream that Uncle Carl's visage visited her when she fell asleep at the bottom of one of our beds while trying to get us to sleep. He told her not to worry, and that the new will could be found tacked to the back of his dresser up against the bedroom wall in his house. The next day she mentioned the dream to his lawyer, who then went to the house and found the new will which designated her and Dad as the sole heirs.

After the funeral, when things settled down, I remember going into his house with Mom where all the walls were heavily stained tan from the cigar smoke, and even his bed sheets and linens were brownish in color. In a very real way his generosity saved our family from being destitute and having to live at the Poor House Hill home. Every Memorial Day Mom would put a bouquet of flowers at his grave, and some of my siblings still do.

At this same time, the drug companies were developing new medications -- especially thorazine and stelazine -- for paranoia and schizophrenia which showed some promise from the trials. It was difficult for Mom to allow the use of those drugs being tested on Dad, but it was presented as her only hope that he would ever be able to leave the hospital and come home. So she agreed, and the combination of those drugs really seemed to turn him around and helped him get better.

At first, we could go to see him at the hospital, and he would come outside into the bright sunshine to be with us. Then, he was allowed to come home for weekends for a home visit, but he had to go back. Gradually, he was allowed to stay longer, and then to be home all the time. Perhaps this transition process was to help him get his life back little by little, and for us to accept him back into the family little by little after such a long absence. Initially, it was strange to have him with us all the time. I never thought of it before, but the younger ones wouldn't have even known who he was.

Dad got involved in a group program called "Recovery" which was run by the Sisters of the Poor. It gave him a chance to talk things through with others who were also trying to integrate into society, and it seemed to help him a great deal. Even so, to me he seemed emotionally distant except for when his anger flared up mainly at the younger children. Looking back, I am in awe of his strength and determination to recover, to fight through this, to get a job, to be responsible for his family again, when there seemed to be so little hope before. In this sense he was a great man and role model.

Death Comes to Me

Death became very familiar to me at an early age. A few of us walked to the corner delicatessen at Heaton and Sixth Streets along with my dog Penny who I really loved. We waited for the light, but Penny jumped into the traffic and got hit by a dump truck, and I jumped into the traffic to pull her back to the curb. She was badly hurt and bloody and screamed out in pain. The car behind the dump truck just happened to be a police car that stopped to avoid hitting me, and the policeman got out and came over and scolded me for not holding her more tightly with the leash and for jumping into the traffic to get her. Then he pulled out his gun and shot her in the head right there. I was in shock with the blast from the gun, and I knew I couldn't ever get her better. I picked her up in my arms and carried her home, crying all the way. We dug a hole for her in the backyard by the fence along the alley, and I laid her in it, crying as we pushed the dirt over her. Even when the small marker disappeared, I always remembered exactly where Penny was, and I can still picture it.

++++

There's a story about how I got my name. Mom and Dad wanted to name a son Thomas or Tom or Tommy for a while, but Grandpa Schellenbach had a wirehaired terrier whose name was "Tommy." Mom had a brother named Tom. When I was born, the terrier was still around. So, in order that it wouldn't be said that I was named after my Grandpa's dog, they chose Mom's brother to be my godfather and named me after him. But I was still kidded that I was named after my Grandpa's dog.

My godfather Uncle Tommy died when I was five. The last time I almost saw him was when he came to the house to wish me Happy Birthday and give me a present. But I was taking a bath to get cleaned up, and I wasn't ready because he wasn't supposed to show up until later. He kept calling to me to come downstairs, and then he came upstairs and opened the door to the bathroom. I jumped out of the tub and ran naked to the back bedroom and hid in the back of the closet crying and angry. I didn't have the chance to get cleaned up for him and put on my good clothes for him and look nice for him. So I stubbornly would not come out of the closet despite him repeatedly asking me to come out so he could give me his present. Finally, he said he came early because he had to go somewhere else, he put the present on the bed and left, and I stayed in the closet for a long time until the coast was clear. He died shortly after of a brain aneurysm.

Accepting Acceptance (2.23.77)

Like a long-remembered godfather uncle,
You come to me Lord, gift-filled hands
Outstretched for me.
And I, not ready yet, washing, naked,
Refuse You entrance.
You, like he, hands outstretched,
Break upon my nakedness,
Gift-bearing.
Terrified, pushing You aside,
I make straight for my dark security
In closet rear.
Despite Your pleas and others' prodding
I remain there, naked, crying,
Not ready to receive Your gifts,
Stance-determined by Your persistence.
Then, trying no more, the gifts are placed on the bed,
And You with others leave,
And I in closet-security cry at being so alone.

Yet, unlike my long-remembered, godfather uncle,
You are present, God, Father,
For Whose coming I need not be perfected,
Whose coming in itself worthies me.
And in whose warm lap-security naked I
Cry at being so love-gifted.

++++

Then my ninety-six year old Great-Grandmother died when I was six. Whenever we all went to visit her, we had to go upstairs to her room where she was fully dressed, propped up with pillows while lying on her Victorian bed. She would extend her hand down to us, and we had to stand in line to kiss it, and then she would pat us each on the head. And only then could we be excused to urgently use the restroom. We would gather back in her room because she expected us to say the rosary with her in German as we knelt on the floor without making a noise other than the "Vater Unsers" and the "Heilige Marias" -- all without fidgeting for an hour. That rosary was quite an ordeal for us, but Great-Grandma was the queen and always got what she wanted.

++++

Then my Mom's dad died. Grandpa Vogt had severe rheumatoid arthritis and had a couple missing fingers which he said he lost while making cigars -- not knowing which cigars got sold with fingers in them. So, he sold Metropolitan Life Insurance after that. He was a kind, handsome man with full white hair. Mom and Dad bought each of us a $1,000.00 life insurance policy which they gave us when we would get married or turned 21. Grandpa loved to hold and caress the babies, but I saw him cry once when his arthritis got so bad he had to admit he couldn't hold the latest one. Also, he used to dispense Life Saver candies to us from the clean standing ashtray next to the old armchair he always sat in.

++++

Then Dad's dad died. Grandpa Schellenbach was a kindly old man who used to visit us all year long wearing a heavily starched white shirt and an impeccable suit. I heard the word "dandy" used to describe him. His father, whom I didn't know, owned a small grocery store called "Schellenbach The Grocer" on Third Street south of High Street. Family legend says that Great-Grandpa was part owner of a grocery store with Barney Kroger in Cincinnati until they had a big argument, and Great-Grandpa sold his share to Mr. Kroger and moved to Hamilton to open his own grocery. Everyone has heard of "Kroger's", but no one has heard of "Schellenbach The Grocer."

Grandpa owned "The Princess Shop" on Third Street where he sold women's dresses. Walking past his shop, we could see the most beautiful wedding gowns through the storefront windows. When he was younger he used to play the guitar for a small chamber music group in the city, and he kept his love of classical music throughout his life. I was amazed at the variety of compositions he would listen to, and which I also listened to later as I broadened my music appreciation. Grandpa got married two more times after his first wife, my Dad's Mom, died at the bottom of the basement stairs. He lived on Heaton Street, and we used to pass by his house as we walked to the fairgrounds, and we would stop and visit for a short while. He didn't seem to mind at all and welcomed our little visits. When Grandpa moved in with Dad's oldest brother, Edgar, in Middletown, we didn't see him much anymore.

We really liked it when Grandpa came over for dinner a couple of times a year, because it was always a special dinner of roast beef, green beans, mashed potatoes, gravy and Mom's special strawberry shortcake. Of course, he wore his best suit with a vest, starched shirt and tie. I closely watch everything he did. Before beginning to eat, he would dip his silverware utensils into the glass of water, then wipe off any spots or smudges, and dry them with his napkin. For one of these dinners Mom had bought the new whipped cream in a pressurized can for the shortcake rather than making her own. It may have been Reddi Whip which had just come into the market. Nobody, not Dad nor Mom nor any of the four kids who tried, could figure out how to work the skinny nozzle at the top of the can; until my brother Jim, sitting directly opposite Grandpa, shook the can vigorously, turned it upside down and banged it on the table. The nozzle bent and swoosh! The whipped cream exploded out the nozzle and blasted all over the front of Grandpa. The pursuing shock and commotion, the wide eyes of each of us, especially Grandpa, brought on getting kitchen towels to wipe him off, continuous apologies, offers to get his suit dry-cleaned, and each of us holding in our bursts of laughter -- because we wouldn't dare laugh. After Grandpa left, the rauchous laughter began at Jim's expense.

++++

Then Mom's mom died rather suddenly after slipping into a diabetic coma. I asked Mom one time why her Mom, Grandma Vogt, never came to our house to visit us like she did to our cousins. She said, "Well, there was always so much pandeminium at our house." I said, "Mom don't you mean pandemonium." She said, "No, it was just a little bit." Mom didn't live in denial, but she did minimize the impact of situations and events. It was her way of coping with reality and surviving. When some of us kids would be together and share memories, especially painful ones, Mom would claim we were remembering things that never happened. (I am sure she would look me in the eye right now and say the same thing about this book).

Anyhow, Grandma didn't seem to want to have much to do with us other than sending us each a birthday and Christmas card with a little cash in them. I never remember her helping Mom by babysitting us. She told Mom that she didn't want to help raise us because she had had enough raising seven of her own. After Grandpa died, we didn't even feel particularly welcomed at Grandma's house. She would tell us to go down into the basement and play on the swing so we wouldn't dirty her house, while she would visit with Mom and Dad in her living room.

And, she didn't want us to ride our bikes out to visit her. We learned to stay away from her.

Dad said Grandma never wanted to permit her daughter to marry him. In fact, there are still actual letters from the early 1940's which Dad wrote to Mom's brother Ferd (Dad's classmate and closest friend), asking for his help to sway Grandma's stance towards him. I like to think Grandpa had more to do with that. But, I wonder if Grandma's approach towards us wasn't just her way of being vindictive since Mom and Dad got married against her wishes.

++++

After each of my grandparents died, I wondered who I could ask about the days when they were my age.

Play and Work

In the alley behind our house we used to play "kick the can" with "Allyee, allyee, in-come free", lots of dodgeball, Lone Ranger and Tonto, Cochise, and Hopalong Cassidy with the neighbors -- trying to imitate our T.V. counterparts with hats, toy guns, and Indian costumes. Ah, yes, we used to raid all the mulberry trees around, picking and eating ripe mulberries until we would get sick, climbing high in the trees to get the best ones until the owners would chase us away. Lots of fun!

Thinking back, I worked a lot and didn't play much when I was doing ten cent yard work and snow shoveling, and going around the neighborhoods collecting huge loads of old newspapers and pieces of metal and iron in our red wagon to take up to the scrap yard to exchange for a handful of coins (never enough to match the effort), and being the ten-city-blocks neighborhood paperboy. I liked delivering newspapers after school and meeting a lot of people, collecting charges each Friday, getting new customers, dropping ones that didn't pay, paying for my papers each Saturday morning downtown at the main office, learning a lot about simple business principles. My younger brother Ed would help when I needed it, even when he had a cut over his eye and pulled in more tips than I did with his sad eyes. We stopped once at Milillo's Pizza after our deliveries. When they burned our pizza and were going to throw it out, we begged for it. They made another one for no charge, and we ate that good one there, and took the burned one home for the others. In all, by the time I was fourteen, I had saved $1,000.00 in my bank account. A lot of money back then for a kid. Mom and Dad made sure each of us had a bank account to put in birthday money, First Communion and Confirmation money, and earned money.

After working hard in her yard one summer afternoon, I told Mrs. Pater I wasn't going to do her yard work anymore for ten cents an hour, and that now I wanted fifteen cents. She got angry and said, "That's not how it works. We agreed on a price before you did the work. I tell you what I choose to give you. You don't tell me what you want after you are finished." When she tried to hand me four dimes for the four hours, I refused to accept it. She placed the dimes under the flower pot on her porch and closed the door, and that is where the dimes stayed, and I went home. In the few minutes it took me to get home, Mrs. Pater had called Mom and told her what happened. Mom scolded me, told me to go right back to tell Mrs. Pater I was sorry and that from now on I would do all her yard work for free -- because "friends are more important than money." So, I turned around and marched over to the Pater's, and apologized, and told her I would do whatever she needed done for nothing. She would not accept that, and said the worker should be paid what he is worth; she had thought about it, and that the next time I would come to work for her she had chosen to give me twenty-five cents an hour. I said, "Thank you," and went back home to eat supper -- realizing I had learned a couple important lessons that day about running a business and about friendship.

Kennedy is Assassinated

One particular day in November 1963 will forever be seared in my memory. As eighth-graders, we took turns answering the office phone for Sister at the Catholic grade school to which Mom and Dad were somehow able to afford to send us. That sunshine filled afternoon, it being my turn, I answered the ringing phone in the adjacent office to our classroom. This lady on the line was frantically crying trying to speak and hard to understand. Finally, I was able to make out, "The President's been shot!! The President's been shot!!" I started laughing as I hung up the phone thinking it was a prank, and was still laughing when I returned to the classroom saying, "It was some crazy lady yelling something like 'The President was shot'." The whole room started to laugh except our teacher, who was the Principal. She resumed our lesson after she got us under control. Not ten minutes later, I got up to answer the phone again. However, this time it was the Pastor wanting to speak to Sister. When she came back crying, she announced that the President Kennedy was dead. It was as if she had slammed all forty of us over the head at the same time with the heavy wooden paddle she stored hanging from the side of her desk. Naturally, we were all stunned to tears and deep shock to hear of such a thing happening in our country to our Catholic President as we sat in our Catholic school, and it took quite a while for the news to really sink in.

When I got home, the Journal News office had called to let me know that I should not deliver the newspapers already left at the usual street corner by the gas station. They would come by and pick those up when they delivered the latest edition of the paper in about two hours. I sat with my brothers and sisters crying zombie-like in front of the television while Mom was trying to get something together for supper. As it was getting past dusk and colder, my brother helped me deliver the newspapers in a hurry that evening. That day and the weeks that followed, with more shootings, and Kennedy's funeral, combined with the threat of Cuban nuclear missile attacks, I lost a great deal of innocence and security I unconsciously had.

++++

Every day, Monday through Friday, we would walk five blocks and over two sets of train tracks to be home for lunch because we didn't have the money for the school lunch. Even when we did have some extra coins, we had to go home to help the younger ones get there and back.

Many times on the way back to school after lunch there was a train parked on the tracks. We had to be very attentive to the sounds the train cars and wheels were making before we would consider whether or not to overcome our fear before climbing through or under the trains so we wouldn't be late for school. Some old lady saw us one day and called the school and ratted on us. Then she called Mom as well. The school principal used it as a teachable moment and let us have it with both barrels -- the one with YOU-SHOULD-KNOW-BETTER!", and the other with "I-DON'T-EVER-WANT-TO-HEAR-OF-YOU-DOING-THAT-AGAIN!" Then at home we got the same message with the same tone from Mom which ended with "JUST-WAIT-UNTIL-YOUR-FATHER-GETS-HOME." Then we were afraid.

++++

For a long time as a young boy I had a strong feeling, and it grew as I got older, that somehow I was different from other boys my age. When I was very young, I had two boy dolls I called Pete and RePete. I often wonder who gave those to me. Girls weren't interesting or attractive to me, boys were, and I seemed to hang around others who were a few years older than I was. Having been asked at what age I felt I was gay, I would have to say as long as I can remember. Although, back then it was a feeling I wasn't like other guys and didn't quite belong. That feeling has determined so much of my life and the decisions that were made.

++++

Oddly, being from a large family, I felt lonely and alone most of the time, but always tried to give the impression to others that I was bright and happy and outgoing. I tried time and again to get a few of my grade school boy classmates together to play, but they were already members of a baseball, football, or basketball team. Never did they initiate a call for me to join them. And my working at side jobs didn't give me much time to join and play on organized teams. Even at school lunch recess I was chosen last for the dodgeball teams or sat on the side by myself and watched. When I tried to join the Boy Scout Troop sponsored by our Parish, I was told we didn't have enough money for the membership and uniform and activities.

> *"Four magic words, we can't afford it, should be a part of every child's education. A child who has never heard those words -- or also has never been forced to abide by their meaning -- has surely been cheated by his parents. As exercise strengthens the body, frugality strengthens the spirit. Without its occasional discipline, character suffers."* -- Jewish Press

Following in my eldest brother's footsteps (he was the hometown Champion one year) I did enter the Soap Box Derby after building my own car with my brother's and his mentor's help. The first year I lost a later race. The second year, after revisions to the car, I was on my way to be champion when in the last race my competitor came into my lane and bumped me, slowing me down. He won the race, and that made me runner-up. I don't know why he wasn't disqualified, but I got the latest model brand new Schwinn bicycle as my prize, and I was happy. Numerous times I would ask Dad to take us all on a Sunday afternoon car ride. His stock answers were: "Maybe later," or "I'm too tired" or "Maybe next week." I got so tired of the disappointments that I would take off on my bike to the country roads, to small towns near our town, and even to the cemetery and be gone for many hours alone by myself pedaling into the wind and sometimes the rain.

Some Quick Memories

When I was very small, after all of us were put to bed and Mom and Dad were still downstairs, I remember getting out of bed and very quietly going down most of the steep stairs and stretching out there on one of the steps and falling asleep. Even the scolding didn't stop me, but getting too big for the step did. I learned that I was growing and getting bigger and had to find another way to get attention.

++++

In summertime, when we were little, we would sit along the sidewalk coping in front of the house on Buckeye St. in shorts and no shoes and boys with no shirts waiting for the French Bauer milk delivery man, Mr. Weaver. We would beg for ice from him, and he would chip off a large piece from the ice he used to keep the milk cold and hand us each a piece of it during those hot summer days. It sure did taste great! One time after he parked, I climbed into the back of the truck to get my own ice, and I then left my little straw cowboy hat in there. I wondered if I would ever get it back, but after all his deliveries of the day he returned to our house to return it to me – he knew it was mine.

++++

I wanted to have a birthday party, so I told the whole neighborhood in the middle of the summer that I was having a birthday party (my birthday is actually in February), and everybody was invited, but I never mentioned anything to Mom. She did find out when one of the neighbor moms came to the house to ask Mom what I would like for a present. When I overheard that exchange, I knew I was in deep trouble and hid under the dining room table until Mom found me and then the paddle found my naked rear end. Then, I had to go around to all the neighbors and tell them I lied, it was not my birthday, and there would be no party. It was a really embarrassing way to learn to tell the truth.

++++

Mrs. Pater used to give me small antique items from her house. But Mom didn't want them in the house, saying, "Get them out of here. Yes, they are nice, but there's no room for them in this house. Take them down to the museum to see if they want them!" It was no use trying to hide them in the house, because she would find them and throw them out. I even asked Mrs. Pater if I could keep them at her house, but she didn't want them there. Once I brought home a very old black typewriter, one of the first ever made, and got the same reaction, "I don't want it in the house. Take it to the museum!" Reluctantly, my younger brother and I took it to the museum, but it was closed that day. I couldn't decide what to do with it. If I left it at the door, someone would steal it. I certainly couldn't take it back home again. We decided to walk about three blocks to take a look at the Great Miami River, which was above flood stage. The muddy river was about two feet from the top of the levee and the bottom of the High Street bridge and flowing very fast, taking trees along with it. We knew it was dangerous to be there, but I couldn't take my eyes off it, and the typewriter was getting heavier. So, I lifted up the typewriter and threw it into the river and let the river carry it away. Don't keep it if it's not useful, don't clutter up the house, and don't accept it if it's not wanted are lifelong lessons.

++++

Of course, there were bullies in our neighborhood. If my sisters or brothers were bullied, they would let me know because I always had their back. I hated to fight, but it made me angry that the bullies would beat up on my sisters or brothers. So, I would go and talk to them and tell them to stop even though they were usually older than me. If that didn't stop them, my anger clicked in, and I would take them down, punch them some, and grab them by their ears and beat their heads on the concrete a couple times.

For a while on Fifth Street, there was a group of five bullies who would taunt my brother and me when we were carrying afternoon newspapers. I told Dad about it, thinking he would go talk to their parents, but he said, "The next time fight them. Fight your own fights." They would lie in wait most every day and come out of their houses when we walked by, then they would come to the sidewalk and call us names and push us around. I had had enough and told them to meet me in the alley behind their houses to fight it out. I delivered a few more papers and told the lady in the last house what was going to happen and asked her to watch it with my brother from her back gate to make sure it was a fair fight. I cut through her backyard, and there the five guys were in the alley. I went out and they formed a circle around me. I told them, "This has to be a fair fight. I will fight each one of you one at a time. Who wants to be first?" They seemed to be as scared as I was, not believing I would actually take them on. The biggest, tallest, and oldest stepped toward me and I rushed at him, caught him off guard, knocked him to the ground. We scuffled a bit on the alley gravel, and I got on top of him and grabbed hold of his ears as firm as I could and started beating his head on the gravel as hard as I could. His buddies ran like hell. I was crying the whole time as my anger took over. I might have killed him if the lady and my brother didn't come out and pull me off him. I stood up as tall as I could. He ran like hell back to his house yelling something about his dad, but no one from that low class tribe ever bothered us again. The lessons I learned were to stand up for my sisters and brothers, to not be afraid to fight so long as I didn't start it, to grow up and be a man, and to fight for what is right and if people are getting hurt.

++++

All through grade school and my "playing Mass", I entered deeply into the parish church, St. Stephen's. I was fascinated initially by the ceremonies, the exquisite German stained glass windows, the hand-carved and painted Stations of the Cross, the Holy Day processions, the sacramental milestones, the good smelling clouds of incense, the goosebump-causing bells, the holiness, the sacredness, the mysteriousness of it all, the incomprehensible Latin, the needed prayer books – which didn't make it much more understandable – the large organ and the choir music. Eventually, I was able to serve, assisting at the beautiful white and gold Gothic main altar for Mass, Funerals, and Benediction. The building itself was built in the 1830's as the German Catholic church for the many immigrants drawn to the land and manufacturing in the Hamilton, Ohio area. It had been remodeled and expanded throughout the years into the neo-Gothic style, with a very tall vaulted and ribbed ceiling having faux marble pillars holding it all up. My whole family and ancestors had worshiped there for many years. My original ancestors in this country had helped pay for and build this Church, and there were many old spirits attached to it. I felt like I belonged there and was involved in something beyond me. It lifted me up. I felt very close to God, being appreciated and accepted. In prayer there, I could pour out my heart, feelings, pain, hurts and loneliness, and my yearning for something more, and leave them there as so many thousands had done before, believing God would figure it all out and it would be better sooner or later.

Franciscan Fathers and Brothers in their brown robes and white rope belts were the Pastors and Assistants through most of the long history of St. Stephen's, and they were fathers and brothers to me. I hung around there and helped and volunteered whenever I could. Early on, I began to develop an attraction to that religious lifestyle and being a Franciscan priest. This was no surprise to anyone who knew me. There was no pressure, but there were growing expectations.

A Priest Sexually Abuses Me

When I was thirteen, one priest took a particular "liking" to me. From the start, I was uncomfortable being alone around him. I had a new and strange feeling about him, and I tried to avoid him or serving for him. He looked at me strangely and always reeked of alcohol. Still, I said nothing to anyone. Friday and Saturday evenings I was assigned to serve at Benediction, and many times he would be the priest doing the prayers and ceremony. I used to stay for a short while after the service to clean up and put things away before I walked home. Then, he made his move one evening. As I was leaving the priest's sacristy he wanted to give me a hug, stinking of alcohol, squeezing me against him, and rubbing me against his erect penis. He made me promise to not say anything to anyone about what just happened, or he would tell my parents what I had done. I broke loose and walked home in the dark, feeling very afraid and totally insecure and disgusted and confused and ashamed and dirty and guilty. Why did that happen? What did I do to make him do that to me? What if he told my parents and said it was my fault? What would they do? I kept all this inside, living in fear and a darkness of not knowing. I said nothing to anyone.

This went on for six months at least, maybe a year, whenever he was there, and I never knew if he would be there. It got to where he would have me fondle his genitals. I felt caught and I had no choice. I had to do what he wanted or he would tell my parents. When my younger brother Ed got to the age where he could serve, we would walk to the Church together and serve Benediction together and then back home together. But when this priest would have Benediction, I would send my brother home alone immediately after Benediction so the priest wouldn't hurt him.

After much brooding about it, and not being able to get to sleep at night, I felt I had committed a mortal sin and needed to go to confession. But, I couldn't go and confess to the other priests in the parish, as they would know who I was. So, I waited until this priest was hearing Confessions and confessed my sin to him. The way he responded sounded like he had no involvement in the incident, like nothing had happened. I really wanted to talk to him about it – I had no one else. He quickly gave me a penance and absolution, and I was out of there. I went to Confession to him two more times, and then he told me to never come to confess to him again because he could not do my confession or give me absolution. Who was I supposed to go to? Was I being rejected? I said nothing to anyone during that time: such deep confusion, such deep loneliness, such deep feelings of being totally alone, and powerless and guilty.

I know why I never said anything to Dad or Mom. I didn't want to hurt them or the family. I was afraid Dad's impulsive rage would have commenced an immediate showdown at the Rectory; he might have threatened to kill that priest and make the incident public to the whole Parish. I know this because when I was six years old one of the neighborhood teenagers on the next street tried to rape me behind their garage. I wiggled loose and ran home to tell Dad and Mom. Dad turned a scarlet red that I hadn't seen before and shot out of the house, and I hid under the dining room table. We could hear him angrily shouting at the kid and his mother a block away. They moved away a month later.

The other things that would have happened: Dad would not have let me or my brothers or sisters near the Church anymore, convinced all the priests and brothers were that way and perhaps pull us out of the parish and the school. Mom's deep faith in the priests and the Church would have been shaken to its core. Our whole family would have been torn away from St. Stephen's school and Church, and perhaps the Catholic Church. For me personally, I would have been forbidden to become a Franciscan and a priest. Before the incident, I had been making preparations to enter the seminary the next year. I was extremely afraid that all that would be taken away, and it would be my fault. So, I said nothing and kept it all inside me, trying to push it down, having to make an even greater effort to seem happy, and all the while becoming even more alone and lonely and guilty and depressed.

It amazes me how, even now, fifty-four years later, that remembering and feeling what happened can still cause such deep disgust and hatred and anger.

High School Seminary Years

After I turned 14, the official home visits with the family, the testing, and the interviews of the parents by the Franciscan priests became more earnest in anticipation of my entering the high school St. Francis Seminary boarding school in the Fall to begin my studies for the priesthood. As something I had been preparing for inside myself for many years, it wasn't a big deal at the time. Devoting all my time towards that goal, being able to be closer to my God, gaining a lot of independence and some separation from family and surroundings, growing up with a large group of boys my own age, and the challenge of the studies and the rules were all something I wanted – to see if it all fit with me and if I fit with it. The buildings and grounds were not unfamiliar to me since a Franciscan priest, a good friend Mom and Dad grew up with, would take some of us to the minor seminary in Cincinnati, Ohio in the summer to swim in the large outdoor pool there.

I knew the idea of my becoming a Franciscan was not something Dad was totally keen on because he said, "Why don't you think about becoming a Diocesan priest? The Franciscans have to take a vow of poverty and can't keep any money. The Diocesans can keep their own money and become Bishops." In his past there was some bad blood between the Franciscan priests at St. Stephen's and his dad and his grandfather that I never knew all about.

That first year, there were 250 students in the seminary and about 70 in our freshman class, which was quite a lot and a bit crowded, but I tried to adjust well. Even in the study hall which was supposed to be silent at all times, watched over from the back of the large room by a professor on an elevated platform, I found it difficult to study and focus my attention with that many guys all around me. We were awakened each morning by a priest clanging a loud school bell through the large dormitory rooms filled with bunk beds. Then, after a quick washing up, we had devout early morning prayers and Mass followed by breakfast, then off to our first classes of the day. All of the classes were taught by Franciscan priests and Brothers who also double-dutied as coaches, groundskeepers, mechanics, tutors, carpenters, and disciplinarians; one even taught radio controlled airplane making and flying.

The food was prepared by some Mexican nuns and some local ladies assisting them in the basement kitchens, and frankly, it was terrible. For instance, eggs for breakfast were baked in stainless steel baking pans until they were way beyond done to the point where we could lift up one edge from the pan and lift up all twelve eggs in a single solid sheet of egg rubber. Vegetables were all cooked to mush, and sections of sausage were deep-fried to almost crispy through and through thus gaining them the moniker of "Rhinos." Needless to say, I lost a lot of weight. My Dad wrote the seminary a scathing letter (he was well known for his letters). I never got to read it, but the head of the seminary told me they had received a letter from him and chastised me about sharing my opinion of the food with my father. That came from a kid who grew up eating anything. Meals were served family-style to each table of ten or twelve, so if I couldn't eat something, one of the other students was glad to finish it off. Mid-morning, during a break in classes, large aluminum baking trays stacked with day-old (week-old?) doughnuts and danish would show up in the recreation room, or on the patio right off of it, to be attacked and devoured by those lucky enough to be at the front of the line or by those ravenous enough to fight survival-of-the-fittest style for them. It truly was a punishment for the class held over by the teacher.

Each one of us was part of a weekly rotating work crew, and this meant daily cleaning of the many restrooms, the large shower rooms , or dust mopping all the long corridors, or dining hall, or dorm rooms, or classrooms, or slaving outside to keep up the grounds, and so on. I learned to take orders from the older student crew chief, how to do a lot of things such as buffing and polishing terrazzo floors, and a sense of responsibility for the job and for others on the crew.

Every weekday evening, we were in study hall for two hours. Saturday afternoons, after a morning of chores, were free for informal sports, hiking in or beyond the many acres of the wooded property, searching for fossils in the stream bed down below, glee club practice, or other activities we were involved in.

One activity I really wanted to be involved in was to learn to play a musical instrument. I asked our music teacher if he could line me up for an appointment with the local teacher who would come to the seminary once a week to give piano lessons. He did, and my first piano lesson went something like this. He looked at both of my hands, palm and back, and pronounced, "Your fingers are too short and too fat. I will not teach you the piano." Getting over that rejection took quite a while, but then I asked our music teacher if he could line me up a violin teacher for lessons. He did, and my first violin lesson went like this. He looked at my hands and said, "Your fingers are too fat and too short. You will never be able to play a musical instrument."

I was devastated, but didn't give up. I thought I might be able to play the clarinet since Dad played it in his high school band and still had the silver clarinet he played. I asked our music teacher if he would teach me how to play it since he played the clarinet. He lent me a mouthpiece with a reed, showed me how to moisten the reed and attach it to the black mouthpiece and how to make a sound. He told me to come back when I could make a song. I tried and tried every chance I got, but finally had to show him I couldn't do it. He suggested I give up on musical instruments and try to sing in the glee club when my voice finished changing. I tried out a couple times my freshman year and my sophomore year, but it wasn't until my junior year that he accepted me as a bass-baritone in the club. He also chose me to be in a quartet and a small ensemble. We won some local competitions and got First Place medals, and then went onto the State competitions. The glee club won First Place, and the quartet and ensemble won Second Place. I was so happy and proud, and decided to play my vocal chords since nobody could say they were too short or too fat.

I ended up taking two years of private vocal technique lessons from him even though he was not a patient man and demanded perfection. At one lesson as he was strenuously trying to get me to practice correct breathing techniques, I said, "If I do it that way, I feel like I'm going to vomit." He said, "Well, vomit a couple times. You'll get over it." I remained his student for the whole two years.

Later on, I thought that perhaps the piano and violin teachers were testing my resolve to learn those instruments; and that if I had tried harder and insisted on it, my passion to play would have convinced them to teach me. I resolved to never take no for an answer, to keep trying to find a way, and never believe I couldn't do something if I was willing to work hard enough for it.

One of the requirements of being in the seminary was that we each had to have a Spiritual Director chosen by us from a list of available ones. This was so we had someone to talk to at least every month about how things were going, about how our praying was developing, what spiritual books we were reading, and to go to Confession. I liked mine. He was a good listener, kind and gentle, and challenging enough to keep me on the right track. At one of our sessions freshman year he asked, "What's up? It seems like there's something deeper on your mind." That was all I needed to start crying and sharing what that priest had done to me at our parish, and my extreme fear of my parents finding out, and the shame and guilt and hatred and anger I had. I had never shared this with anyone, and was shaking when I shared it with him, but it felt good to get it out -- like lancing a severely infected wound. He asked if I would be willing to remove that from the confidentiality of Confession so something could be done about it, so he could see to it that no other boy was abused by that priest, that it was not my fault and I had done nothing wrong; he would never use my name, and no one would ever know it was me, and my parents would never know.

Reluctantly, I agreed, mainly because I didn't want another boy to go through what I went through and was going through, and I gave him the priest's name. The next day he called me into his office, and told me he talked to his boss who was the head (the Provincial) of the all the Franciscans in the Cincinnati Province, and that the priest was removed that morning from St. Stephen parish in Hamilton, and that he would be placed in an administration job and would never again have Mass in any parish or ever have any contact with any boys or even be allowed near any children ever again. I thanked him for handling it the way he did, and I walked out of his office feeling happier and relieved and a little proud of myself.

After religious Sunday morning Services, the afternoons were scheduled with organized team sports of seasonal baseball, football, basketball, and the less team sports inclined students played volleyball, dodgeball, handball, and tennis, which were more my style. The moniker for all this was "forced fun." Once a month was Visitors Sunday, when parents and families could come and visit with us. I watched out a window waiting full of hope for mine to come. Mom and Dad and the brothers and sisters came whenever they could and brought goodies from home that could be stashed in my locker. Those afternoons were fun as I played with the little ones and heard news of home; but each time, it took days to get over the homesickness.

Most of the time, I was lonely despite being part of the group. My closest friends were Hispanic and Anglo students from the Southwest who were also lonely being so far from home. We hung out together all the time and eventually had to be warned by the disciplinarian about having "particular friendships." There was never any explanation of what that fully meant, but we took it to mean that we were getting too close and perhaps exclusive – which we weren't. There was another student who came from quite far off who became my close friend. We would take walks through the woods together and sit there and talk and have a great time. One afternoon I halfway jokingly tried to get him to show me his penis so we could compare sizes. He froze and started calling me a queer and a faggot and ran back up to the building. I was so pissed at myself and hoped I didn't lose a friend. I walked back up to the building, showered and cleaned up, and went to stand in line for dinner. All of the students in the corridor started to laugh at me and point at me and derogatorily called me "Faggot" and "Queer." Even those I thought were my friends took part in shaming me and attacking me like a pack of rabid dogs, and there was no getting away. After taking it for a while hoping the doors to the dining hall would open, I decided to skip dinner and slinked away and went to the chapel. With my face in my hands I cried more alone than ever. I realized I had not only lost one friend, but I had lost most of them.

The name calling didn't stop in the corridor that evening as some of the more vicious dogs would whisper "Faggot" and "Queer" loud enough to be heard by others on our way to classes and in the recreation hall. I would remove myself and go to the chapel and pour out my shame and hurt in prayer and crying. Later that day, I made an appointment with my spiritual director to do some damage control, thinking he should know what was going on. After I told him what I had done and about what the students were doing, and that I was terrified of being expelled, he said that the faculty was not aware of what was going on, or he would have heard about it already, and that I should not worry about being expelled. If the faculty hears about it, and if someone wants to make it an issue, he would handle it.

As for me, I clammed up from then on, shut out everyone, hid in my studies and books, would not share my opinions or thoughts if asked, became my own prisoner inside never to share or express any of my feelings. I became very aloof and very strict on the outside, like a granite statue with no expression, not allowing anyone to touch me, not allowing myself to give anyone cause to expel me, to make fun of me, or call me names ever again. No one could have been a more perfect seminarian. This severely changed my life, and it became who I was through the rest of the thirteen years of study and college and into the priesthood.

Music, studies, playing gloveless handball, walking in the woods alone and spending time alone in prayer closer to my Lord became all I was interested in doing. Glee Club practices and performances, getting private vocal technique lessons, and listening to all the classical music as loudly as I could from the vast record collection in the music room were the best ways for me to express my feelings and passions without involving anyone else. Studies on every subject taught with a focus on two years of German (language, grammar, and literature, even the old script), and English (literature and especially poetry and writing short stories) were my concentration. I was quite good at playing handball with one other student and it was a great physical workout summer and winter.

I also developed intestinal problems or "nervous stomach" as it was called, and had some pretty strong bouts with the flu. Once, I had a very high fever that wouldn't come down for a few days. I got delirious and shaking, but do remember a doctor being called in to the Infirmary and some talk of being sent to the hospital. Instead, the doctor told them to take off all my clothes and to douse me with rubbing alcohol to see if that would force the fever down. The shock forced me to pass out, but I did wake up the next morning feeling totally weak and a little better and with the infirmarian sitting next to the bed. He said he had been there all night keeping an eye on me. Since I couldn't remember much from the day before, he told me what was done and how serious it was and that I would be in bed for a week until I got all my strength back. Later I found out they never called my parents to let them know.

On Thanksgiving, Christmas, and Easter, I was allowed to go home for a few days during the vacation time. Feeling sorry for all the students from the Southwest who couldn't go home during those times, I would invite some to come home with me and share the holiday with our family, with my parents' permission of course. The guys really appreciated it, especially being around my budding sisters. On returning to the seminary after one Easter, we were informed that one of our classmates had committed suicide by hanging himself in the shower room. He was a jokester, always happy and trying to make us laugh and help us in every way. We just couldn't imagine it, and found it unbelievable that he would kill himself, although I was not unfamiliar with the feelings and thoughts that would force him to make that decision if it was intentional. I was particularly saddened and upset because I could have invited him home with me for Easter, but did not.

++++

During summer vacations, one of my brothers had to vacate his bed so I would have a place to sleep with twelve others in the small house the family had moved to while I was away. In fact, I didn't know they had moved until I was dropped off for Thanksgiving vacation at the house I grew up in on Buckeye Street. No one was home, and the house was empty. It was disheartening, to say the least, even though I knew they were going to move, but I didn't know when or where or how far. The neighbor across the street kindly let me use her phone so I could call them. Mom very apologetically came to pick me up.

The reason for the move was that our neighborhood was going down, there were more and more houses converting to rental apartments, and crime was increasing in the area. One of Dad's friends was a realtor, and he spoke with him about a house with a very large yard on the southern outskirts of town. The price was right, the payments were low enough, and it was far away. Mom didn't want to move. She didn't want the hassle and disruption of moving, of leaving everything she had been familiar with her whole life, of removing the kids from school, and leaving the parish where she and all of us had grown up. She could understand the reasoning all too well and saw that the area was not the best place to raise the kids, and she eventually agreed that moving was the best thing to do. The new Catholic parish was too far away from the new house for them to walk to, but it did have a school. Dad and my brothers remodeled the old house into two apartments, and he rented them for a while, using those payments to make payments on the new house. In fact, my oldest brother Dan and his new wife moved into one of the apartments. Dad showed a lot of foresight in pushing to move the family in the right direction. Yes, the new house was a little smaller, but Dad saw that as the kids moved out and got on with their own lives, it would be just right.

++++

One summer, I got a job at the Capri Motel in my hometown folding laundry, making beds, cleaning the pool and adjusting the chemicals, keeping the landscaping up, and whatever needed to be done. I had that job until one day I was told to change the words on the marquee along the highway to read: "Let Us Arrange Your Next Affair." My parents made me quit the next day.

++++

Dad tried to teach me how to drive when I turned sixteen by driving me to the cemetery, then I got behind the wheel of our old green station wagon and practiced. He was a nervous wreck, telling me not to hit the tombstones when I didn't turn the curves tightly enough. Back in town, he let me drive around the city block we lived on, and afraid I wasn't going to stop at the sign, he yelled "STOP!" and shoved his foot through the glove compartment. He was a mess when we got home and swore he would never take me out to practice driving again. I was glad.

A Plane Crash First Responder

One sunny, Saturday afternoon of late May when I was seventeen driving back home, I noticed a single engine plane which seemed to stand still in the sky, just for a second, then it plummeted straight down towards the cornfields behind our house. After I got home as quickly as I could, I told Mom and Dad what happened and to call 911, and I took off running through the cornfields towards where the plane should be. Perhaps half a mile back there I could see the total wreckage with the nose of the plane buried in the field and the fuselage a little elevated off the ground. No one else was running to help. I ran up to it looking for survivors, but there was no movement and no sounds. The scene was very gruesome, total carnage, and it was very hard for me to determine exactly how many passengers there were, but I was able to guess that there were five young men all smashed together and intermingled. Without touching any of them I didn't notice any of them breathing or moving. It was an insignia outside the plane on the ground from the local Catholic high school which clued me into the possibility that they might be Catholic, and perhaps it was my being in total shock after seeing such carnage that impelled me to take off running and running as fast as I could to the nearest church rectory to find a priest to administer the Last Rites for these young guys. Fortunately, the priest answered the door, and between breaths I told the priest exactly how to get to the wreck. I crumbled to the ground to catch my breath, then knowing there was nothing else I could do, I walked slowly, crying all the way home while hearing police, ambulance, and firetruck sirens in the distance on their way to the wreck.

One very sad part of all this was that on the News that evening the crash victims were identified without being certain that each of their family members was notified. We knew this because, to our total disbelief, one of the victims was the brother of my sister Ann's date that evening. There was no way Greg could have been informed or known what happened. We all hoped and prayed that they did not listen to the radio on their way home. When they returned to the house later about 9pm, as had been planned we all ran upstairs, while Dad feigned interest in Greg's car and wisely asked to look at the keys and took them, then told Greg that his parents were trying to get in touch with him and he should call them right away. Somehow we got Greg home right away. The news said that all five of the young men had just graduated from Badin Catholic High School, one of the boy's father owned the airport, and his son who was a pilot got the group together to celebrate their graduation with a ride in his plane. Of course, there were theories of how the crash could have happened, from the plane being overloaded, to it running out of fuel, to the fuel line getting plugged, and so on. Nothing could assuage the deep grief, pain, and sorrow of those families and the whole town which grieved the loss of such fine young men who had so much life to look forward to. In all, that was the kind of deeply emotional scene that my reality nightmares were rooted in.

Draft Card and Vietnam War

When I turned eighteen during senior year, as was every other eighteen year old man, I was required to register for the Selective Service with the government and to get a draft card. 1968 is when the Draft Lottery was reinstituted to fill the ranks of the military to fight in the Vietnam War. There had been plenty in the news for the last four years about the Vietnam War, and how the United States was handling its involvement, enough to convince me it was an unjust war, we had no business being there, and that I could never fight in or support the war.

Knowing I could never kill another person, I actually started looking at maps and which routes I could take to escape to Canada if I needed to flee as a conscientious objector. It turned out that the seminary administration and I filled out forms for a ministerial exemption, and it was granted with a draft card stating such an exemption.

When the draft lottery actually took place, each day of the year was pulled up randomly, and everyone born on that date would most certainly expect to be sent to Vietnam. The first date pulled was my birthday, and I kept my exemption draft card in my wallet with me at all times for the next fifteen years. I heard of so many of my grade school classmates and seminary high school students who had left who were sent to fight in Vietnam, and many of them never returned. There were three choices for me: stay in the seminary (continuing my choice to serve the people and my God), join the Vietnam War protests and be arrested (but it was not who I was to be public with my aversion to the war), or get to Canada as soon as possible (the adventure of a new life was appealing, but I couldn't leave everything I was familiar with or bring shame to my family). Even though I had thought of leaving the seminary during very lonely and stressful times, now I felt I needed to stay and choose it once again. These were very turbulent times.

++++

During High School, boarding there and only going home for Thanksgiving, Christmas, Easter and for the summer, I was basically growing up apart from my sisters and brothers as they were from me. Later in life they reflected:

> *"You were gone the majority of my life."*
> *"I have often felt you were robbed of your childhood."*
> *"I remember going to the seminary on Sundays once a month for donuts – and to see you."*
> *"I remember visiting you at St. Francis. I always thought it was pretty cool but I could not understand how you could do it. I admired the discipline and devotion."*
> *"I really wished I had gotten to know you better on a different level. I never really got to know you until later in life."*
> *"I regret not getting to 'grow up' with you. I still don't think it was fair plucking you out of the world as a high school freshman. Way too many things we did not get to share and see together."*
> *"You learned about 'family dynamics' so much later in life than should have been possible."*

I graduated in June of 1968 with respectable grades, but not with any special recognition or Summa Cum Laude honors for me. However, it was an excellent education with much credit to the professors and staff, and I did a lot of growing up into a man there.

Chapter Two
College Years

Racial tensions and the resulting riots and burning of the city were breaking out in sections of Detroit when I moved to Duns Scotus College seminary in Southfield, Michigan. The turmoil and burning and destruction and looting were on the news everyday, and I could see the smoke whenever I left the college to go downtown, which was not very often. Here, too, all the classes were taught by Franciscan priests. This first year we were Lay Seminarians and were housed in the newest section of the huge building. It was the first time in my life when I had my own semi-private room; and when my first roommate decided to leave the seminary, and the second was asked to leave, I had a private room to myself for the rest of the year. Despite the reverberating noise and talking in the uncarpeted hallway, I could concentrate on my studies and reading and learn more how to pray even with distractions.

Something totally new to me was being able to choose which courses I wanted to study for each semester, so long as they fit the basic curriculum and totaled at least a minimum number of credit hours and were approved by the academic advisor. Each semester, I took an extra course for more credit hours. We all had our monthly assigned rotating chores, but if we wanted to get a baseball game together, or a hockey team, or a handball partner, we did that on our own. There was no "forced fun." There was no study hall, no standing in line, no one looking over our shoulders. We were required to participate in morning prayer, Mass, classes and evening prayer. Otherwise, the responsibility was on me to swim or sink.

I used to help the Brother with a heavy Eastern European accent in the orchard, and he taught me horticulture and trimming of apple trees. That and doing extra jobs and snow shoveling were part of a work study program to help my parents pay for the tuition, room and board.

Honestly, I don't know how they could afford my education in the minor seminary or during this year with ten children still at home. The $1,000 in my bank didn't last long, but I suspect they were helped by the Pastor at St. Stephen's and some generous friends.

The building itself was a wonder of architecture with a definite Italian monastery flavor. It was built of red brick, red clay tile roofs, had corridors with arched windows and brick walls and red tile floors, huge vaulted refectory, featured an extensive open two-story library with shelves to the ceiling and many ancient books some dating to the 1500s, small individual living cells, and a most beautiful chapel to rival any rich parish church. The chapel was my go-to place where I would sit for hours in the oak choir stalls. Here, I would learn Gregorian chants for the Sunday high Mass, listen to the organist practice, sing in the Schola choir, pray and trust God with my life, marvel at the predominantly blue stained glass windows, and be awed by the huge marble high altar covered by the tall marble baldacchino which separated the students and friars in the stalls from the laity in the benches.

Even though the whole building was a bit on the dark side, it fit who I was at the time, and I liked it there. My depression was getting worse, and I took to worrying a lot, but I repressed that with even greater determination and resolve. One nice break to all that was my friendship with a very good looking classmate who would ask me to work out with him, lifting weights and wrestling with him, after which we would lie on the mats all sweaty and talk late into the night. We never carried it any further, but I yearned for it and hoped we would.

After the first year, I had the option of staying for a second year as a lay seminarian, or going to the Novitiate for a year of intense study in the life of St. Francis and the Franciscan way of life in religious community and prayer. I chose the Novitiate, mainly because of my family's financial situation. Most all of my classmates opted for the second year.

Novitiate

Entrance into the Novitiate was preceded by a weeklong retreat. Then we were bussed to a late 1800s monastery in Oldenburg, Indiana where I was invested with the Franciscan "habit" on the Feast of the Assumption August 1969. The habit was a brown robe tied at the waist with a white rope having three knots signifying poverty, chastity, and obedience in one of the rope ends. A detached hood or cowl was slipped over the head to complete the uniform.

I felt a definite calling by the Lord into this religious community: a band of spiritual brothers, something beyond us. This was the beginning. I felt set apart, and ready to start the instruction. That lasted all through my Franciscan life, but the bubbles began to burst soon after this graduation to the next stage of my formation and the investiture. Since I was the only one of the novices studying for the priesthood, and following tradition, I was made the prefect of the class with added responsibilities. When the novice master or the assistant master of novices were not around, the class was supposed to check with me if something was needed, and I was supposed to coordinate with the kitchen, check to see that the assigned chores were actually being done, and then to report (snitch) to the novice master what had happened while he was gone. While not setting myself above the others, I soon felt excluded from the group, alone again, not supported, not belonging. My understandings, my goals, my ideals, my reality would need readjustment. Talking with the novice master and my spiritual director helped a lot because they shared what their long lives had been like as Franciscans and as Priests. I asked the novice master how to become a Franciscan, and he said, "Be the best follower of Christ you can be, and you will turn out brown" (an allusion to the brown habit). I was encouraged to read all I could about the life of Christ, the life of St. Francis, the writings of Francis and what others had written about him, the histories of the Order, and the history of the Province, and especially Scripture.

With some of the novices, those who were very serious about their vocation, and following the rules and instructions, I felt a kinship and sharing. Some other novices totally isolated themselves from the group. One even spent the whole year writing out in longhand the entire Bible. This was a reaction to some of the other novices who disregarded nearly everything that came from the novice master. In one way or another, they were able to get alcohol and food supplied to them from the outside. One even rigged a pulley system from his room window to the sidewalk below and then hauled up the delivery in a large basket. He also set up a hot plate in his room to cook. The beer and alcohol were lowered into an ice cold well in the basement. Of course, this behavior was strictly forbidden.

This entire disregard for Franciscan ideals disheartened me, and I complained to the novice master about it a couple times, and he ignored what I said. Shortly before Thanksgiving, all of it came to a head when at one of our daily classes, the novice master, Fr. Edwin, totally exploded like a volcano with fire and brimstone. "I have had enough of you! As far as I am concerned, you can all just go hang yourselves! I will no longer have classes for you! I will no longer have morning Mass or prayers from the Office with you! You are not required to do anything! You already do your own thing anyhow! You can go kill yourselves for all I care! You can go to Mass at the parish church or another Mass or not at all! You are the most immature infants I have ever had! You are on your own!" And he stormed out of the room his face bright red in a rage. I was so angry at his rampage that I walked right out of the room and followed him to his room. His door slammed shortly before I got there, but I started to knock on it as loudly as I could, pounding on it until he swung open the door and yelled, "What do you want?!" Trembling a little, I said loudly, "You just called us a group of immature infants, but for you to do what you just did shows me you are more immature than any of us and the most immature person that I have ever met!" Enraged even more, he slammed the door in my face. I was afraid I would be expelled.

Fr. Edwin did continue with his regular Mass for those novices who wanted to go to his. Maybe half of them did. Perhaps I was a bit too emboldened after my confrontation with Edwin, but I also started to call him out during his homilies at Mass. Politely, I would raise my hand when he was speaking. He would acknowledge me, and I would ask him how he came up with those conclusions (because it sounded like a bunch of b.s. to me), and he would explain or rethink the statement. He also got to inviting the others to ask questions, and the homilies became discussions among ourselves – so much more meaningful.

He kept to his word, and basically lived his own life. The assistant novice master took over our instruction. At one time, he had been the Chancellor of the Archdiocese of Santa Fe and recounted many great stories. The Southwest stories and the Santa Fe stories and the Chancellor stories enchanted me, and I decided I would make it a goal of mine to have the job he had. Eventually, the novice master would ask some of the class if they wanted to go on a hike in the countryside with him. I was not included in the invitation. So, I lived my own life taking hikes by myself into the hills behind a local farmhouse. I found a quiet and peaceful grove of walnut trees from which I could look down on the steepled town and would sit there for hours thinking and praying. One day, as I was exploring around there, I found a bed of fossils that had been exposed by some recent erosive rains. Imagining myself to be a paleontologist I found some hard sticks and began to carefully expose the fossils from the hard clay even more. What a treasure trove it was with many different kinds of extinct sea life. One cone-shaped fossil was easily six feet long with a diameter of two feet on one end and tapering down to a dull point on the other. I looked it up in a fossil book back at the library and found it to be a large crinoid. Excavating it completely and transporting it back to the monastery became an obsession for me, a strenuous and muscle building chore, and just plain something to do.

Despite, or perhaps because of, my intense reading and study and rigorously following the rules, I found myself feeling alone most of the time and very lonely. I did become good friends with one other novice, an Apache from Arizona. He felt more alone than I did and terribly missed his family and tribe. There was a psychic connection between us, and mostly we did not talk, but still knew what the other was feeling and thinking. He had a deep connection with a mysterious world, and he would teach me about the Native American traditions, beliefs, ceremonies, and spirits of his world and the Apache tribe he came from. Somehow, I could understand what he said and what he taught, and I could put myself in the small village in Arizona as he described it, being transported into an existence I had known nothing about. He was a very spirit-filled man, and it nearly broke my spirit when he told me he had to leave. His parents and tribe had written him letters threatening to totally disown him if he took vows as a Franciscan. They would see it as a rejection of their family and tribe if he became a member of the Franciscan family and tribe. After much thought, he decided he had to leave and to go back to be with them – he could not live being cut off from them. It hurt, but I understood.

Again more alone and more lonely, and bored as hell, I continued to cut the grass, weed the flower beds, tend to the rose garden, learn how to maintain the pool and use the right chemicals, learn how to help with plumbing issues, volunteer more for the kitchen cooking meals and washing dishes, and to learn to bake breads and cakes and cookies in the bakery above the kitchen.

A local potato farmer and apple orchard owner named Tony would frequently ask the novice master for help, and I would always volunteer. The harvesting was hard, dirty work on a crew of men and boys picking up freshly tilled potatoes out of the great smelling earth and bagging the spuds. There was great comradeship with lots of kidding and laughter, and I loved the lightheartedness and exhaustion at the end of each day when my pay was a bag of potatoes to lug back to the kitchen until the cook said, "NO MORE!"

There were about twenty bee hives out in the orchard, and the farmer taught me how to open the supers, smoke the bees to calm them before I removed the frames filled with honey, brush the bees back into the supers, and insert another cleaned frame in the slot. Then, I took a hot knife to skim the surface sealant on the honeycomb to release the honey. After the extractor whirled the frames for a while, the fresh honey would run down the inside to a spout which would empty in a clean stainless steel bucket. Never have I had such wonderful honey like that before or since. Sent home with two pint jars of honey, I gave one to the cook and kept one for myself for whenever I needed a sweet taste of sunshine.

Picking a variety of apples for hours and hours was hard work too, but not quite so dirty. And every day Tony's wife made the best apple pie and served the best grape wine that warmed me up for the chilly walk back to the monastery right before sunset. With my experience the year before at Duns Scotus, I would go over and help him trim the apple trees all winter long. At the end of the day, the offer of dessert and wine was always accepted. When early summer came, he asked me to help him clean out his huge underground fruit cellar with the vaulted brick ceiling that smelled like fermenting apples and rotten potatoes. Going through each crate, we sorted the good apples from the mushy fermented ones, and the rotten potatoes from the still firm ones, with the intention of taking what was still good to Cincinnati for the Sisters of the Poor who ran a nursing home and retirement home for the poor. His herd of cattle would come to the fence to observe and get the thrown out tasty morsels. So, Tony and I started having some fun by throwing the rotten apples at the animals and watching them lick the sweet cider apples off each other with their long sandpaper tongues. I sure was happy to get permission for the trip to the real world of Cincinnati and away from the monastery to deliver what we could salvage to the Sisters. It was my first time in almost a year away from the difficult living situation in the too small German village.

Also, I found a "greenhouse" in a small space that had been excavated under the attached old parish church. It hadn't been used in years, but still had the shelves, trays, pots, boxes of compressed peat discs to start seeds, and "Gro" fluorescent lighting. It was damp and cold, especially after New Years when I started to plant flower seeds to mature for the Spring outdoor planting, and I had to crawl on my knees or sit down in the dirt to work there. Not ten feet from me was the large brick covered tomb of Franz Josef – the founder of the parish – enshrined under the floor of the sanctuary above. I used to talk to him, but he never carried on the conversation.

The evenings and nights were the hardest, and when I was most lonely and depressed. With all my work, I quickly wore out my only pair of jeans and decided to make my own jeans by deconstructing the old torn and ripped pair, using the parts as a pattern, and tediously machine-sewing some green Army canvas I found in the tailor shop. It took me a month of sewing, and the fabric was a lot stiffer and uncomfortable, but the jeans were warm in the winter and lasted through the next eight months. It was stupid, but it was an escape from the boredom. I learned to tailor and sew better and to gulp my pride enough to avoid asking for another pair of jeans. The room next to the tailor shop was a large classroom with a cabinet containing a stereo record player and about fifty classical recordings which I listened to mostly every day as loudly as I could. My favorite quickly became Saint Saens Organ Symphony. It calmed my spirit and gave me hope on such dark lonely nights both inside and outside as I watched the lone headlights inching down the country road in the rain and into the village.

The Provincial came for visitation. He talked with all the novices individually. The first thing he asked me was, "Are you planning on switching over to the Brothers and not seeking to be ordained also?" I told him I had considered switching about a year ago, but that I have definitely decided to work toward the priesthood. He said that all the reports about me had been good, and he saw no reason why I shouldn't continue as a cleric, that I have the capability, and he thought I'd do a good job of it.

In August of 1970 I professed "simple temporary vows" of poverty, chastity, and obedience for three years with no hesitation, and then headed north to Duns Scotus again.

During the whole year of Novitiate, we had no access to TV or radio, and thus no access to the news. The lack of distraction felt good, but not knowing what was going on in the rest of the world, other than what I could glean from letters, was a real deprivation for me, especially regarding the Vietnam War. The war was still front and center when I got back to college. The devastation, the killing and the carnage over there were too harsh to be believable. The war protests were still going on here, and some of my fellow friars even drove to D.C. in 1971 for the march on Washington.

It took a while and some effort for me to get back into the groove of college life and studying the groundwork of theology and extensive philosophy. After trying and studying very hard, I still only got mostly "Cs", even on the courses I enjoyed the most like humanities and music, English literature and Scripture, six semesters of ancient to contemporary philosophy, and four semesters of psychology. I took sixteen to eighteen credit hours each semester. Of course, I still made time for my vocal technique classes at the end of the class day all six semesters. My voice teacher, retired from the Metropolitan Opera and an excellent accompanist, mentioned that I could leave the Franciscans and the priesthood goal, and move on to the Cincinnati Conservatory of Music. He said I was a fine lyric baritone with perfect pitch. I did not want to give up on my goal, and I would not have had the money on my own to make such a move. I just didn't think I was good enough or as good as he thought I was, and didn't have the self-confidence.

Each January, we were to take a month of intensive independent study on our own, directed by a faculty member, and then present our results to the faculty at the end. Once again, I took it way too seriously, while most of the other students proclaimed it to be "Winter Sports Month", a month of ice hockey, downhill skiing, and cross country skiing. I couldn't understand how they could do intense study while they were outside playing all day. Also, I couldn't understand why I wouldn't allow myself to be outside with them and enjoy playing. I was afraid I wouldn't have enough time to get the study done and then fail, which I did one January. Perhaps the projects I chose were too much to fit into the month, such as tracing the complete history of and implications of "Volk" in Germany. Perhaps I was afraid of being chosen last for the teams.

After two years of high school at St. Francis Seminary, my brother Ed decided to give the Franciscan life a try as a Brother. The Brothers program was at Duns Scotus at the time, and it sure was good to see Ed around the building. I could usually find him in the garage repairing the car fleet. His director was very demanding of him and verbally abusive, and that was very hard for Ed to take. Sometimes, he would come to my room for beer and pretzels and talk. After a while, he just couldn't take it any longer; thinking that if that's what his life as a Brother would be like, he didn't want any part of it. So he left, and I sure did miss him.

I still had my share of the rotating chores of dusting and cleaning the building (one building with many wings all connected), washing windows, doing dishes, mopping and polishing the floors, waxing and burnishing the terrazzo floors in the chapel, and I got more involved in learning to cook institutional style. Each year, I would put on a big German menu with German beer on tap, but I never got down the knack of making dumplings which, after enough beer, were used as baseballs and bounced off the walls of the dining hall. At breakfast one day, one very intelligent philosophy professor came into the student break room to ask me if I would teach him how to make his toast. Their cook was off sick, and he didn't have the slightest clue.

++++

There were two very significant friendships I developed over those three years. Steve was a year older than me, but we had the same ideals and study habits and prayer habits. We spent a lot of time together and became very close. For the first time in my life I felt I could actually say I loved another man. Then he got sick. He showed me the sores under his arms which got progressively worse. I tried to encourage him to go see a doctor about whatever it was, but he wanted to wait and see if they got any better after applying a number of salves. He lost energy and a lot of weight and then decided to go to the doctor who put him in the hospital right away. I never saw him again. Numerous times I tried to go see him, but I was told he did not want any visitors. Then I was told his parents did not want anyone to visit him. I kept holding onto the hope that he was alright and getting better. When he died (probably of leukemia), I just could not accept it. How could someone die at 23 years old? How could God let this happen? How could God not listen to my prayers? And another first for me: Was there actually a God at all? The funeral was extremely tough on me, and I sobbed all through it. There I was -- alone and empty.

++++

The other friendship was with Tom, and it happened kind of suddenly. After a very nice Feast Day meal at which wine flowed freely, the Master of Clerics asked me to help an intoxicated Tom to his room. I did, but he didn't want to go to his room. He wanted to go to my room which was directly across the corridor from his. After he flopped on my bed, I was leaving to go back to the festivities when he grabbed my arm and pulled me to sit down on the bed. Then he grabbed my head and started to kiss me, and I began kissing him. All kinds of feelings started to explode in me. I had never kissed a man before. He was a very attractive and well-built Hispanic man from the Southwest who I tried not to notice before. I'd thought I could never be in his league, so we just passed each other in the corridor or in and out of classes.

Because he couldn't remember anything the next day, he asked me what had happened the evening before, and I told him the story about his getting drunk and my helping him to his room and my room and that we kissed, nothing more. He thanked me, apologized, and said it wouldn't happen again. And it didn't, until about two weeks later, when he had been drinking again, and I found him in my room again, and we kissed again, and my feelings exploded again. A student in the room next to his got suspicious and jealous and began to stalk me wherever I went. Again, I was afraid that he would tell the master of clerics or the administration, and I would be asked to leave. My confessor was a wise elderly priest who would absolve me each time, and told me it was natural. I never could shake off the other creepy student and totally ignored him. (I strongly suspected that the creepy stalker snitched on Tom to get rid of him.) When Tom decided to leave the Franciscans because he acknowledged what he really wanted, we talked a lot about allowing each other to be free or perhaps leaving together; but the expectations I put on myself, and others put on me, and I had been living with since I was young, forced me to stay. My heart ripped in two when he left, and my half was forced deep into the cave of the worst depression and anger at myself and loneliness and being alone I had ever been in.

I wasn't possessive of him. It was just too hard for me to deal with myself. We stayed in touch for a while, then lost contact. Fifteen years later, when I heard he was living in San Francisco and dying of AIDS we spoke on the phone a couple times, and I drove all the way there from Albuquerque to visit with him. For final directions to his place, I called and spoke to his friend taking care of him. He told me Tom had just slipped into a coma the night before, and he didn't think Tom would want me to see him that way. I asked him to give Tom a kiss for me and hung up the payphone. It was a downcast and lonely twenty hour drive back to Albuquerque. In the weekend newspaper obituaries, I read that Tom had died the day after I was there to visit. Since the funeral was to be here in Albuquerque, I went to the visitation and sat in the back of the mortuary chapel by myself for a while and remembered before I left.

++++

After he left Duns Scotus, I again had to work harder to repress all my emotions and feelings, and related with no affect to others; I just lived on the surface. The only place I could allow it to burst through the surface was in the music practice room where I worked on perfecting my voice. Franz Schubert's Lieder were good for that. Listening to classical music filled my spirit otherwise. In fact, one night I stayed up by myself to listen for twelve radio hours of the complete Ring cycle of Wagner. For me, music was and is a necessity.

In a classroom late one night, working on a Sociology term paper for a course I hated and just could not get into, another student was smoking Winston filtered cigarettes. Already I had been smoking cigars for a year, but lately I had begun to inhale the smoke and chew on the stub for hours. The cigarette smoke smelled so good I asked him if I could buy one from him. He gave me the nearly full pack and said he was planning to quit anyhow. He wouldn't accept my offer to pay him, but he did bum those cigarettes off me into the wee hours of the morning. The cigarettes seemed to calm my nerves some, and they were more acceptable to others than cigars and less detectable than cigars to my voice teacher who would raise hell with me whenever he smelled cigar smoke previously. This experience was significant, because I have been addicted to cigarette nicotine ever since and now for forty-six years.

Field Education - Hazard, Kentucky

To give the students for the priesthood a better idea of what life would be like after ordination, we were assigned to parishes that had shown some interest in mentoring us for the summers. For the three summer months after my second year, I was sent to Hazard, Kentucky to help out an ailing Pastor. I had no idea where Hazard was, and I was given no information about it, or what I would be doing, or about anything. But, there was a parish which the Franciscans staffed there. After a two week vacation with the family, Mom and Dad drove me down to Hazard, which is about a five hour drive south from Cincinnati. What a surprise we found when we finally discovered on a hillside that the church and the rectory were very small, more like a mission than a parish. I soon realized how ill the Pastor was, and that about all he could do was have Mass weekday and Sunday mornings. He would be gone to Cincinnati a number of weeks for doctors' visits, but would always be back for Sundays. I led Communion services on the mornings when he was gone. Cooking meals and cleaning the house and keeping up the yard around the place were tasks I took upon myself. The Presbyterian minister and his wife, Ross and Lorena Blount, were friends of the Pastor, and they invited me to assist them in running a teen summer recreation program for the city at the main park Monday through Friday mornings. Boredom has never been my friend, so I eagerly accepted.

Never having done anything like that before, it was quite a challenge for me to relate to a group of unruly teenagers, to play along with them, and have them relate to me as an authority figure. I felt that somehow I was supposed to be having fun with the group, but I didn't. Not feeling I was offering anything to the program, I still stuck with it because it was something to do, I was representing the Catholic Church there, and because I had become such good friends with Ross and Lorena. They lived deep into one of the "hollers" in the Appalachian mountains east of town off one of the many old coal-mining roads. They took me to their home one afternoon to show me how to get there. It was like entering the deep dark woods of fables and legends. Deciduous and pine trees filled the steep hills on either side of the path, a small stream the color of iron rust ran along the roadside. There were stories of the evil strip-mining companies destroying the land and poisoning the rivers and streams, leveling the tops of the mountains to access the coal, efforts to take a stand and trying to effect a change which never happens – and then arriving at a small clearing where the four room log house with a porch facing the road half rested on the mountain and half on supports seemed to be holding on for dear life. Actually, in a rustic sense it was very nineteenth century romantic, which must have been when the cabin was built along with another old two-story log house across the clearing. Ross and Lorena were renting this place as a suitable environment to raise their three young boys, the watchdogs, and the countless chickens. After this initial visit, I volunteered to babysit the boys if Ross and Lorena needed to get out of town for appointments or R&R.

One very memorable time was when Ross asked me to come to the house in the holler to help them butcher some chickens. When I got there early in the morning, not knowing how I ever found it, I found Ross trying to catch the chickens with a hooked coat hanger to snag their feet and the boys trying to corral them while Lorena was boiling water in a large tub outside on a wood fire. Catching them was frustrating fun with very slow progress, but finally we snagged eighteen of them, tied their feet and hung them upside down on the fence. Next, there was a very civilized discussion on how to kill the chickens more humanely with less pain. The options were: grab the head and snap their neck then cut off the head and let them bleed out while tied upside down to the fence, or grab their head and chop it off on the butcher block and let them bleed out with wings flapping and blood spurting while tied to the fence, or hypnotize them by drawing a chalk line on the butcher block and placing their beak on the line and then chopping off the head and bleeding them out on the fence. After a few trial runs, we decided the most civilized and easiest way for us was to do it the old fashioned way of just chopping off their heads and hanging them on the fence to bleed out, but some of them never made it to the fence and they ran all over the yard with wings going wild and blood spurting and the three boys having a wildly great time trying to catch them. (The scene reminded me so much of Dad killing the turkey for us.) Immediately after the bloodletting, we dipped them in the hot stinking water and pulled all the stinking feathers out, then slit them, took all the innards out, and cut up the carcasses to package for freezing. It all had to be done very quickly so the chickens wouldn't spoil, and we were exhausted when we finished by noonish. Lorena fried up some of the chickens for our lunch, but I just couldn't eat it, and I wasn't able to eat chicken for at least six years after that.

For one three week stint, the Pastor was to be gone for meetings and vacation, and a substitute priest was sent to take his place. The priest had been one of my Latin professors in high school seminary, and I thought we would get along fairly well until he didn't show up for Mass in the morning, and I had to go back to the house to wake him up. The first time he said to go on without him, as he wasn't feeling well. That evening, he asked me to wake him up half an hour before Mass each morning. The next day I went in to wake him and found that he had vomited on the floor. I figured he must have been really sick, and after cleaning it up, I went over to the church, explained that the priest was sick and led a prayer service and Communion. That evening, I noticed the priest was drinking alcohol heavily and chain smoking as he always did while we watched TV. Before he got too drunk, I helped him to bed, and then I went to bed realizing what was going on and deciding I was not going to enable his alcoholism.

The next morning I went into his room to check on him and wake him up for Mass, and I found him lying on the floor asleep in his vomit with an empty liquor bottle in his hand. It was tough on me, but I decided to leave him there as he was, and that I would not wake him in the mornings anymore. Later that morning he came into the kitchen and yelled at me, "Why didn't you wake me up?! Why didn't you help me clean up?! Now go in there and clean up the floor and do my laundry!" I stood up angrily and said, "Look, Father, you have a problem, it is not my problem, and I am not going to take responsibility for your problem! If you want to get drunk every night and sleep in your puke, go right ahead, but I am not going to help you to bed or wake you up in the morning or clean up after you!."

The next week was hell, and he barely spoke to me. He took to leaving empty liquor bottles next to his chair and all over the house, and I did not pick them up when I cleaned the house, not even when the Mayor of Hazard came by unannounced. I had only lost total respect for the one other priest who abused me at my boyhood parish and now this one. I felt that, all over again, I was being abused; only this time I *knew* it was not my fault. I was guilty of nothing, and I was not going to stand for it. After another argument, I confronted him again and asked him to leave the parish since he wasn't helping us at all. In his rage he said, "How dare you speak to me like that! I am a priest and you are not my superior! Wait until you get my evaluation of you! Now I am telling YOU to GET OUT!" So, I did and went to stay at Ross and Lorena's house for a couple days to try to figure out what I had learned about being a Franciscan friar and priest. I felt stronger and realized I wasn't a boy any longer. I was a man, and men stand up for their convictions and take control. When I went back to the parish, the priest was gone with his belongings and never returned. I was gladly alone this time and immediately scrubbed the house. When the Pastor returned, I told him everything that went on while he was gone, and told him I thought he ought to talk to the Provincial about that priest's problem.

Lorena and Ross and their family have remained my close friends to the present day. We have been sharing our lives irregularly now for forty-six years. They are the kind of friends that even if I haven't seen them in years, when we meet again it seems that no time has lapsed in between. They are always a blessing.

At the end of the summer, after I returned to Dun Scotus, my superior called me in and showed me the scathing evaluation from the alcoholic priest. After I explained the situation, he ripped up the papers and said he would find a better parish for me the next summer.

Simple vows were normally professed for three years with the expectation that at the end of that term, the friar would profess final solemn vows of poverty, chastity, and obedience for the rest of his life. But, I still had my doubts. My mind, my faith, my hopes, my dreams and ideals were all saying, "Go for it. You should do this"; but my feelings, my emotions, my body, my desire for wholeness were all saying, "You're not ready. Wait to see if it all comes together." There was a huge disconnect, perhaps because through the years I had worked so hard to create the chasm between the two approaches. I was given another year to decide.

After earning a Bachelor's Degree in Philosophy with emphasis in Psychology and English Literature from Duns Scotus College in June of 1973, I moved on to the major seminary run by the Franciscans in Dayton, Ohio to begin my Theological studies. As in the minor seminary for high school, I had received a top notch education throughout college from the professors, most of whom had received their Doctoral degrees from the best universities in Europe.

St. Leonard Theology Seminary

The summer after graduating was not another field experience in a parish, but rather a total immersion into Scripture, Hebrew, Greek, canon law and moral theology classes. It was intense, and I got the impression that these professors at St. Leonard College really meant business. With the adjustment to a new town, a new college, a new staff, a new focus for study, a much newer and brighter facility and grounds, perhaps that initial structure was a good thing; but I was worn out with studies and needed a break which wasn't in my future any time soon. However, along with the usual rotating chores the students were expected to do, I got more involved in taking care of the grounds by tractor-cutting acres of grass, trimming bushes, keeping algae out of the swimming pond with copper sulfate, and shoveling and plowing snow in the winter. Working outside in the sunshine or gray skies and doing a lot of manual work was good therapy for me and helped me to focus on coursework. Most of the rooms on the third floor of the college were reserved for college, staff, and students' guests. Somehow I was put in charge of making sure these rooms were kept clean, well-vacuumed, thoroughly dusted, with fresh linens at all times. When I was not off somewhere for field education, I was the hospitality director for three years. This meant not only checking on those rooms all the time and making sure the student crew was cleaning them, but it also meant actually doing the cleaning and set up most of the time by myself because the crew was off campus or just plain lazy. Other students were generous in helping me before and after celebrations and high guest volume.

The thing I enjoyed the most for sanity retention was cleaning up the small forest on the property. There were a number of dead beech, walnut, oak, wild cherry, and maple trees still standing, and even more that had fallen. The discussion was whether to leave it natural and "virgin", which it wasn't anyhow since the large trees had already been sold some time ago and removed, or to go ahead and clear out only the dead trees and branches. Fortunately for me, the administration gave permission for option two so long as I would keep the four main fireplaces well stocked, and the Brothers appreciated my help with what needed to be done. For four years I would take the Stihl chainsaw and the truck out to the woods, cut up, split, load, and drive back and unload the wood along the back of the building into "cords", rows four feet wide by four feet high and by eight feet long. About an hour away, my oldest brother Dan lived with his family, not too far from Mom and Dad's house where most of my younger sisters and brothers still lived. I borrowed his hydraulic wood splitter frequently to split the larger diameter logs. I never kept count of how many cords of wood I cut, but there got to be so many I asked for permission to start selling it to those who came to Mass at the chapel at $80.00 a cord delivered, and the customers were glad to pay that for such fine hardwoods. The college made a lot of money from this over four years, and I was happy to have something to do to fill in the lonely and boring times, especially in the winter months.

The courses that first year ('73-'74) and the next three years were all geared toward ordination, but with a definite practical focus of leading, preaching, and teaching the public and living what I preached. My goal was getting closer and within reach and so were the doubts and reluctance. The purpose and application of each course was obvious to me, as were the field education assignments. During the fall and winter semester of the first year, I taught at an adult learning center in Dayton and worked as a counselor at a medical clinic in Springfield, Ohio.

The Xenia, Ohio Tornado

The EF5 tornado that leveled Xenia, Ohio the Spring of 1974 was the one I saw from the library windows at St. Leonard's about 4:00 pm April 3rd. A large black thunderhead with a small yet very distinct tail traveling from the southwest collided with a large white cloud coming from the northeast, and then all hell broke loose. The tornado grew so rapidly; the lightning exploded constantly, the deafening thunder shook the windows, and the tornado took off to the northeast. I knew right then it was going be really bad for the towns, the structures, and the people in its path. The Sheriff's office called the college about 8:00 pm asking for immediate help in Xenia to dig through and remove debris while looking for the dead and injured. Six of us squeezed into a sedan and drove as fast as we could down the back country roads and the shortest route to Xenia. The closer we got, the more silent we became as we saw the total destruction along the roads. The Sheriff Deputies stopped us about a mile from town at one of their roadblocks, asked who we were, told us where to park, and said to run and try to help.

I was very familiar with Xenia since I drove right through downtown twice a week on the way to Springfield, only now there was very little left of the historic town: the old Catholic Church was gone, the trees were gone, a large yellow bus was sitting precariously about thirty feet up in one of the few trees left, the buildings were gone and the rubble filled the streets, in places even the pavement on Main Street was sucked up. I was in total shock, which was enhanced by the total darkness and eerie silence. There was an elderly man with a flashlight wandering down the middle of the street, not knowing where he was going, but needing to go somewhere. I asked if I could help him, and he said, "Please help me find my wife. She's an invalid and can't get around on her own. We just finished having dinner, and I took her plate and turned around to the sink to get her a glass of water and I heard this noise and turned around and the whole side of the house was gone and she was gone. Please help me look for her." He was obviously in shock with a mission. He had to keep moving. We went back to his house and looked around outside and tried to move some of the rubble for hours, but we never found her. We walked back downtown searching all the way for her and others. A Red Cross worker came up and asked if we could use some help. The man told her his story, and she took him off to one of their tents for something to drink, and I sat down on the street curbing not believing what I was looking at. It looked exactly like photos of the bombed cities in Europe from WWII. We searched all through the night until the sun came up and found not a single soul. We left at dawn in total silence and shock.

The President of St. Leonard College announced that classes would be suspended for the next two weeks for anyone wishing to go back to Xenia to help in whatever way they could. With my trusty chainsaw, a large gas can, oil, an extra chain, a chain sharpener, safety glasses, gloves, and a sack lunch, I headed up to Xenia each day and spent the next two weeks cutting up trees blocking the streets and surrounding roads. It was the only thing I could do to feel like I was offering something to the city and to keep the horror of that first night from creeping up on me. At night, it was a different story altogether, with recurring nightmares for months and months and months.

Independent Study Summer

During the summer of 1974, instead of going out for field education in one of the parishes, I was allowed to do independent study on the writings of the early Doctors of the Church while staying at St. Leonard and doing groundskeeping. Most all of the other students and some of the staff were gone that summer, so there was no stress, and it was a much needed and welcomed break. I really needed the break from the pressure of having to do what others wanted me to do, and who they wanted me to be, and from who I expected myself to be. Conversely, there were few distractions, and loneliness came out of its cave and grabbed me hard. At times in the evenings and at night it seemed like I was the only one there in that huge building as I wandered the halls. I listened to loud classical music in my room, did a lot of reading and study, and spent extra time in prayer alone in the chapel. Perhaps this break was an inkling that something deep was working its way to the surface.

One day I was walking in the staff wing and got a whiff of some god-awful scent. I notified some of the staff, who traced it to a retired priest's room. When the room was unlocked and opened while I was still there, I about passed out. The priest was on the bed in such a state of decomposition and rottenness with maggots and flies that he was unrecognizable. I knew I couldn't help in any way so I left. It was later determined that he had been dead for five days in the summer heat. That was the last time anyone had seen him at prayers or meals. His absence was not noticed. I never have and never will get that smell of rotting human flesh out of my nostrils and head. The experience was horrifying and got me thinking: he was one of our Franciscan brothers, and he wasn't cared about, wasn't noticed, died alone in his room rotting for five days, and is this what I am getting myself into?

This was also when Fr. Edwin, my immature novice master of 1969, was named the Guardian of all the friars at St. Leonard. What a transformation he had over the years! He even thanked me for being the only one with courage enough to confront him in the Novitiate, and apologized for writing us all off. Now he was a solid caring man of 65, and we became great friends. He saw himself as my mentor even when I was not into being mentored. He was good to talk with and share what was going on in our lives; but, he also tried to fix things for me and strongly "suggest" what to do, trying to protect me from going through what he had gone through in life. What I needed was someone to listen, not someone to make it better. While I don't think he ever understood how to handle that dynamic, we did remain close though his lifetime.

++++

Gradually through prayer, wanting to know the Lord personally and feel him in my being, I felt being pulled more into his being. I had taken two courses in mysticism at the University of Dayton the semester before, and two approaches rang true to me. One was John of the Cross' Dark Night of the Soul; the other was the Anonymous The Cloud of Unknowing. Now I felt I was being hesitantly pulled into the cave, a place of loneliness, a place of darkness and fear, a place of repression and oppression, a place where I thought I could seal off thoughts and feelings and bury them forever. Not so. There is no bullshit with God. I was being taught that in order to know the being of God, I must know, understand, and eventually come to accept the totality of my own being. Entering the cave was a lot like slowly entering the tropical ocean littered with old rotting shipwrecks and ghosts of the past. Over time, I was less and less afraid to remember my life on those ships when at full sail, and more able to remember the fear which made me sink each and every one of them hoping they would be gone forever. The more meditation I did in the cave, the more I came to discover small bits of treasure among the shipwreck ruins. It seemed that proportionally the more I faced myself the more I could face the Lord. My spiritual director, Fr. Joe, who also taught Pastoral Counseling and Spiritual Direction at St. Leonard, was a great help in this process.

Solemn Profession

August of '74 was decision time regarding Solemn Vows and Profession in the Franciscan Order, no more delays or extensions. I felt I was finally ready and decided to go for it. We had a month-long July retreat at King's House in Henry, Illinois in the middle of cornfield country. Fr. Edwin was the Director of the retreat and gave daily conferences and Mass, and listened to my questioning, my doubts, my encroaching episodes of depression, and also my deepening spirituality. In fact, it was in weighing my love of the Lord and wanting to serve Him on one scale against my doubts and misgivings on the other scale that convinced me to request Final Vows on the Feast of the Assumption in the middle of August. We had a huge celebration at St. Leonard, and my whole family came for it. My joy and happiness also reflected theirs. I could feel their love and pride in my giving my life totally to the Lord forever. As far as I was able to at the time, I chose it freely, and was ready to live this Franciscan life more diligently for the rest of my life.

++++

In the Fall of 1974 I took a short course on suicide prevention then volunteered for six months on the twelve hour, 8:00 pm to 8:00 am night shift of the suicide prevention crisis hotline for field education two nights a week. All night long, one phone call after another kept two of us busy listening intently and asking: How were they going to do it? Did they have the means to do it? Was alcohol involved? Was there anyone else in the house with them (to whom they might turn their anger)? Through these questions, we were trying to surmise if this was an emergency which required police or medical response, in which case we tried to keep the caller on the line long enough to have the call traced, or if we would be able to help them by talking them through this crisis, recommending long term help, letting them know of available resources. By each morning, I was totally exhausted and a bit sad. I had no idea that people were going through such severe life situations, such crises of pain, hate, anger, and depression. Each story was different, each reason individual. Some would give us their address so we could send help, while some would actually kill themselves while I was on the phone with them. Age made no difference, as callers ranged from pre-teen through old age. Just living life for these people was a real internal war zone. I could certainly empathize with them and understand why suicide for some was a moral choice and for some perhaps the only choice.

Psychological and Emotional Break

Dealing with other people's crises on the prevention hotline soon foreshadowed my own personal crisis. After I turned twenty-five in February 1975 the first sign that something very seriously wrong was going on was when I started to lose interest in cutting wood and cutting grass. I couldn't understand it. Forcing myself to do something which before had quickly given me such joy and peace, my loss of interest also seemed to undermine my study habits and created an inability to focus on the courses at all. Everything became a strenuous effort, like cliff-climbing out of an abyss that was pulling me deeper into it. Then, it hit. I could no longer be around anyone or listen to music as the noise was too offensive. I just could not go to any meals with the other students and friars to dig something out of the trough they called a buffet. I tried to eat something from the refrigerators in the break room at night when no one else was around, but the kitchenette was filthy and even eggs or cheese or bread didn't taste good. Oddly, I couldn't take walks outside around the facility after dark, because I was afraid of the moon and afraid of everything. I couldn't sleep at night even with the lights full on, couldn't read, couldn't bear the darkness, couldn't shower, couldn't function. I was terrified of night time, because that's when the demons would come and laugh at me and taunt me and rip out my insides. I began to shake uncontrollably.

Everything imploded and exploded inside this rusting iron sphere that was me. It seemed I spoke every day with my spiritual director, sometimes even at three o'clock in the morning, about this "dark night of the soul", my thoughts of going completely crazy, my inability to pull myself out of the cave, or to go deeper in the cave, or even to be in it at all. I would not have made it through this without Fr. Joe. Perhaps I was being tested in the furnace-fire of the Lord. Perhaps I was having the same experience as Job's trials. I was unable to do anything about it at all, and I was powerless, helpless. All I could do was let it happen and fight it all the way until I was exhausted and stopped fighting. Whenever I entered the ocean, the wrecks were deeper into the darkness, there was no light, and now there were destroyed battleships, and pleasure boats, and corpses of the young and old.

From the experience of watching Dad go through a nervous breakdown I was afraid, and I knew that was probably what was going on with me. And this went on in varying degrees for at least six months. My director thought it best for me to go see a doctor who could prescribe something for my nerves. The doctor's prescription: "You should leave that place and go find a woman and get married. You don't belong there. Get out of it. But, anyhow, here are some pills to help you sleep better." I left his office very confused. What the hell was he telling me that for? He doesn't know me. I went there to feel better, not to feel worse and question everything all over again. I took the pills for three nights then stopped. They didn't make me sleep at all. All day and night they just made me see strange colors and shapes, and when I tried to walk I felt like I was being blown away in the wind.

Through all this, I felt I had to put on an exterior image that everything was fine and normal. It took every energy and effort for me to squeeze it out to the façade. Daily Mass and Liturgy of the Hours were primary but became torturesome. Never did I share any of this with anyone in my family, even during visits to their place an hour away. My professors could tell something was up and were sympathetic to a degree and tried to cut me some slack. I was so sleep-deprived, sometimes not sleeping at all for a week. Not interested in eating, I lost a lot of weight. With my head down on the desk, I would fall asleep during class and not wake up until the class was over and everyone was gone, or sometimes I wouldn't show up for class at all. I didn't trust myself to drive, so I couldn't go out to buy something to eat. Nothing sounded good anyway. I ended up at night searching the backs of cabinets in the break room and in the kitchen like some inner-city rat looking for crackers someone may have left there a year ago. Literally, I was a wreck, and my life was a wreck at rock bottom. Not needing any added pressure, I was advised not to make any major decisions during this time: like deciding to leave the Franciscans or college for a while.

Clinical Pastoral Education

Honestly, I don't know why or how I started coming out of it. Maybe it was the weather getting warmer and sweating in the sun again or laying on the warm grass for hours. Maybe it was initially being able to sing in a choir and a few short solos in the background again. Maybe it was the requirement of my education to participate in a unit of Clinical

Pastoral Education (CPE) at Harper Hospital in Detroit while living at Duns Scotus that summer.

There had been a lot of war stories about CPE from other students who had taken part in it at other locations. So, I was very apprehensive about going, knowing how fragile I was emotionally and psychically at this point in my recovery and being very afraid that the darkness would hit big time again and I would crash. But I decided to go and see how I would respond. If I crashed again, I could get appropriate medical help at the hospital I would be working at, or check myself into their psyche unit.

Being away from St. Leonard that summer of 1975, living with the friars at Duns Scotus in a very familiar surrounding, dressing in lay clothes with dress pants, shirt and tie, and being in a professional public situation for three months all helped and felt like a short leave of absence. Our CPE group of ten worked in a hospital setting and was run by four chaplains training us to be with patients to listen to them, to comfort them where possible, and to bring a religious presence to the families, and especially to work with the doctors and nurses in coordinating the patients' care. All ten of us were assigned to the stage four terminal cancer ward for eight hour days, five days a week for three months. For the patients, it seemed like life imprisonment, not that they were convicted of anything, but that the only way out was by dying, or being given a pardon to leave to die at home, or for the very lucky few who improved to be given parole. For me, at times it was like talking to and listening to the living dead. They knew they were dying since it was the policy of the hospital and doctors to let the patients know this, and the approach of the staff and chaplains to help the patients in the transition. Their voices were distant; their eyes were focused elsewhere even though they were looking directly at me.

One lady was overjoyed when I went into her room to visit. "Oh! Elton John! You came to see me! I love your music and your voice! Please sing me a song and give me your autograph!" Even though I initially tried to correct her, she insisted I sing for her and give her my signature before I left. I went along with her, and sang a song, and told her I had run out of photos, but I would be happy to sign the hospital menu for her. And I did sign it "With Love, Elton John" in the most flamboyant longhand I could channel from Elton. A few visits after that I met her family, who assured me I did kind of look like Elton John and that singing for her and forging his signature meant so much to her as she was showing it to everyone. I saw her a few more times, singing for her each time, before she died the next week.

Each morning the whole group would meet at 11:00, sitting in a circle, discussing <u>On Death and Dying</u> by Elisabeth Kubler-Ross, and sharing what had happened during our visits with the patients for a kind of group therapy session. The chaplains were confrontational and specifically nailed me for not speaking up or sharing. I was told I was distant and cold, like a fortress not giving up a glimpse of what was going on inside, and when I did speak it was more like a guarded pronouncement that couldn't be discussed, not letting the group in on how I reached the conclusions. I could accept that from the chaplains because I needed their acceptance and affirmation, but when the other group members began tearing at the stone walls, I would get angry since I didn't need them and felt they had no right. One of the chaplains very gently found chinks in my armor, and I could trustingly open up more to her in the group. As the chinks widened and my interior reinforcements could no longer hold the gates closed, I melted down and sobbed uncontrollably spilling out the pain and hurt and loneliness I had been hiding in my life. Extra time was given for me, lunch was delayed, and I was excused for the rest of the day. The experience wasn't freeing, nor was it shaming. It was more like, "What the hell happened? What all did I say? What will be the repercussions?" The next morning I was used, not in a shameful way, as an example of why ministers are or can become ineffective and unrelatable.

The three month CPE was tough -- focusing on death every day. A doctor working with our group said, "Once cancer is found, it will always be the cause of death sooner or later. There is no cure. Cancer drugs make you so sick you regret begging for those few extra months of life. If I ever found cancer in me, I would not have it treated. I would live what life I had left with the quality of life I had as long as I could." After my experience there, I decided I would do the same.

One day, right after lunch, we had to witness an autopsy of a middle aged man who had died of cancer in our ward. It was hard enough seeing this friend I had visited numerous times in his room, but to see him cut up, and the brain removed, right after lunch, I found a trash container quickly and lost my lunch. I left the room before I fainted.

In all, as the patients shared, I learned a lot about physical pain and suffering in others, and the emotional suffering of letting go, and the strength pulled up from somewhere as they tried to hold onto life, and losing this life and the ones loved and loving, and slipping away, which could only be done totally alone. As I focused on being with and helping others, I could feel that I was healing. I felt I got more from them than they got from me. Some squeezed every breath out of life fighting until the end without saying a word, while others peacefully passed on with a smile on their faces, getting the last laugh. I began wondering if there was anything beyond this life. "Is this all there is?" And then, "Why not?"

Jemez Pueblo

September of 1975 three of my classmates and I drove out west, all four of us assigned to different parishes in the northern half of New Mexico for field education. It was the first time I had been west of the Mississippi, and everything was new to me, with the cornfields of Kansas as far as I could see, the sky getting less and less gray and more and more a seductive blue, the landscape getting less and less green and more and more brown, seductive in its own way. We left the large cities behind with smaller cities ahead; and oh!, the mountains in the distance became more majestic with each passing mile. The people and the cultures spoke to me.

I was assigned to Jemez Pueblo, a small Native American village of mud brick houses and dirt streets, and a native culture that stretched back centuries and centuries. The two-story mission friary was established on the far west edge of the Pueblo since Anglos were not permitted to live in the Pueblo proper, and to keep the separation enforced. In fact, when the Pueblo people had secret ceremonies, the roads were blocked to and from the mission, and we were told to stay inside from dusk to dawn. But, when there were public ceremonies, feast days, and native dances, everyone was invited from all around. Anglos flooded into the central village plaza from Albuquerque and Santa Fe and tour buses, and natives came from the other Pueblos and tribes in the area to watch perhaps altogether 500 dancers from the Pumpkin clan and Turquoise clan stretched in long lines praying the Harvest Dance, Buffalo Dance, and various feast day dances punctuated by deep, heart-pounding drums and ancient chants.

In front of the friary was a small one-room post office which had been run by Brother Tom as the postmaster until he died earlier that year. He had been in Jemez for a long time and was much loved by the people. There was also a small Catholic school run by some Franciscan sisters. I used to teach religion in the school and fill in teaching the regular classes if one of the sisters needed to be absent. I had never taught children before, and it was a challenge to get down to their level and strip everything I had learned down to the most basic concepts and understandings. I also taught catechism four days a week, one place each day, to the children at Santa Ana and Zia Pueblos in the public elementary schools there, and at the very small Spanish mission churches of Ponderosa and Canon. Just trying to keep order and control the kids took most of the most time, the sixth graders being the worst, and it seemed it was more of an after-school daycare than them actually learning anything. I hated it and felt it was a futile waste of time.

The friars themselves were a good group of men: there were two Priests and three Brothers. We got along well, and they were most willing to share their insights into the Jemez ministry and ministry in general. I really liked living there and felt included at all times. However, at times, boredom and loneliness took over, and I would steep myself for many hours into the large library of New Mexican, southwest and Native American history books, asking the friars to embellish on what I read. If I needed a break, I would take off and walk around the pueblo, greeting and talking to everyone I saw. I became very good friends with a couple of families and used to help them peel the dried corn from their fields, and then to shuck the kernels, or go up to the mountains for firewood and Christmas trees. They would share words from the Jemez language with me, though they were not supposed to, only to find out later that they were teaching me the words a woman would use and a man never would. We had great fun over that joke.

++++

One older man stood and spoke with me in English one evening in front of the friary about his hunting with his grandsons in the mountains and what he had seen and what he had killed that season. He told stories of elk and deer, of black bear and brown bear, of mountain lions and wildcats, of eagles and owls, and how each one was important to their culture. When I asked if he was ever afraid being out there around wild animals, he painted this picture: "Imagine there is an owl and a cougar in that tree. You are afraid. Both of them bring death. You can throw stones at them to chase them both away. Or, you can make friends with them so they will not hurt you. Or, you can throw stones at one and try to chase him away, and make friends with the other one so he will never hurt you. You must decide which of the fears to throw stones at and which ones to make your friend." I thought of St. Francis in Gubbio, Italy making a friend of and taming the wolf who was terrorizing the people, and the many wolves inside of me I had to make friends with and tame.

++++

61

On Halloween, I decided to dress in a costume to scare the children when they walked down to the mission in total darkness to beg for candy. Not knowing the taboos and customs, I dressed like a witch ghost all in white, carried large bags of fallen leaves to the small porch above the front door, and would make moaning noises and much rustling of leaves as I threw them down on the kids below before they got a chance to ring the doorbell. I was going to run down the stairs to pass out the candy; but, totally terrified, they all ran back up to the Pueblo crying and yelling and screaming. Very soon after that, four of the Pueblo leaders showed up and told me to get down and stop that because I was scaring the people. They spoke with the Pastor and told him the people thought I was the ghost of Brother Tom come back from the dead to haunt them. I took off the costume and apologized to the elders, and they left to do damage control with the people. I learned that even if something sounds like a good idea or a joke, always find out and anticipate how others might take it first.

++++

As it got closer to Christmas, I worked with the choir and guitarists at Canon to make the Christmas Eve Midnight Mass something really special. I practiced with just the small choir in the late afternoons, then those ladies would go home to make dinner, and the four male guitarists with fine voices would show up after work to practice. I got to be very good friends with Orlando, one of the guitarists, and with his young wife Velma, and their son and daughter. They treated me like family. At the last practice, I asked them all to be at the church at 11:15pm so we could sing Christmas carols before the Mass. The bonfires were burning brightly outside around the church with smells of cedar and pinon, and the bagged luminarias were placed to light the path for the Christ Child, and the stars in the heavens shone electrically from one horizon to the other. At 11:15pm, everyone was there except Orlando. His wife explained that Orlando, who was a Highway Patrolman, had to work a little late since there was an accident on the main road down by San Ysidro, and he would be there soon. So we started without our lead guitarist leading the carols. At 11:45pm, his wife knew something was not right since he was never that late, and she left with the kids to find out what was wrong. At midnight, I asked the priest if we could wait to start until Orlando showed up. The church was packed, with many standing in the back and outside the front door and around the bonfires. At 12:15am the priest sent one of the servers to tell me he hoped everything was alright, but he was going to start the Mass. He did, and we all sang in Spanish and English, and it was all very nice except for the empty spot. At the very end of Mass a Highway Patrol Officer showed up at the door and told us that in Orlando's hurry to get to the church he didn't negotiate a curve and went off the road into a deep ravine. He wasn't expected to live. The shock was indescribable, and those that could cried and wailed, including me, as the priest led us in prayers for him.

When we got back to the friary about 2:00 am, the Brothers had a "light" Christmas Eve luncheon spread for a small army ready for the six of us. Cookies, cakes, candies, lunch meats, drinks, decorations, candles and lots of small gifts were displayed so sumptuously that a picture of it could have been in the Good Housekeeping Christmas issue. After the news, none of us were much in the mood to feast, but we all had a drink and nibbled and talked until 3:00am.

++++

As exhausted and sad as I was, I just could not sleep at all, and besides, I wanted to be in the Pueblo plaza at sunrise to witness the buffalo, deer, antelope, and eagle dancers coming down from the hill to the east and into the plaza.

I stood alone in the plaza about 6:00 am, waiting. Sunrise came and went; there were no dancers coming; there was total silence in the plaza on this freezing Christmas Day. There was so much for me to think about and pray about that I didn't mind. Very faintly at first, then louder, I heard a man shouting and knocking on doors, then he appeared at the far end of the plaza knocking on each door, shouting in the Jemez language what I presumed was a wake up call like a town crier. He saw me and came over to talk, asking what I was doing there so early. I did not recognize this man, but he seemed very familiar with who I was. He said, "This is good to see you alone. I wanted to tell you something. We wanted to ask you to dance with us today." I was almost knocked off my feet, and he picked up on my surprise and confusion. "That's alright. We will take care of everything for you," he said. When I could speak I said, "Thank you very much. That is a great honor, but I don't know how to do the dance, and I might mess it up. I know every step must be precise, and I do not know the steps. Tell you what I will do. I will stand right here and be with you as you are dancing in your way of praying, and I will stand here and pray with you in my way of praying." He pondered that for a while and said, "That is what we like about you Brother Tom. You respect us. There was a priest here before who was not invited to dance with us, but he dressed up like the dancers and went out with them and danced with them. We would never tell him not to dance. Besides, every dance needs a clown."

> "*Every dance needs a clown.*
> *Never dance without one.*
> *A smile arises from a frown,*
> *As fear and stress are outdone.*"
> *Tom -- 2000*

++++

I am still great friends with some of the Jemez People, and am personally invited to the public ceremonies, dances, and personal family celebrations. Of course, there is some expectation that I will be there, but it is always a joy and deeply moving experience, especially on Christmas Day.

The day after Christmas, I flew back to Dayton, Ohio and St. Leonard, and then I drove to Hamilton, Ohio to spend a few days with my family for the holiday. It was another adjustment to go back east with so many experiences and lessons learned. I knew I wanted to spend the rest of my life as a Franciscan priest in the Southwest working with the Native Americans. When I got back to St. Leonard, I received a phone call from the Pastor at the mission in Jemez Pueblo to inform me that Orlando did not make it, that he had died that morning. Despite all my prayers and hopes for his recovery so he could go back home to his family, he never would. I went to the chapel and shouted my grief and extreme anger at God, demanding an answer, demanding that He be held accountable. All I got were the echoes off the walls. He had promised me that all things would be alright – be not afraid, I am with you, ask and it will be given you and all that – and now he had broken His promises again. This was the second time I seriously doubted there was a God at all. There really was no one there. I was on my own.

> *Either God wants to get rid of evil, but he cannot;*
> *Or God can, but he does not want to;*
> *Or God neither wants to nor can;*
> *Or he both wants to and can.*
> *If God wants to, but cannot, then he is not all-powerful.*
> *If he can, but does not want to, he is not all-loving.*
> *If he neither can nor wants to, he is neither all-powerful nor all-loving.*
> > *And if he wants to and can -- then why does he not remove all evil and suffering?*
> *Epicurus (341 BC-270 BC)*

Ordination as a Deacon

The Spring semester of 1976 through June of 1977 was filled with cramming in the courses and studies for my theology degree, ordination to the Diaconate, field education at St. Louis Parish, Batesville, Indiana; followed by internships at Acoma Pueblo, New Mexico and St. Rita Parish, Fairborn, Ohio. There was a lot of anticipation, joy, internal struggle, doubt, fear, re-commitment, highs and lows in ministry, learning, and recognition.

This time is also when I started to write down my thoughts, feelings, prayers, poems, anxieties, dreams and highlights into a journal of sorts. I was not very consistent with it, but it seemed to help somewhat to get significances on paper. Diary of a Country Priest by Bernanos influenced me quite a bit and touched me deeply. Reading it was like talking and feeling with an old friend whom I had not recognized for a while, or whom I was ashamed to meet again, and whom I knew I would not meet again for many years. Each paragraph, each page touched something deep inside me, and reading the last page was very sad, because by then I realized the friend was me and I was no longer ashamed to meet him and cry with him.

The closer March 20th of '76 came, the date for Diaconate ordination, the deeper the anxieties and doubts became. This was a serious milestone for me to be ordained into the hierarchy of the Roman Catholic Church. Was I really being called by the Lord for this? Was it just a hoop to pass through on the way to Priesthood? How much does personal choice actually have to do with it when you feel you are being called by God? How much choice did the Prophets have when they were called? Could I be a precursor paving the way for the Lord? Or was all this a sham, something I had been working towards most of my life and had to go through with it, something I needed to do for me, something to show I was not afraid of long-term commitment, something to be somebody, to be a good man, to be rid of all the feelings of being no good? Was this about God, or was it all about Tom?

When the date arrived, I already had the flu for a week, and it was getting worse. I was so physically sick I couldn't walk, was a bit delirious from high fever, coughing constantly, and had no energy whatsoever. Fr. Edwin suggested having the Archbishop come to my room and ordain me there, or get me in a wheelchair and take me down to the chapel to be ordained with my class. Even though I knew I couldn't participate much in the ritual, I knew my whole family would be there for the celebration. I opted to be wheeled down. There I sat sweating profusely waiting to pass out, and two friars helped me up the altar steps for the Archbishop to lay his hands on my head for the actual ordination. I am sure I took part in the luncheon in the hall afterwards with my family, but I didn't remember much at all. When I got to feeling better in the weeks that followed, I wondered if my illness was a psychosomatic response to all the anxiety; my body saying, "If you're not going to deal with this, I will sabotage this to make you realize you really don't want to do it."

Being out among the people of God and ministering to them during field education is where I felt most comfortable. If only I could just skip the rest and go out to them, I could feel like I was offering something and focusing on something other than myself. But, _me_ always caught up with me somehow.

++++

The summer in Batesville was stressful: the Pastor felt I was being too independent and making decisions for the parish; my comfortable friendships with the parishioners threatened him. A friend of mine from Duns Scotus, Bro. Walter, who was running the parish school, felt misunderstood by the Pastor who would not allow him to run it as he thought best. I had to have two wisdom teeth pulled and dealt with the pain, the swelling, and the sleepless nights; the Pastor did allow me to preach, but would dissect each effort to the point where I didn't know what I could say. At night as I looked out my bedroom window, I felt like a prisoner looking out on a world I was not part of and yearned to belong to. Beyond the Pastor, it felt good to be working in a Midwest parish where I could be in a culture I grew up in, one that was familiarly easy to be in.

Journal entry August 1976
   "Odd what a force passion/lust is. I have been saddened twice last night. The depths of passion, the power, the uncontrollable urge, the extreme release, the indescribable darkness and fear. Oh, to build myself up one night and tear myself apart the next. Jesus, teach me discipline and control of my body. God how much I lack it, how much I need it. Lord, give me peace as I commend my body, mind, soul, and spirit into your hands."
   Or ...
   "God, make me chaste; but not yet." St. Augustine

++++

The Pastor of Acoma Pueblo, Acomita, and McCartys in New Mexico said he would like to mentor a deacon for their internship. So that is where I went for the Fall semester. We lived with three others friars who also ministered in the area. The old fifteen room white-painted and stuccoed friary was directly across the dirt road from the small school and convent in San Fidel, which was an old, dying, very small Western town on the original Route 66 until the Interstate by-passed it. It felt and looked like a half-ghost-town, with many adobe homes and small businesses abandoned for years, boarded up, deteriorating and crumbling in on themselves. The other half were ranchers and struggling families who grew up there and didn't want to leave.

My role there was to assist the Pastor in his ministry to the Pueblo Peoples and other missions, to teach religion at the school, to fill in teaching grades when the teacher was absent (which happened for two months while an old nun was sick), to take my turn cooking and cleaning, and to learn more about the parishes and ministry near there. The kids in school were a delight, and we hit it off fairly well, but I soon realized how much I did not like to teach. The Pastor did not want me to visit the kids' families, so I would visit the families near the friary and befriend them. He actually told me, "Look, you are only here for a short while, and I don't want them to end up liking you more than me. So I am forbidding you to go out and visit anyone anymore." He also would not allow me to preach because the people might like my preaching better than his. I have never met such an old man in a young man's body, and I didn't understand him at all.

However, I did remain close friends with a family down the road from us. I learned how to butcher a steer, and I drank some of the fresh iron-tasting blood and ate the fried fresh liver. They saved the hide to tan later. They also taught me how to saddle up and ride a horse and told me to feel free to come anytime and ride her. I took them up on that offer frequently, practicing in the pastures, and running wild on the unfenced open spaces of the desert. She enjoyed it, and I enjoyed it, and we were both exhausted by the time I would take her home and brush her down. Other than that, there was very little for me to do, and I got very bored and lonely. One of the other friars showed me the back way up Mt. Taylor, an extinct volcano, to the very top where I could see hundreds of miles in every direction.

"I've been out West now for about a month and a half and have climbed Mt. Taylor two times. This time I didn't go to the top, but stopped short

on a butte, Vista Point, and layed there. It kept striking me that mountains are not male but female. So gigantic, restful, absorbent. I can heave my spirit into the mountain, and she keeps it folded, as in a womb, and does not throw it back." -- October 1976

"You love me, Lord. Others love me. Why do I not love myself? I feel this day I have really begun to love myself, just for who I am, Tom. I've always contended that my greatest enemy was myself, but I never knew how to go about making friends with him again. You, Lord, help me to grow in accepting and loving your gift of me to myself."
-- November 1976

"Love of myself - it has much to do with ministry and what I feel I have to offer to the people. It had to do with self-consciousness, a fear of being put down, of not being wanted or needed or seen as important. In the past I see that I acted so much out of fear, out of defensiveness. I used to think that loving oneself would be selfish, would be a turning in on myself, and you know Lord I do enough of that already. But it hasn't turned out to be that way at all. Loving myself, I go more freely out to others. I don't know why that is, and I don't care." -- November 1976

"Something has been going on in me, and I really don't know what it is. So, Lord, I'm writing this down so we can look at it together again. I guess for over a year now I've been more nervous than ever before, and I never knew why. Well, something came to the top today. Perhaps it is a feeling of wanting to go out on my own, to just take off, to bolt. You see, Lord, I'm tired of being under someone, of being controlled, of taking orders. Guess my own self identity is so weak that lots of things strike me like they are putting me down, saying I'm not important. I find when I'm alone I don't feel that way (except when others' expectations weigh heavy on me), and I'd like to believe that later after ordination I will be pretty much on my own. But even then, someone else will be pastor/superior or .... Lord, I don't know the answer of where you're leading me through this whole thing. Sure, I've thought of leaving the Order and the Priesthood behind and striking out on my own, but I want to serve your people. I want to be with them in their experiences of our human weaknesses. I guess I need to talk to someone about this soon, or maybe ride it out alone for a while with just your silence always before me. By the way, I wonder if you really realize how much that hurts me at times not to feel you very close to me when I'm down." -- December 1976

Preparation for Ordination to the Priesthood

Back at St. Leonard for the Spring semester began the flurry of studies, practicing the celebration of the Liturgy (in Latin and English), writing theses, studying for final written and oral exams, and settling on the Liturgy, booklet, and invitations for ordination to the Priesthood on June 11,1977 and for First Mass the day after. As hurried and stressful as all that was, I could handle it. But, as I had expected, my struggles within myself continued. My spiritual director encouraged me to put my trust in God, resigning myself to His Will. He had gotten me this far, He wouldn't let me down now, and He won't let me down in the future. I also went and spoke with my moral theology professor, told him about the doubts and struggles, the thoughts about leaving, and the desire to be in a relationship. He said, "Honestly, Tom, it's a good thing you feel that way. If you did not have those thoughts and feelings and struggles, if you did not feel you were on the fence trying to make a decision and could go either way freely, I would say you should not be ordained. Also, it is the man who is so sure of himself and absolutely committed to being ordained, almost to the point of believing he deserves it, who should not be ordained as it would be all about himself. Tom, your struggle shows your humility, that you cannot do this on your own, and it is not of your own doing, and your ministry will not be about you. I would say it is a good sign, and you are ready to be ordained. Besides, ordination is not imposing something on you that you did not have already. It is a blessing of the Church and the People of God in recognition of whom you have become. " With those reassurances, and a bit relieved, I decided to continue on.

During this time, I also had to decide what ministry I wanted to be involved in after ordination. I toyed with the idea of going to the Philippines and being a missionary over there in our missions. What I really wanted to do was go to the Southwest and work with the Pueblo missions. Along with Jemez and Acoma, there were five other Pueblos around Santa Fe that the Franciscans ministered at, but I was told there were no openings at any of them. While one of the friars from the Navajo Reservation was visiting (recruiting?) the students, I asked him a lot of questions about the people and their culture. When I asked him about having to learn the Navajo language, he said, "Oh no, they all speak English." I was relieved, especially since he had been there for twenty five years and knew nothing more than a few common phrases. So, I decided to request from the Provincial a ministry among the

Navajos. He told me there was a need for another priest at the Chinle mission, so I accepted. Fortunately, I was familiar with the Pastor, Fr. Kevin, and he seemed like a pleasant guy to work with.

++++

After studying heavily for two months through each of the courses over the last four years, I did end up passing my exams. The oral exam in front of the whole faculty was particularly grueling. Each faculty member could ask anything he wanted to from any of his courses over those years. I was extremely nervous standing in front of them, but I seemed to answer and explain my conclusions to them satisfactorily. I was asked to wait outside the conference room while they debated my fate for a much shorter time than I anticipated. I was called back in and was told that they decided to accept me as a Master of Divinity and to give the go ahead for Ordination to the Priesthood. Then they all stood up and applauded me. Even though I was told previously not expect any surprises after I had made it this far, I was so relieved I had to sit down. Two of them wrote special poems for me, and handed them to me as I left the room.

Tom -------

Peaked sails filled with wind,
Strong man at the tiller,
Foaming sea cut in twain,
Salt breeze in his hair.

And Jesus was a sailor, too;
God's cause among the lost --
Healing broken seamen and
Leading them into deep waters.
                    Aaron 5/77

Tom Schellenbach, the Solid Man

He's durable--though made for more--
This man of chopping wood and steady air,
A swinging-ax, Franciscan man.

You're NOT just tree, some weed or flower--
You're ALL the orchards, fields and streams--
That clash of love where Mother Earth
Meets God the Father's ancient seed
To grow in restless edge of seasoned time,
For our communing with each other
(Like burning logs you cut for fireplace love).

The human kindness that you make derives
From quiet power wrestled into life
From fears that want to make you die--
But prove to be the Passion which brings spring
Each splendid year--your goodness born
Each push you make towards sleety veils
That locked you into patterns of a too-long winter;

You grow as thoroughly as nature under God.

Joris

Chapter Three
Embracing the Priesthood

Having participated in a number of Ordinations and First Masses of upperclassmen, witnessing, observing, singing, serving the Bishop's Mass, setting up and serving the luncheon afterwards (a traditional task for the Deacons), I pretty much knew what to expect, or so I thought. The evening before we had a splendid party thrown for the seven of us (four of us from the original freshman class of eighty-two at the minor seminary thirteen years earlier) and for all our families, guests and visitors. We even put on a small talent show, and my segment was an excerpt from college of my role as Papageno the bird-catcher looking for a wife, with his love interest played by my classmate Alan as Papagena from Mozart's opera The Magic Flute, in full costumes, with another classmate playing his recorder for the flute and Fr. Edwin playing the score on the piano. When Alan came out on stage wearing a full length flowery dress and a blonde wig and heavy rouge on his checks, I lost it and just could not stop laughing, but we made it through the skit. The crowd loved it and roared with laughter and applause! I was disappointed that no one from my family came. I went to my room early to get some rest for the next day.

There was nothing that could have prepared me for the personal experience I was to have. The early morning of my ordination day it had been raining, but it cleared up about 9:00am with a radiant full double rainbow in the West - a good sign. The seven of us gathered in the large sacristy for congratulations from the Archbishop, the Franciscan Provincial, and a great number of priests and deacons who came to join us in the Liturgy. We were all vested in our appropriate garb, the Archbishop offered a prayer of blessing, the opening music began, and we solemnly processed down the side aisle to the back of the chapel, then up the center aisle to the main sanctuary and high altar. I was glad to see Mom and Dad and all my brothers and sisters in the front pews, although I knew they would never have missed it. I was so thankful to them for their love, support, encouragement, and understanding through these years of preparation for this moment. In contrast to my diaconate ordination when I was very sick, I was able to totally participate in the ceremony and receive the laying on of hands by the Archbishop and all the assembled priests. I deeply felt I was being blessed personally by the Lord, and by everyone, to the point that I silently wept a bit through most of that part of the ritual. I was in total awe. We were invited up to the altar to gather around the Archbishop so we could con-celebrate the rest of the Mass with him. I especially remember the music, with everyone singing, the organ, and the choir, to be overwhelming. The whole experience was such a high.

Everyone gathered for a luncheon afterwards where I could introduce my parents and family to those around us and to those who came up to congratulate them and me. Then, I went up to my room to gather what I would need for my First Mass and for a week of vacation. I rode home with Mom and Dad, and we talked the whole way about how wonderful everything was.

From my Journal, May 1977
"Lord, I want to be the best priest around. I want to serve the people with everything I've got. I want the liturgy to touch their hearts. And I want to touch them and heal them to wholeness and unity, to wipe the mud and sweat and blood and tears from their faces -- to hold them with my arms and my heart -- to wrap them with my/your Spirit -- and somehow bring the peace they need. I want to commit myself to the wounded and poor.

I should ask them to lay hands on me. I should ask them to absolve me of my sins, my lack of love. I should ask them to assure weak-faithed me of your forgiveness. And, Lord, if they weren't at the Eucharist I would wonder if the bread and wine really were Your Body and Blood. It is they who consecrate it with their lives, their work, their suffering, their struggle to follow You, their belief in Your love. And, yet, I am called to lead them closer to You, to unite them so they can be Your people and You their God."

Soliloquy of a Seed
Something tells me
To surrender
All I am
And hope to be,
And to descend
The dark earth

To be transformed
Into a tree;
But to go up
Dare I go down
And think a tree
Can fit in me?
-- Gloeggler

Shortly after 1:00pm on Sunday June 12th my whole family, extended family, and friends gathered at St. Stephen Church in Hamilton, Ohio for my First Mass. Even though the Pastor and Associate Pastor did not participate, many priests did join me in the rectory to vest in order to con-celebrate with me; we processed over to the church with all the church bells wildly ringing a happy song. After Mom's wedding to Dad thirty-four years previous, she had her satin wedding dress made into Mass vestments for a priest. They had always hoped one of their sons would be a priest, and I was proud to wear those vestments this day. After all, how many other priests could say they wore their mother's wedding dress? I was nervous I would make a mistake on my first go around with the Mass, but there were plenty of others with me at the altar and in the sanctuary to catch it if I did. Everything went very well. The music, singing, organ, and choir were fabulous. Fr. Edwin's sermon was deeply meaningful. So many people attended that I recognized from my youthful years at the parish.

After the Mass, I stayed in the sanctuary to bestow my first priestly blessing individually upon the heads of anyone who came forward, beginning with Mom and Dad, and there must have been at least a hundred others who did. While I was doing this, my sisters and brothers were setting up the dessert reception in the parish hall. I didn't want to have an impersonal caterer handle the reception, and since my sisters had offered in order to have something to contribute, I gratefully accepted them handling everything – even baking cookies and cakes and all kinds of goodies. Some of the parishioners even brought their favorite desserts. After the blessings, I joined them at the hall, greeting and meeting all those who attended. We had a wonder-filled time as there was so much happiness and joy, and I was so totally overwhelmed, thankful and exhausted afterward. Mom, Dad, and the family gifted me with my first gold chalice and bowl pattern.

++++

My brothers and sisters reflected on my ordination thusly:

"I remember thinking you were closer to GOD, that your answers were gospel! You had the connections!"

"I always felt that mom and dad regarded you in high esteem because you chose to devote your life to the priesthood. I felt you were special having chosen that vocation and I was quite proud of you."

"Mom was very proud of you, and it seemed she took advantage of any chance she could to let someone know she had a son who was a Franciscan priest. Because of her deep rooted faith, this meant a lot to her."

"I always felt you were a reincarnated St. Francis."

"I am frustrated by the intellectual side of you. You are so smart and such a deep thinker, aloof at times. I often wished you could let go and be stupid sometimes. It was as if there was a wall, and you couldn't jump over it to let loose. I often wished you could communicate more openly instead of reasoning behind everything."

"I absolutely love your singing voice and the homilies that you gave at Mass. (They had substance, something to take home and reflect on)."

"I always thought about your motivation for taking vows like poverty, chastity and obedience. I just know I didn't like the sound of any of the three. I wondered if you felt you were chosen to go that route. If you were certain God called you to that ministry. Or you found it as a way to escape the craziness at home and get recognition and acceptance."

"Being at your ordination was very meaningful to me. I know one thing for sure, I was so very proud of you. My brother is a Priest."

Navajo Reservation Years

The week of vacation was way too short. It was spent mainly enjoying the company of family and their children and our relatives. But, then again, I was very anxious to begin my new life -- the ministry on the Navajo Reservation in the northeast part of Arizona. I drove out West with two other Franciscan priests who were beginning their ministry in New Mexico among the Hispanic people. After dropping them off where they needed to go, I continued on to Chinle, AZ., located at the mouth of Canyon de Chelly. While driving there, I had so many thoughts running through my mind about everything that happened in the short prior month that had brought me to this point, trying to go over it in detail so I could remember it forever; but then, I would take a break and focus on the beautiful and desolate landscape which kept changing and unfolding with every passing mile during the four and one-half hour drive from Albuquerque.

When I arrived in Chinle at 2pm, I was exhausted, it was boiling hot, and there was a bad sandstorm as I drove up to back parking area of Our Lady of Fatima mission. I had never been there before, but I had no trouble finding it on the map. The Pastor, Fr. Kevin, opened the back door for me, dust blowing in, telephone in his hand, and motioned for me to come in and have a seat at the kitchen table, and I did, and he forced the door closed. Since he took a while on the phone, I sat there thinking, "What the hell did I get myself into?", and I cried to myself.

Kevin came in and offered me some coffee and cookies (something I was soon to find out was offered to everyone who came to the back door), and we chatted a bit. He showed me the room on the first floor I was to be using, helped me unload my things from the car, and then gave me the grand tour of the mission. The pink-painted friary/rectory was over a hundred years old and built of adobe and stucco with cracks in the walls, a curling wood shingle roof which had to be coated each summer with a mixture of turpentine and linseed oil, a porch around three sides, and it seemed that with the slightest jiggle the whole house would pulverize and come crashing down. There were two bedrooms, a bathroom, living room, dining room, front office, and a very small front entrance room (which doubled as a "counseling" room) on the first floor. Two bedrooms took up the roof space on the second floor with a small storage room between them. With four friars there now, there wasn't any room for privacy or quiet other than our own rooms. The inadequate swamp cooler (aka evaporative cooler) didn't work so well, and it was stifling in there.

The sandstorm had died down a little, so Kevin and I walked over to the yellow-painted church closer to the road in front of the friary. Built of concrete block, it was a very simple rectangle that might hold two hundred people if you stretched it. On the front wall was hanging a beautiful Navajo rug with a crucifix hanging on top of it, and other Native American symbols decorated two walls. The two side aisle walls were full of clear glass windows which radiated abundant light – and heat – into the church. At the front exterior of the church a short steeple with a great sounding bell was attached to the side of the church. Nothing was paved around the mission.

We walked around the back of the friary down a short dirt incline to the parish hall, which was a large steel-framed Butler building with steel panel sides and steel panel roof. Inside and to the right was a storage room, to the left a large kitchen, and straight ahead an expansive wood-floored space used for basketball, roller skating, Sunday evening bingo, parish functions, and some civic functions where perhaps three hundred could be seated at tables and chairs. Two large classrooms for religious education occupied the front second floor above the storage room and kitchen.

There were four other buildings on the property: an old maintenance shop built of hand-chiseled red sandstone blocks; the original church, now unsafe to use whose walls were bulging and built of the same red sandstone blocks, was used anyhow as the teen center; the sisters' house, built of the same stone and used by three Franciscan sisters; and a long narrow squat adobe building about to fall down, but used now as a thrift store selling (practically giving away) donated clothing and small items. Perhaps one hundred years earlier a German Franciscan Brother taught the Navajos how to chisel the sandstone into blocks. The thrift store was the original chicken coop for the mission, but had been fixed up for use by Sr. Bonita for her ministry to the people who came steadily all day long. Sr. Quinta cooked and served dinner for us at their house most every Monday through Friday. After praying Vespers, we would walk down to their place and have a very nice meal complete with dessert. During dinner we would talk about how our day went and share stories, and the Sisters would share how their days went, and Sr. Viola would share her experiences at the Chinle Clinic where she was a nurse practitioner.

After dinner that first evening at the Thunderbird Lodge, which Kevin liked despite it being a small cafeteria that served tasteless food, Kevin and I and the two Brothers chatted into the evening. Being so tired, I slept well and late into the next morning. During coffee and breakfast, Kevin told me about St. Anthony Mission at Many Farms eighteen miles north of Chinle which he wanted to turn over to me as the Pastor there. I would be having Mass there on Wednesday evenings and then again on Sunday mornings, picking up people along the road who needed a ride to the church, and then dropping them off again on the way back to Chinle, have religious instructions, and get a teen program going there again.

On Wednesday evening, Kevin took me to Many Farms, which was a very small "town" and which would be next to nothing if the large boarding school was not there. It seemed the Navajos did not live in towns, but rather at their own homesteads and sheep camps miles away from each other. St. Anthony Mission was one smaller Butler building of steel frame, steel sides and roof, divided into one-half church which might seat 100 if it was really packed, and one-half gathering room with a very small "apartment." Again, nothing was paved, and it seemed that if you weren't on the main road – very little was paved at all. For Mass that evening, only five ladies in their fifties, two Navajo three Anglo, showed up, four of which were glad to meet and welcome me. The other gave me a very cautious vibe, and she just stood off to the side and sized me up, almost like I was invading her space. I could feel the coldness and suspicion in her.

On our way home, I had so many questions about that mission and the area around it. Kevin tried to answer what he could and was surprised I picked up on the vibes from the suspicious woman. He explained that the previous priest was not much involved in the place and had let everything go downhill, and he had pretty much turned over everything to that lady who turned all the people away. She even took it upon herself to preach and have Communion services when that priest was away. I understood that my first task would be to deal with her presence there.

++++

Perhaps out of boredom, sometime during that first week, I asked Kevin what I should be doing for the parish other than administering the mission of St. Anthony's and having Mass there twice a week. He said, "Tom, I could tell you what I do or give you a whole list of things that you could do, but maybe those wouldn't suit you. So, why don't you take six months to see what you feel needs to be done, what you have to offer, and what suits who you are. Then we can talk about it again." Here I was fresh out of the seminary asking for something to do, raring to go, and he says to do nothing, observe, be aware, take it all in. At the time I was really disappointed by his answer, but I came to see that it was one of the best pieces of advice I had ever gotten. It literally changed my life, my ministry, my spirituality, my preaching, my approach to others – everything.

++++

I began ever more intently to listen to everything the Navajo People said and didn't say, to watch what they did, how they lived and related to each other, always asking myself what I could bring to that. I felt I had been sent there to help them be saved, but from what, for what? Once, I asked a ninety year old Navajo man, the Son of the One Who Talks a Lot, blinded in one eye with a thick cataract, if he had ever been baptized, and he answered in Navajo, "What for?" Rather than giving him the stock answer about salvation being found in Jesus, etc., I found I couldn't answer him. I pondered his answer in the months that followed. There is truth to his comment. What did they need baptism for? They surely believed in God, a higher power, an intricate spirit world. Would the Lord condemn him if he wasn't baptized? I knew He wouldn't.

This same old man asked me once if I would like for him to make a pair of Navajo moccasins for me to use. Not expecting much, I said, "Sure." After handing him the two sheets of paper he asked for, he traced each of my feet on the papers, and trying to fold the papers neatly, he finally just stuffed them in his pants pocket. About three months later he showed up with his granddaughter and with two new ankle-length moccasins. His granddaughter explained that he had tanned and molded the thick cowhide for the sole by hand, had himself tanned the deerskin for the upper, had hand-sewn them together with sinew, and even made two new 1976 quarters into buttons. He beamed with pride when I tried them on, and they both fit like a pair of gloves, and they even had an arch molded into them! I marveled with surprise at his craftsmanship. All he asked for was ten dollars, but I gave him twenty-five. Well worth it as I wore them many times for church services and ceremonies, and I still wear them on rare occasion now forty-two years later. They just won't wear out or come apart at the sinewed seams!

The Navajo had their own ceremonies, refined over hundreds (thousands?) of years, their Navajo religion. I needed to respect that. What did they need another religion for? Perhaps the ceremonies of the Catholic Church appealed to them because some saw their own religion being lost and abused by maltrained medicine men, tourists wanting sacred sand paintings for souvenirs, or the younger Navajos' disregard for their beliefs. Perhaps others saw the old ways as ineffective in the modern world against modern problems and illnesses. I know some of the other churches demanded that the people give up their ceremonies and medicine men.

++++

One medicine man told me of his experience with the Mormon elders who came to visit and teach his family. After many visits, the elders decided it was time for the man to be baptized as a Mormon. They arranged it for the next week and told him to have a large fire ready, and to have all of his Navajo paraphernalia and items he used for ceremonies ready. Next week they showed up, saw that he was ready, and told him he must first take all the items and throw them into the fire. The man replied, "No. You must first tear out all the pages from your Book of Mormon and throw them on the fire." The elders were shocked and started to babble, "We can't do that. The Book of Mormon is what we live by. We couldn't live without it. It would be a great disrespect to our God to burn it." The medicine man said, "It is the same with me." The elders left and never returned again.

++++

Perhaps another reason the Navajo might come to the Catholic Church was to use it as an alternative, a have-all-the-bases-covered "just-in-case-there-is-something-to-that-religion" alternative. Shortly after my arrival, Kevin asked me to take care of a funeral scheduled for 9:00am the next day. I had everything all ready for them, but no one showed up. After waiting for another hour, I blew out the candles, extinguished the incense, turned off the lights and locked the doors. At 3:30pm, the mortician knocked on the friary door and said the family was here for the funeral. When I told him I thought that the funeral was to be at 9am, he said, "You were right, Father, but the family wanted to have prayers at the mortuary, then we didn't leave Gallup until 9am, then we drove the two and one half hours to here, then they wanted to have a service at the Presbyterian Church, then at the Mormon Church, then at the Full Gospel Church, then at the Lutheran Church, but the family wanted to have the last funeral service at the Catholic Church because they knew the priest would go to the cemetery with them and bless the grave." It was also my first experience with "Navajo time."

Of course, while most all would say they were Christian, there were some who really believed in Jesus and felt that the Catholic Church was the best spiritual way for them and were fully committed to it. But, what about the ones who didn't? How were they relating to Christ and the Church? What would be my role? I got my answer during one of the scripture readings at a Mass during Advent: Emmanuel means "God with us." I was being called to be the presence of God with His people. All I had to give was myself, who I was, who I had become. All I could do was be with them, to preach mainly by being present – in much the same way that St. Francis would preach by walking through a town, not saying a word. God with us. Me with them. This would be the mold, the template, the standard for my ministry. If the People could not experience the Lord through me, with me, and in me, then my preaching and ministry would be in vain.

I realized that in order for me to be with them, I had to know them and they me. I had to study Navajo culture and history to be with them in who they are and how they had come to the present day, to learn the worlds of emergence, the four sacred mountains, the four sacred colors, the four directions, the four everything. I had to hear and understand the stories, the significance of Spider Woman/Changing Woman, how clan relationships influence so much of their lives, the coyote stories and morals, when to speak and not to speak and to whom, the taboos contributing to harmony and survival, the taboos surrounding death and its hold on the people, the pain of the Long Walk and Sheep Reduction Act – all these and so much more and how all these things have formed the Navajo today.

++++

First and foremost, I had to learn the Navajo language. Not to do so would be unthinkable. They did not "all speak English", and even the ones who did also spoke Navajo. Never to be able to speak with them in their own language, never to understand them when they spoke, I would never be able to be with them in any genuine way or be with them in one of their favorite activities of joking with each other or "just saying it." So long as one attended to their place in the family-clan, and who they could or should not joke with, it seemed anything could be the topic of a joke so long as they were "just saying it." This meant they were just kidding, and meant no harm, and others got a good laugh.

I did learn to converse fairly well, and to read, and write Navajo within four years of study at Navajo Community College. I was never able to understand word for word what I heard or read, but very able to grasp the meaning. After finishing all the Navajo Studies courses, I graduated with a certificate to teach Navajo language. I laughed at that presumption when they handed it to me, but then maybe the college was "just saying it."

Once, I went to a celebration where there was lots of food and the best tasting lamb. After I finished my plate, I went back up to the serving tables and asked in Navajo for some more meat. But, I forgot to pronounce a nasal "i" at the end of the word. So, instead of asking for more meat, I asked for the daughter. Everyone was so shocked, but then roared in laughter, and never let me forget that. I got to purposely mispronouncing words just to get a big laugh.

I did end up teaching it on a small scale to some Anglo boarding school teachers who wanted to converse in and write in Navajo with their students. Very few Navajos were able to read or write their own language, so I very gratifyingly taught a group of Navajo women who wanted to read the Bible in their own language to the point where they could read the first two readings at Mass while I would read the Gospel also in Navajo.

The only other three Franciscan priests on the reservation who spoke Navajo and I spent two years translating the Eucharistic Prayer from the Mass into the Navajo language in order to have it approved by Rome. That was quite an arduous task and involved a lot of meetings among the four of us and some trusted Navajos who helped us translate. I agreed to type the whole document and the many revisions along the way. Each phrase was given a page with: the Ecclesiastical Latin, below that the English approved translation of the Latin, below that the proposed Navajo translation, below that the word for word translation of the Navajo, below that the flowing meaning of the Navajo. The slightest mistake and revision required the complete re-typing of the whole five-lined page (before computers). Rome required perfection, and the four of us were perfectionists. It took another year after we sent the final document to Rome to get the final approval – without a single correction requested! As if anyone in the Roman Curia knew Navajo! The very sad part of getting the approval was that only the four of us knew enough Navajo to actually be able to use it at Mass.

++++

Meanwhile, I was administering Many Farms. Getting that one lady, an Anglo teacher at the boarding school – I will call her Connie – to accept me and my style would prove to be extremely difficult. She was belligerently against everything I would try to accomplish and would even sabotage my efforts. Over a stretch of nine months, my stomach would lock up as I drove to St. Anthony's not knowing what confrontation I would run into. She increasingly interrupted the Mass, and would stand up and speak or yell while I was preaching. I would not allow her to have even the slightest involvement in the management of the parish, which made her even more angry. I asked her over and over again to please sit down and be quiet so the rest of us could pray, which she would not do.

During one of my personal meditations at home, it occurred to me that perhaps I was dealing with something or someone more than just Connie -- something that was working through her; some other power that wanted to pull the rest of us at St. Anthony's apart, a spirit of division, some power that did not want us to worship the Lord. I called upon the Blessed Virgin Mary and all the Saints to help me. The next day, a Wednesday, I went there for Mass prepared with a box of rosaries. As usual, Connie was there, and as expected she began to interrupt the service. My plan was that if that happened, I would stop the Mass, hand a rosary to the other few who came, and we would begin to pray the glorious mysteries of the rosary together. Even though Connie's attacks intensified initially, by the second or third decade of the rosary, amazingly, she would sit down and be very quiet for the rest of the service, or she would storm out of the church in a fit of anger. I shared this with Fr. Kevin and the Sisters Bonita and Quinta during dinner, and gave them updates, and they all supported me. The Sisters even started to join us for Mass at Many Farms on Sundays after the Mass in Chinle, and then again on every Wednesday. They couldn't believe what Connie was doing or the transformation in her as we prayed the rosary. I very much appreciated the Sisters being with me for support at those services.

However, she never stopped doing it…

> "Lord, if the demon, the spirit of evil is to work anymore havoc among my people, let him, try to convince him to take it out on me and let my people go. I offer my body, feelings, emotions, intellect, and even my sanity to your disposal -- if he will only let my people go. They are so weak from dealing with this, Lord, just learning to stand. I have stood for a while, and even if I can stand no more when he is done with me, I can remember your love for me and the experience of your power in my life. This grace I beg of you that they may know and be convinced of your love for them and learn to respond to that love. Amen." Journal entry December 1977

As small as Many Farms was, everyone knew everyone's business, and everyone knew what was happening at the mission. The Navajo Chief of Police for the Chinle District was a member of the Chinle parish; and I met with him one day, described what was going on at Many Farms, and asked for his guidance about what could be done. I figured it was time to make it officially public and bring in the big guns (so to speak). He said he would be willing to come to Mass there to witness Connie's antics firsthand. He showed up in full uniform the next Sunday with his wife and family, and got an unbelievable eyeful and an earful. She put on quite a show. Afterwards, when everyone had left, he spoke to me about issuing a Cease and Desist Order for Disruption of Religious Services to her. It didn't take much thought, and with a sense of relief, I agreed with him to go ahead and get it done.

The next day, Monday morning, the police chief showed up at the boarding school, went to her classroom with the Principal, and took her to the school office. He handed to her an Order, signed by a Judge, to Cease and Desist Disruption of Religious Services. Later that day, he told me what he had done, and that she really let her sparks fly after that in front of the Principal, who told her that if there were any more outbursts she would be fired. Whoa! Thanking him for how he handled it, I asked what would be next if she didn't abide by the Order which I fully expected her to disregard. The next step would be to issue a Restraining Order to her, that she would never be allowed near St. Anthony's again. Gratefully, because I feared her getting physically violent, he also told me he would station an Officer at the church every time we had Mass for a month. But, my stomach would still cramp up every time I drove to Many Farms, but never again did she disrupt the Mass. In fact, sometimes she didn't show up at all as she went to Chinle for Mass. Kevin told me she never disrupted the Mass there, but she did complain to him about me overreacting, having her embarrassed at her place of work, and threatening her job. Kevin merely told her he agreed with me about how to handle the situation. Still, every time I saw Connie at the church there was such a sense of pure evil about her, and her eyes flashed intense vengeance toward me without a word. Never before had I experienced such a physical embodiment of evil, and, in fact, I was not inclined to believe it existed until I experienced it.

"I have never believed in the concrete reality of the devil until this year when I saw it so clearly personified in a person, and experienced it, and felt the effects of it on this person, the community, and on me. The force to divide, the spirit of division and alienation, the power to control and pull us away from our relationship with you, Lord. ...Lord, I get scared

when so many images, visions, feelings, gross and horrible actions are thrown up before me (as if the devil were vomiting in my mind and imagination). Give me strength and your peace in my fear at these times. ...Spirit of Evil I know the power of my Lord, his power for unity and peace – and it is in His hands that I place my life, my security and my only hope. ...Oh, how I want to be most wholly holy." Journal entry February 1978

++++

The Exorcisms

About this time, some strange things started to happen at the friary in Chinle. Fr. Kevin was on vacation and there was only Brother Eric and me there. At midnight, I was awakened by some banging noises, and I got up to investigate. The noises stopped, but I checked the doors to see if they were locked and if anyone was trying to get in, then went back to bed. The next morning, I asked Eric if he heard anything, and he said he did but thought it was me. The next night, it happened again, only this time much louder with the hallway door swinging and banging. Both Eric and I got up to investigate, finding nothing. The next night, I taped all the exterior doors on the inside along with the swinging door, and I dusted flour on the floors by the doors, to determine if someone was getting in the house. That night it happened again. I immediately got up to check. The swinging door was still swinging, the tape was broken on that door, there were no footprints in the flour, and the exterior doors still had the tape intact. Then we knew there was some disturbingly evil spirit causing the noises. I told Eric not to say anything to anyone about this.

I knew the house was being possessed and the evil was focused on me, and I had no doubt that Connie had everything to do with it. That morning, I called the Bishop's office in Gallup to make an appointment with him to discuss the situation, without divulging anything to his secretary, just saying it was a personal issue. After checking with the Bishop, he told me to come right in and the Bishop would see me. I got there in the middle of the afternoon after the two and a half hour drive to Gallup from Chinle. I shared with the Bishop the history of what was happening at Many Farms and the most recent incidents at the Chinle house. He was a very understanding and spiritual man and said he definitely felt an exorcism needed to be done on the house and on the church at Many Farms.

He gave me an old tattered black book on the Rite of Exorcism, told me he was assigning the ability to perform the exorcisms to me as a Franciscan priest, but to keep it absolutely confidential: no one must know about it other than Eric and me, and to report back to him after the exorcisms were done when I return the book. We prayed together and read Scripture, and spoke of the danger of the evil attaching itself to me; he laid his hands on my head and prayed for me and gave me his blessing. When I told him I was afraid, he said, "Be confident in the power of the Lord that is with you. His power is stronger than any evil, and He will not allow any harm to come to you. Trust in the Lord and his love for you and His people. In Christ you can do all things. Be firm and strong." He suggested that at midnight Brother Eric and I receive the Eucharist and pray the Rosary, and then perform the Rite precisely as it was in the book.

That night, Eric and I sat in our living room and began with the Bishop's instructions with a small altar set up with blessed candles burning, and a crucifix and a bowl of blessed Holy Water, and incense burning before us. Then we began. After Communion and the rosary, I held the Rite of Exorcism book in my left hand and began reading the words exactly and strongly. Eric held the Holy Water, and we both used our right hands to splash the water on all the walls of each room including the closets, and the hallway, and doors with my non-stop reading of the exorcism getting louder. Then we took the blessed incense and blessed the whole house. Then we took the Holy Water and incense and blessed the walls and doors on the exterior of the house The whole service was very exhausting, but very effective. Never again did we experience or sense any evil in the house. In fact, a very peaceful calm that was not there before penetrated the house and the surrounding area.

The next Sunday, I got to St. Anthony's in Many Farms two hours before Mass and kept the doors locked in order not to be disturbed while I performed the exorcism of the church building in the same manner as at our house. At the beginning of the Mass, I blessed the people with Holy Water and incense. The peacefulness and calm afterwards was noticeable again. Connie was not there nor did she ever come again. I heard that a week after the exorcisms she quit her job, packed up and moved to Phoenix.

After all that, the people started to return to the church cautiously little by little, and after some time it got to be quite a thriving little mission, and the church was full for Sunday Mass. The makeup was about one third Anglo/Hispanic, mainly from the boarding school, and about two thirds Navajo. Some of the teachers would bring some of the

Catholic Navajo students over to the church for Mass, activities, and religious education. While I tried a number of times to get a teen group going, they had all they could handle at the boarding school and the high school in Chinle, so I would go over there for some of the games and activities and talk with the adults and kids. We did have religious education taught by the Sisters and a couple of ladies after Mass on Sundays.

++++

Some of the people from Rough Rock, one half hour West of Many Farms, asked me to start having Sunday Mass there in one of their homes. Some others from Nazlini, forty-five minutes South of Chinle, asked me to come down there and have Sunday Mass in the Chapter Meeting House. So, I would have an early Mass at 9:00am in Rough Rock, then back to Many Farms for Mass at 10:30am, then back to Chinle for a lunch sandwich and soft drink, then down a very rutted, bumpy, dirt road to Nazlini for Mass at 2:00pm – if all went well. Always, I offered them the Sacrament of Confession before each Mass. Very few ever accepted the Sacrament.

I formed a lot of contacts and friendships with the people, and we got to trust each other more and more. One lady asked for Confession one Sunday, and we walked away from the group and sat on some boulders in the bright warm sunshine. She confessed that twenty years ago she had an abortion before she got married, and that she had never told anyone about it until now, including her husband. She held the secret and pain and guilt and shame inside all by herself all these years, and it was like the dead fetus was still in her mind and heart all this time; it was like she was still carrying the dead baby in her womb for twenty years of grieving. I was in awe of this woman and said nothing, just held her hands as she spoke and sobbed, letting out her sorrow and grief. We spoke for a while about her life during those twenty years, her life of love with her wonderful husband, not being able to become pregnant again and have more children, and the deep personal love that the Lord has had for her. She gave me the great gift, the great honor, of being the one to assure her that the Lord forgives her through absolution for this sin. It was as if this huge boulder which held her down for so long rose above her head and evaporated into the sunshine, as if she had been raised from among the dead, the mountains were leveled and the valleys filled in and the roads made straight for her in joy. I will never forget this, and I am still in awe of her.

++++

In May of 1978, our Franciscan Provincial came to Chile to visit personally with each of the friars, as was the custom every year. When he met with me, I shared everything that was going on at Many Farms and the other missions, and some of what was going on inside of me. He told me that Fr. Kevin was going to be moved to St. Michael's Mission, and that he will need a new Pastor to take over Chinle. Then he asked me to accept the Pastor position. I was more than a little floored that he thought I could handle it after only one year of ordination, traditionally a new priest was never assigned as a Pastor until he had been ordained for at least five years, so I thanked him for his confidence in me, but told him I didn't feel I was ready to be a Pastor yet and would like to turn down his request (which one does not normally do to the boss). I said that if he would appoint me as pastor, I would accept it out of obedience, but I would prefer he find someone else. He said he would let me know.

Why did I turn down the offer? There was a growing anxiety, depression, and confusion going on inside of me. Wondering where all this was leading me. Feeling alone. Wondering if I could be using my gifts better elsewhere, perhaps back East where there were more people and bigger parishes to minister to. I was committed to this life, to the Navajo people, but there was something going on, and I couldn't nail it down yet.

"This last week I was wondering just what use my ordination has been, seems such a waste out here. I could be teaching in one of our high schools, studying to be a prof at St Leonard or Scotus. I have abilities not being used. I'm not doing much here, no great results. Then You led me to Is. 49 – and like Isaiah, I felt I had "toiled in vain, exhausted myself for nothing." Yet You reassure me that great things will come. You call me a "restorer of the people, a light, a salvation instrument." You call me further, broaden my ministry. Can the greatness you meant for you suffering servant Isaiah be meant for me too?" Journal excerpt May 1978

++++

June came, Kevin left as did one of the Brothers, and I got a call from the Provincial informing me that a priest returning to the States from the Philippine missions had agreed to be Pastor at Chinle, and that he would be arriving in a month. I was in effect pastor-for-a-month, having Mass every day in Chinle, another on Wednesday evening, another on Saturday evening, and four on Sunday. Having to study the different readings for each Mass during the week and prepare a homily for each one and another for the weekend was tiring. After each preparation, I would pray, "Ok Holy Spirit, I did my part. Now take that and You do Your part." But, it got me wondering what were the people coming to Mass for? What did they really need to hear? What were they looking for? What would make a difference in their lives? When I asked them that during one homily, I got a lot of varied answers: a time to connect with the Lord and friends, to pray for their families, to pray for the sick people they knew, for healing, for the relatives who drank too much, for relatives who were dying, to be healed from the hurt and pain in their lives, for peace in their families and in the world, and on and on. They had a reason, a purpose, an emptiness which they expected me to help them fill. I prayed I could say even just one small thing that would mean something to just one of them each time. Then my preaching would be worthwhile. After one Mass, a lady came up to me and said, "Father Tom when you were preaching this morning I felt like I was the only person in the church and you were preaching directly to me." I said, "I was."

The new Pastor showed up in July and seemed like a nice enough guy, perhaps twelve years my senior. I showed him around the mission, explained the activities we had going on and the participation of the laity, the financial books, how the parish was run, the relationship between Many Farms which I took care of and Chinle which he would take care of, introduced him to the Sisters and a number of people around town, and everything else he would need to know. However, it didn't take long before he would show that he was going to take control and be "the boss."

For example, Our Lady of Fatima Parish had bingo every Sunday evening in the parish hall. It was run by the parishioners: the tables and chairs for 200 were set up by the parishioners, the concessions were run by the parishioners, and the number calling and verifications were run by the parishioners – which they were happy to do. Fr. failed to set up a schedule for the bingo helpers, which was the custom, and publish it in the bulletin for a couple of Sundays. Some of the helpers came to me and asked when they were going to be needed. I told them to come on Sunday for bingo and ask Fr. if he wanted their help. The people usually came on Saturday afternoon to set up the tables and chairs for the event, but he told me to do it. Since he was in a bind that week, I swallowed what I felt and did it for the people.

The next Saturday, he again told me to go down and set up all the tables and chairs. I said, "Look, I don't know what your problem is, but before you came the people were glad to do this as their way of supporting the parish. You are turning them away. You knew the bingo workers' schedule needed to be published in the bulletin for Chinle. You haven't been doing that. So, this is your problem, not mine. I will not be ordered around. I will not be your slave. If you want the tables and chairs up, get the people to do it again or do it yourself." He turned red and slammed the back door as he walked down to the hall. Strangely, he did set them up every Saturday afternoon. On many other occasions he tried to tell me what to do, not ask, not discuss, just <u>tell</u>. He tried to take control of St. Anthony Mission in Many Farms, telling me what to do and how to handle this and that, especially regarding Connie. I figured I had a hell of a lot more experience with the Navajo and that parish than he did, and I very curtly said, "Back off, and lay off!"

A wall seemed to be growing between us, and he shared only what was necessary, and even then very coldly. It seemed to me he was very threatened by me. Maybe he never had to work with or live with someone like me, and I certainly never worked with or lived with someone like him. As much as I tried to talk with him, or include him, or show interest in him I would always run into that wall. I just could not understand him at all. I didn't know where he was at in his head, what he was thinking, or what any of his plans were for the parish. He was a passive aggressive. It got to the point where there was no "working with", just the two of us ministering totally separately. It also got to the point where there was no "living with", just the two of us in the same house talking very little and sharing even less. The Brother living with us did his bidding -- that was how he had been trained to relate to priests.

Needless to say, all the old feelings of loneliness and being alone and having no support came creeping back in a big way, like cockroaches on a summer-heated evening. I called my spiritual director at St. Leonard, and we spoke for a long time. His thoughts: don't give the situation or persons power over you, who you are, to make you unhappy; take it easy on yourself, when you're down – get out; be realistic and use common sense, if life there is unbearable, seek out persons you can live with at this time in your life.

I decided to take vacation in August for two weeks and drove back to Ohio to visit Mom and Dad and the family. The time away from the reservation and Chinle was much needed, and working in their yard was good therapy despite the heat and heavy humidity. I helped out with Masses at Sacred Heart Church and enjoyed preaching there to a full church. I visited those I wanted to see, and vacation was over too soon. My sister Mary Clare had never been out West, so the two of us packed too many ham sandwiches and hit the road on a Thursday, driving straight through to New Mexico so I would be there for the weekend Masses. The plan was to take the next week and show her around the Southwest and then drop her off at the airport in Albuquerque.

Dad Dies

But – at 3:00am on Sunday morning -- I got a phone call from home telling me that Dad died. His death was a shock for my sister and me since we had just been there four days before. I had the Sunday Masses, we packed and got in the car and headed for the airport in Albuquerque. During the four hour flight back to Ohio, I was feeling and thinking about the man who was my Dad, now dead at 60 years old. Honestly, I had to admit we were never really close to each other, I never really knew him, and I never remembered him saying "I love you" to me. When I was young, he was not the kind of Dad I wanted or felt I needed. He didn't go with me to play baseball at the ball diamond like the Dads of my other classmates did. He just wasn't around or involved much in my life, and I dearly yearned for that. He did take the family to LeSourdsville Lake Amusement Park near Middletown once every summer for Kroger Days, or to Coney Island Amusement Park near Cincinnati. I remembered him buying reams and reams of ride tickets, and he had such real joy and pride dispensing them to us as we ran to the rides we wanted to get on. At Christmas, he was happy passing out gifts to the young ones, but never did I see him get down on the floor and play with them. He loved to have a good time with his high school classmates, and wanted to have parties at our house with them, but money was always an issue – to take it for that would mean taking it from something else that was needed more. I am sure he was down and depressed for not being able to make enough money to live the grand life, only making enough to support his wife and large family with very little left over. Honestly, I don't know how he ever did that, but he did. He was a constant worrier and a fighter beyond his limitations and got it done somehow or other. He was tired all the time and rested less than he would have liked to. After all, how could Mom keep all the kids quiet when Dad wanted to rest? She couldn't.

I asked Mom once why she and Dad had so many children. "Well, we just took what the Lord gave us," she said. "Did you ever try birth control?" "Oh no, the Church would never allow that." "Did you ever try the rhythm method?" "We did, but it seemed to work the opposite way for us." "Did you ever try abstinence?" "I did, but your father wouldn't!"

Mom asked, "And which one do you think we should have stopped at?" I quickly responded, "Well, me of course!"

He had very painful eyes from glaucoma, and at least one operation on his eyes to release the pressure. In fact, his right eye eventually went blind for some time before it got horribly inflamed and had to be removed and replaced with a glass eye. Shortly after that, and perhaps because of the tremendous emotional and physical pain and trauma, he had a stroke at 54 years which partially paralyzed his left side, making it difficult for him to walk and express himself clearly, especially in the evening when he was tired, and he seemed to be in constant pain. He couldn't drive after that and had to quit his job. His frustration and depression would erupt into verbally abusive outbursts for the slightest reason and often at the younger children, grandchildren, and at Mom, and at me, particularly when he did not take his medication. It seemed we walked on eggshells to not upset him. He gave up the fight, except for the one deep inside of himself, and perhaps even that. All this destroyed the man he was and his self-worth, and he turned to alcohol for relief. If I said realistically that he was an alcoholic later in life, some of my brothers and sisters would disagree.

Needless to say, it was very hard for me to have his funeral Mass. In my memory, it is all a blur, except that at the cemetery after the prayers were finished and the others had left I wanted to stay while the caretakers lowered his casket into the ground as was the custom on the reservation. I stood there sobbing until my brother Ed pulled me away. It was too much for him.

++++

A few days after the funeral, I flew back to the Southwest with some anxiety about what my life was becoming and the decisions I needed to make. Knowing the Navajo reservation and being with the Navajo people was the right place for me at this time, how could I be with them more, minister to them more effectively, while being away from the friary house as much as possible? I prayed a lot for guidance and was led to re-read the writings and life of St. Francis. To live as poorly as possible, to be an itinerant minister, to be open to whatever the Lord would present to me, to rebuild His house not of stones or mortar but inside hearts and minds, to be His presence to His people as a Franciscan priest, never staying in one place, to work for what I needed and beg if necessary; this was the way of life I felt called to more and more. I had no idea what this would bring. I had never been so drastic in trying to live the life of Jesus and St. Francis, to give everything away and go follow Him.

"Somehow I am made to be lonely, to sink to the dark cave of earth time and time again and speak to Lady Loneliness and hold her and comfort her and lead her gently, firmly, out into the light again. She has so much to offer – She has the ability to sink to the dark heart-caves of others, and in there to transform them, to be with them, to bring them peace through saying nothing. She looks into others' eyes and understands their hearts and broken spirits. So often though she is not wanted. She is not beautiful, and others are afraid to acknowledge her in themselves, so she enters into her own Loneliness to understand once again.

My Lady, present in winter and springtime alike, teaching me, guiding me, making me whole, healing my brokenness. I find the more I am with her, the more I am like her, searching the depths, wanting so much to heal, to be peace-bringer, and yet feared and hated and abandoned.

She has a Sister I would like to know better. She has made overtures to me, but I seem to be playing hard to get. Strange, as I get to know Lady Loneliness more, I feel I know Lady Poverty more. In fact, perhaps Lady Poverty is there first wherever Lady Loneliness and I go. She takes so many forms and is so hard to understand or even touch. She even scares me a little; and when I hear her calling my name, I try to ignore her, but she too strikes my heart, and Lady Loneliness helps me to understand her call.

Lord, Lady Loneliness seems to be leading me to a very deep relationship with Lady Poverty, as if Lady Loneliness were the herald only. In truth, right now I feel called to, guided to, even deeper love of Lady Poverty. Help me to see who and what she is, how we can work together for the wholeness of others in absolute dependence on You." Journal excerpt October 1978

I explained to the Pastor what I was thinking and what I wanted to do. I got no understanding, no encouragement, no response from him.

Itinerant Ministry

It was a joyous day when I received permission from the Provincial and his counselors in Cincinnati to embark on an itinerant ministry. Initially, I would leave Chinle on Monday morning in the old Chevy Suburban with no direction in mind, stopping at any house and hogan (traditional six or eight-sided log home) I came upon to visit the occupants and pray with them and bless their homes. From my studies, I had learned that the proper way to approach a Navajo's home was to pull up to the home and sit there for a while (5-10 minutes, and sometimes even more) until all the dogs calmed down and there seemed to be some movement inside. If the occupants did not come outside, then it would be appropriate to knock on the door four times – and wait. If there was no response, usually no one was home or they didn't want to be disturbed, I would get back into the Suburban and move onto the next home I came upon. Most every single person and family was very surprised and happy that the priest in the long brown robe was coming to their home as no one remembered that ever happening before, no one from the church had ever visited them. How sad.

Letter from Mom Spring 1979

Now for the letter you sent: I have read it and reread it and each time I cry. Not a sad weeping but a humble one. I know being permitted to live the lifestyle you have set up for yourself will not only be difficult, lonely, and dangerous, but also will take complete trust in God. I feel you have that special gift. I know that in the past over-indulgence, over-spending, and selfishness in the Order irked you. Your insight, now that you are older, that some can and some can't and you must is a gift.

After reading your letter I don't see how the Definitors, etc. can deny you at least a try. The people don't come to you. You must go out and invite them, just as the Lord did. It's hard to believe that there are people that have never heard Bible stories, never read the Gospels, in their language. Your trips to Nazlini showed you for sure there was a need.

This would be a difficult and sometimes discouraging mission. The God who seems to consume your whole being at times can also seem so very far away. I hope my prayers will help in these times.

It's hard for me to formulate the right words as to how I feel also, but I don't think I ever loved you more than when I read that letter, or was as proud. It was inspired. Now, here it is almost 15 minutes gone by and I've been serious all that time. That's not like me...   *Love and miss you -- Mom*

Week after week, Monday morning through Friday evening, I would herd sheep while avoiding the rattlesnakes, chop wood, haul water, join in butchering a sheep and drinking a little of the warm blood before it coagulated, pray with the Navajo, read Scripture in their language, and play games with the children, all dependent on how comfortable they were with me being there, and sleep in the rear of the Suburban, or in their homes, if invited. After a number of months ministering this way, the Pastor told me he didn't want me to use the Suburban anymore. There were two other vehicles at the Chinle friary, a nice four-door sedan and a truck for his use, but there was no explanation.

However, not having a vehicle now didn't stop me. In fact, I got closer to the people that way. I would take off on Monday morning with a small knapsack over my shoulder, walking down the roads hitchhiking in my brown robe. When someone would stop and ask, "Where are you going Father?", I would say, "To your house." Always surprised, sometimes laughing, thinking I was joking, "just saying it", but always saying, "Alright, get in," or "Get in back." I found that the best way to see the Navajo reservation was from the back of a pickup. So many friendships were formed, and word got around quickly. The teenagers nicknamed me "turtle." When I asked why, they said, "Well, your last name is 'Shell-on-back' (Schellenbach), and the Navajo name for a turtle means 'the one who is tired of walking'." It sounded good to me, and we laughed every time. The older people said Turtle was a good name because it meant "long life." I didn't get the connection and asked about it. "Well," they said, "turtles live a long time, they look really old, and it takes them a long time to get there." Ok, then, that explained it. I also took to giving the younger children rides with them lying flat on my back and me crawling v-e-r-y slowly on the ground like a turtle. We always had a lot of fun.

++++

On weekends, some of the people who lived quite a distance from Chinle would come to the house and ask for me to come to visit their families. They would show up on Monday morning and take me home with them, sometimes wanting me to stay all week, during which time I would also walk to the nearby homes to visit with those families. One such family from Nazlini asked me to come down because the Grandma wanted to be baptized. I told them I would have to give instructions for a while before I could baptize her. That was fine with them, and I climbed in the back of their pickup with some of the grandkids. Also, I took along a handheld cassette tape player and some instructional tapes of the Catechism which one of the other Franciscan priests had recorded in Navajo.

When we got to their house way out in the boonies, the Grandma sat in the middle of the sofa on the west side of a rather large room, with daughters on either side of her. She wanted to wait, and we small-talked about their lives while all of her children and grandchildren gathered in the room and sat on the floor. There must have been thirty of them of all ages. I offered a prayer, and everyone else who wanted to offered a prayer. After I spoke a sentence in English, the daughters would translate it into Navajo for all to understand. If there were any questions, the daughters translated into English for me. I would respond, they translated, questions, translation, my teaching, they translated, back and forth, on and on for most of the day. Even when I played the Navajo tapes, there were questions, and translations, and further translations, etc. It was a tedious and exhausting process, but I was encouraged by the questions and the desire to truly understand, and I was very surprised how well-behaved and quiet the grandkids were. When I told the Grandma we would do this for two months, she said one of her children would pick me up in Chinle every Sunday afternoon. They drove me back to Chinle in the early evening.

(I learned that Grandmothers were in charge of the families, most everything went through them as they called the shots; if anyone in the family crossed them, they were reprimanded. In this matriarchal society, when the young woman got married, the new husband would leave his family and go to live with hers, but he should not speak with the mother-in-law. All land was handed down through the women of the family, and all children were born into the mother's clan.)

On Sundays, we followed the same procedure all afternoon. On the last Sunday after the two months, Grandma was dressed in her finest silver and turquoise jewelry, deep blue pleated velvet skirt, deep blue velvet blouse with silver buttons, a concho belt, deerskin moccasins, and her hair in a traditional Navajo bun, and everyone else was dressed in the best and cleanest clothes they had, the girls' hair combed back in a bun, the boys' hair slicked down and parted. Other relatives were there cooking frybread and mutton stew, and they had even butchered a sheep for the occasion. When I asked Grandma if she was ready to be baptized, she said yes, and that she wanted all of her children and grandchildren baptized too. I baptized Grandma first, then the thirty-five others. After each one was baptized, she or he returned to their place on the floor and waited until I was finished with all of them. It took quite a while for the mass baptism, and it was one of the most deeply spiritual moments of my life. Then the feeding took place with the youngest being fed first and on up the age ladder. The daughters wanted me to go through the line and eat first, but I told them I would eat with Grandma, so they prepared a plate for her and brought one to me also with bowls of delicious mutton stew and plates of all the other food. Their fry bread was the best! After the celebration, now stuffed, they carted me back to Chinle.

++++

On a Sunday afternoon in February of 1979 one of Grandma's daughters came to the back door of the Chinle house and said her mother wanted to talk to me at the truck. She wanted me to come down to their house to pray for her sister. I got into the truck for the dusty washboarded road ride to Nazlini. When we got there, all the children were at the house, with a couple newly arrived great-grandchildren, and Grandpa. The daughter told me that her father wanted to talk to me first. After meeting him for the first time, we stepped outside in the warm sunshine. After the appropriate standing there in silence, the conversation went like this:

> Grandpa: "Father, I want to ask you a question." (in broken English)
> Tom: "Ok. What's on your mind?"
> (pause)
> G: "I know what the law says. I know what the other preachers say. But, I want to know what you say."
> T: "Alright."
> G: "Can I keep my two wives?"
> I indirectly stared at him off to the side (one never stares at anyone in the eyes or even looks them in the eyes for more than a few seconds). I thought inside, "Is this a trap? Is he a Mormon? A Cop?" But I could see the sincerest pain in his face, and it melted my suspicion and a good bit of my legalism. I stared at the ground, then crouched close to the ground, I began to trace a circle in the dust with a stick and I asked,
> T: "Do you love both of your wives equally and in the same way?"
> G: "Yes."

T: "Do you love the children from both of your wives all in the same way?"

G: "Yes."

T: "Do you take care of both of your wives in what they need?"

G: "Yes."

T: "And do you take care of all the children in what they need?"

G: "Yes. I don't have much money, but I do the best I can." (pause)

T: "Then I have a question for you, How can that be wrong?"

Glancing up at him, I could see the pain had left his face, and I also noticed Grandma flanked by all the children in the doorway behind him. The daughter came outside and said, "My Mother wants you to come with us and pray for someone." They all poured out of the house, and I followed them for a short walk across the desert in the warm February sunshine, under the bright blue Arizona sky, up a small hill to a one room gray-stuccoed wood-framed house. Everyone packed into the small space with me being the last to enter. I noticed the photos tacked on the walls, a framed picture of Jesus, the Pendleton blankets folded neatly and hanging from a clothes rod, the little pot-belly wood stove to the right of the doorway, and Grandma standing next to the bed to the left. As I wedged to the bedside the children squeezed aside. Lying there was a conscious, but very thin and fragile Navajo woman, Grandma's sister and Grandpa's second wife, perhaps in her sixties (although it was always very hard for me to tell a Navajo woman's age). She appeared to have been sick for some time, but I did recognize her as one of the three in the front seat of the pickup when this family had come to the Chinle church a number of months ago asking about baptism.

Grandma unbuttoned the sleeves of her sister's deep purple velvet Navajo blouse and revealed her arms. The skin of the woman's face, neck, and hands while gaunt was smooth, but her arms looked worse than prunes. I immediately asked if she had been taken to the clinic to see the doctor. "Yes, many times. He gave pills and creams, but it didn't help," said the daughter. "Did you take her to the medicine man and have a ceremony done on her?" "Yes, but it didn't help either." I felt an anger deep inside that nothing had been able to help this lady who was literally and obviously shriveling up and dying. "My Mother wants you to pray for her sister."

I felt a power rising up within me.

I asked one of the teenage boys by the door to run and get a large bowl of water and some salt. He returned quickly, and as he held the bowl I put a small amount of salt in my left hand, prayed aloud over it, and blessed it. As I slowly sprinkled the salt into the water I prayed over the water and blessed it, spreading the water four times with signs of the cross. I told everyone that I would bless the house and all of them first, as I proceeded with much difficulty through the group. Beginning with the doorway, then clockwise around the room, I threw dripping handfuls of the holy water at the walls, beyond the bed, over the heads of everyone, praying aloud for peace, harmony, and good health, and material things needed and a good life, the power of the Lord to drive out all evil and show His love for us and His healing for this woman. I taught them all how to make the sign of the cross on themselves after dipping their hand in the water, calling on the Father, Son, and Holy Spirit to come and be with us in this room. The bowl was passed around; some did make the sign of the cross fairly well, others took some of the water and breathed into their hands and ran the holy water over their faces and through their hair, and the youngsters were just thirsty and drank some of it.

I wedged back to the bedside and began bathing the lady's face and hair, and arms with the Holy Water, leaving tiny puddles in her deep wrinkles, like miniscule canyons after a rainstorm. With Holy Oil for the Anointing of the Sick I made the sign of the cross on her warm forehead, the top of her breastbone, the palms and tops of her hands, and on the bottoms and tops of her feet. Then I told as many as could to come near the bed to touch the lady or the bed or the person in front of them to form a connection with her from the front of the room to the back. We all prayed the Our Father together, and I prayed aloud for her good health as I laid my hands on her head. Then Grandma began to pray with tears and sobs for her sick sister, on and on in Navajo fashion, and then the daughters took turns praying, as did anyone else who wanted to. Then I prayed the Navajo HolyWay Prayer from the Blessingway Ceremony:

> In Beauty I walk
> With Beauty before me I walk
> With Beauty behind me I walk
> With Beauty above me I walk
> With Beauty all around me I walk
> It has become Beauty again
> It has become Beauty again
> It has become Beauty again
> It has become Beauty again

Then I instructed them to give her something to eat as the little ones began pouring out the door into the early darkness, and we all followed with Grandma, Grandpa and me being the last to leave. We could hear the always silent children laughing and having fun. As we stepped outside into the cold, crisp evening, it was snowing heavily with already three inches of snow on the ground and everything was covered in white. Beauty had returned. Leaving our footprints in the desert, Grandma leaned toward me, touched my arm and said, "It is good. It is a good sign, Father."

++++

A month later, Grandpa and his two wives (Grandma and her sister) and a truck bed full of children pulled up to the back door of the Chinle friary. As I walked over to greet them I saw the transformation of Grandma's sister. Without a word she pulled up the sleeves of her blue velvet blouse to show me her smooth skin, and smiled broadly as I ran my hands over her arms. Beauty had returned for her. Grandma reached over, took my hand, and said in Navajo, "Medicine Man Priest", and handed me a "bird rug" she had woven just for me. I still cherish it in our house.

The greatest blessing for Grandma's sister and Grandpa's second wife was feeling the love of her family, and knowing she didn't have to leave it, and knowing that she was worthwhile and acceptable once again. She could feel like she was an important part of her family again. She walks in Beauty.

+++

While I was ministering out among the people, I discovered that the real way to learn the Navajo language and culture – the do's and don'ts, hospitality, kindness, firmness and gentleness, care for each other especially the children, living with so very little, not planning, rather waiting and taking one's time – the real lessons, the real teaching, came when I would go out and stay with the people. One of the highest praises for how well I spoke Navajo came from an old blind man who refused to believe I was a white man. Then again, maybe he was "just kidding" and "just saying that."

Participating in Native Ceremonies

I was invited to a Native American Church meeting that takes place in a large teepee and begins at nightfall and ends at dawn the next morning, sitting cross-legged on the dirt the whole time. These meetings are sometimes call Peyote Ceremonies where peyote is eaten and smoked, and the tea from it is drunk. The peyote is the "sacrament" of the ceremony to cause light hallucinations, and is also an emetic, with the intention of elevating one to another level of spirituality. Each meeting is led by a Roadman, a "priest." For the one I attended, an elderly visiting Roadman, who was also a very respected and sought after Medicine Man from Window Rock, was invited to preside. When he entered the teepee and saw me in my brown robe and a stole, with tears of joy in his eyes, he said, "For sixty years I have prayed for this day when I could have a Catholic priest present with us at one of my meetings. Now that day is here. My prayer is answered. I can move on now. I am ready to die." All during the night the participants took turns tapping the taut wet deerskin covering the mouth of a medium-sized Navajo pottery jug with a little water in it, a water drum, with a special stick with one end bent into a perfect circle while they sang their lengthy personal songs, then it was passed clockwise to their left and it was that person's turn.

When it came to me, I beat the drum in their fashion and sang the Our Father in chant. There were so many in the teepee that the drum never made it around a second time. When it was time to imbibe in the sacrament in the three forms, I did as the others, but was disappointed that it had no effect on me whatsoever. I was so glad I went to the meeting. It was a perfectly crisp, clear night with stars thickly covering the sky from the East horizon to the West horizon, and I will always remember the drumming, the warming fire and its smoke rising through the smoke hole, the smell of Navajo juniper incense, the respect for the sacrament, the focus and intensity of the Roadman and all there, how we were all one, and the blazing sunrise and its significance to the people.

101

"For the Navajo, song is a necessity." I can't remember where I read this, but I found it to be absolutely true. I began singing the Eucharistic Prayer at all my Masses. For the Navajo People, it seemed to me that just saying the words was not enough. The words needed to be sung to tap into an underlying meaning and to bring forth a greater blessing.

Whenever I was invited to attend a ceremony, I would make every effort to go. Twice, I was asked to attend "Blessingway" ceremonies at which the Medicine Man invited me to assist him in making the sandpainting, which involved pinching the colored sand between my right thumb and index finger and drawing very thin lines on the ground inside the hogan with everyone watching as the picture was formed. It was quite an honor, and a lot of pressure to get it right! Under his direction, it had to be perfect, or the ceremony would not be effective for the patient. All Navajo religious ceremonies and dances are intended solely for healing a patient or to help them on their way in life, never to celebrate a feast or occasion as the Pueblos do. Even traditional weddings were packed with relatives giving lengthy instructions, warnings, advice to the young couple to help them in their new life; and to assure them they would never be alone, that the family and the relatives would always be watching and helping them along the way.

++++

The people at Many Farms mission wanted a hogan next to the church so they could have traditional ceremonies and weddings there. We organized a group of men to help with and oversee the building of it, and a group of women who would provide a lunch each day we worked on it. The large old hogan parish hall at Lukachukai was being dismantled, so we went up there with a truck and flatbed trailer for a number of weeks to get the logs, most of which were at least a foot in diameter, twelve feet long, and extremely heavy. Building the hogan took about three months, beginning on the Spring Equinox so the doorway would face perfectly East and the rising sun rays on that day would shine directly through the door and onto the West wall. It was eight-sided, but we did not make the traditional domed roof of logs which had to be placed so precisely rising from the walls on to the top crowned with an open smoke hole and covered with bark and dirt. The weight would have been too much. Our roof was framed with two-by-six lumber, covered with plywood, roofed with asphalt shingles, and peaked with an open smoke hole. For the hogan blessing after Sunday Mass we had a Medicine Man member of the church do a blessing and place the four sacred stones under the threshold, and I did a Catholic house blessing, and we all had a very nice lunch and celebration afterwards. Before I was transferred, I used it once to have the Wednesday evening Mass there, all of us sitting on the dirt floor in Navajo fashion, with a small altar near the West wall. However, I was told later that it was never used again for anything except storage. I was saddened.

++++

The situation at the friary was becoming more and more tense for me. I was becoming more and more lonely and more and more resentful. After asking the Pastor whether St. Anthony Mission could borrow money from Chinle to have their parking lot paved, I was simply told no. It turned out okay anyhow. We had three very lucrative yard sales at the church, and I asked some benefactors back East to pitch in, and the contractor who just happened to be repaving the highway out front needed somewhere to dump the ground old asphalt. I made a deal with the contractor to dump the asphalt on our dirt lot if he would absorb half the cost of paving the lot. He dumped the asphalt as substrate, graded it, packed it firm, and paved the whole lot for what we had raised -- no more having to push vehicles out of the sticky mud.

++++

For Christmas, I asked a Chinle parishioner who knew how to read Navajo if the Pastor had asked him to read at Chinle for the Mass. He said no, and I asked if he would come to Many Farms to read there for Christmas Eve Mass. He agreed, and when the Pastor found out, he yelled at me for not checking with him first since he was going to ask this guy. So, I went to the man and explained that he couldn't read for us, that the Pastor wouldn't allow it. So when the Pastor did ask him, the guy told him no, that he didn't want to get in the middle of this. And I went ahead and read all the readings in Navajo from then on at Many Farms.

++++

Not remembering the exact month or year, in perhaps 1979, Fr. Edwin came out to visit. He helped me a lot by letting me tell him about my life as we took a number of hikes. When the week was up, I drove him to Albuquerque to catch his flight the next day, but we went out to dinner to a nice place that evening. Towards the end of dinner I began to feel very badly, every noise and voice seemed so amplified I had to plug my ears with my fingers, and cover my eyes because the lights seemed blinding. Then I stood up to go to the restroom to get away, and don't remember anything after that until I came to in the hospital not knowing who I was or when I was born or any of the other questions they were asking me in the emergency room. When Edwin got there, he told them that after I stood up I ended up on the floor rolling violently and flailing my arms and legs, and losing control of my bladder.

The doctors gave me an EEG, found irregular brain waves, and started me on medication, phenobarbital and dilantin, for epileptic seizures. I was so weak I slept for three days at the hospital and then was released to go back to Chinle. The Provincial called and said that epilepsy used to be an impediment to celebrating the Eucharist, but with medication to control it, I could still have Mass. Actually, the medication didn't control the seizures very well at first. Without warning, I had three more grand mal seizures at the house at Chinle the first two months after the diagnosis, and I got pretty well banged up. The medication was increased each time until the seizures stopped. The problem with the medication was that it left me very tired and with no energy, and it forced me to take a lengthy nap in the afternoon for the first time in my life. Of course, the situation knocked my self-image off kilter for years.

A different doctor suggested that the seizures were stress induced. Dealing with everything I was going through, my brain and my body were saying, "Look, if you aren't going to deal with this in a constructive and positive manner, we will force you and shut you down. Get out of the situation now and get away from the stress!"

++++

I felt like I had to do everything on my own with no support or help from the Pastor, like slogging in foot-thick mud and getting nowhere very slowly. I spent more and more time at a secret shallow cave I found on the south rim of Canyon de Chelly praying, crying at times, trying to make peace within myself. One afternoon, I went out to the cave and lied down to take a nap. The sky darkened and the wind picked up. It started to get really cold, but I couldn't leave because it was raining so hard. Shivering, I scooted against the back of the cave, still with a full view of the canyon and the waterfalls developing down the red walls. The rain stopped, and there appeared a brilliant rainbow with one arm reaching all the way to the bottom of the canyon. It was as if I was being hypnotized by the Beauty of the Lord, feeling His presence with me with no doubts. As the rainbow faded, it started to snow heavily sticking to everything, dressing in white the red rocks, the cedars and pinon trees green and white. All this and snow, too? I did nothing. This was all given to me.

> *"Consider the lilies of the field, how they grow; they toil not, neither do they spin; yet I say unto you that even Solomon in all his glory was not arrayed like one of these." Matthew 6:28*

++++

I believe it was in 1979 that we got word that there was trouble at the Lukachukai Church. Someone had torched the Sister's house and shot the Pastor. The objective was to kill the pastor, but the rifle bullet through the window lodged in his spine and paralyzed the bottom half of his body for the rest of his life. The two-story chiseled red sandstone Sister's house was a total loss, but the Sisters were not harmed in any way. Despite the Navajo Police and the FBI doing a thorough investigation, no reason, no motives, and no suspects were ever found. There were some leads and lots of gossip, but not enough for prosecution, and it remains a great unsolved case. The Diocese and the Franciscans closed the mission fearing the deranged person or persons would harm others. From then on, Sunday Mass was served by the priest from Navajo, New Mexico.

During the two years Lukachukai was vacant, the Franciscan Brothers Work Crew surrounded the property with a six foot chain link fence topped with barbed wire, renovated the friary, and gutted the inside, making everything inside new and up-to-date and modern, to the tune of $150,000.00. True, the old house did need remodeling and new furniture, but for that amount? The reasoning given was that what was done would attract another priest to come and reopen the mission, and that he would be more secure. Another addition to the property was two doberman pinschers trained to attack. The Brothers did nothing to fix up the Church. Personally, I was appalled and felt the whole thing was scandalous. This outrageous, expensive effort was totally against everything we were meant to be as followers of St. Francis, who would make every effort to be totally accessible to the people no matter the danger, would live in total poverty, trusting totally in the Lord and His love, and not living in fear. Jesus promised us: "Be not afraid for I am with you."

There was so much going on inside of myself at this time, so much turmoil in my thoughts, feelings, depression, sexuality, ministry, anger, living situation, etc. etc. The spectre of acting out on any of these issues scared the hell out of me, and I never did, while suicidal thoughts scared the hell out of me even more. My being seemed split: the giver on one side, the taker on the other, This Tom versus the Other Tom, the exterior battling the interior. The interior needed to be kept in a glass jar with the lid tightly screwed on. I could not let him out. I could not hear him squawk. But I knew he was watching my every move judging fake me.

No amount of busyness in my ministry, no amount of prayer, no amount of faith, no amount of trying to control my life worked anymore. I needed a total change. I needed simplicity. What I really needed to do was to open the glass jar and make a friend with the Other Tom, accepting each issue, having the Lord bless them, having me bless them, no more throwing rocks at them to make them go away, and bring it all into the harmony and wholeness which was ME.

Why So Soon Winter?
Cool Spring and windy dry months of Summer and hot,
One whole month and half left alone, abandoned, not wanted,
Even by self at times as self played havoc within
Afraid to admit me as "he."
Fearful images, dreams of breaking-in, thoughts of losing,
And painful growth in one-liness,

Then admitting and knowing of gain..., and hurt so deep to be healed.
To be met by frost in the Canyon and tamarisks yellowed
And Fall winds, and Sun sleeping later and sooner
And talk of cold (and its Ceremonies) (and heavy covers at night)...
Why so soon Winter?   — Tom August 1981

Journal entry August 1981
"I admitted today, after 20 years of running and hiding and denying, that I am GAY. It feels good just to write it here, I find myself thanking the Lord that I am GAY, that I can now begin to accept me more. Along with admitting the urge and deep desire to have a gay relationship with a man is even more profound than before, along with the emotional and intellectual need to have someone I can talk to about this with no judgements, and even someone I can work with in this ministry. Relationship and this ministry go hand-in-hand. I am not

made to do this alone. I have prayed to find someone to do this with me, but even the prayer is too much to bear." — Tom

Moving To And Reopening Lukachukai

The Pastor of the Shiprock parish, Fr. Larry, and I began sharing our hopes, ideals, and goals in our ministries and our lifestyles. We both had a deep desire to go back to our roots as Franciscans, back to radical poverty, chastity, and obedience, depending totally on the Lord. When there was talk of finding someone to take over Lukachukai again, we talked about it and prayed about it, and thought this might be the perfect opportunity to live the life we felt called to. When we spoke to our Definitor on the Provincial Council, Fr. Kevin, about our moving there, he was very supportive. Our provision was that we could live as closely to the Gospels and Rule of St. Francis as possible in poverty and living as simply as we could. We both received our new assignment to move to Lukachukai effective December 1, 1981.

The three weeks before December, Larry and I were able to go there with one of the Brothers to get the keys and to see what we would be dealing with. The first order of the day was to keep the loose angry dobermans at bay. We told Brother that we did not want the dogs there and to have them removed altogether. We were given a tour of the remodeled "Big House" and agreed that it was too nice, that the Brothers had done a super job, but that we could not live in it. After explaining the way we wanted to live, he showed us a two room log cabin in disrepair at the rear of the property and opened it for us. It needed some roof repair, storage stuff in there for years needed to be removed, and it needed to be cleaned, but Larry and I agreed it would be the perfect spot for us. It had electricity and a gas wall heater (unsafe and never used), but no running water or sewer. It felt like our "little portion", our Portiuncula. We thanked Brother for showing us around, and asked him to please take the dogs with him. He came back a few days later to pick them up.

Larry couldn't get away from Shiprock until December 1st, so I spent the next week repairing the roof, replacing decking which had rotted, laying down tar paper, and rolled roofing on top of that, hauling up supplies from Chinle. To pay for it, I used up some monetary gifts to me to make sure Chinle was not charged for anything. There was a building on the property which had been used as a clinic staffed by the Sisters. It still smelled of smoke from the fire, but now it was cluttered with old medical tables and furniture, other storage items, and a small cast iron half-potbelly stove with the word "FATSO" on the front of it.

Somehow I got heavy old FATSO to the cabin so it could be used for heating and cooking on its flat top surface. I also cleared out the junk from the cabin and put it in the clinic, and gave the cabin a thorough cleaning using some of the cleaning items I found in the clinic. I soon found out there was a family of skunks living under the floor of the cabin, and I spent a day gathering and laying large stones around the perimeter and sealing up two large holes leading underneath. It took awhile for the smell to dissipate.

My many friends from Many Farms, Nazlini, and Chinle did not want me to leave them, but understood I was needed in Lukachukai which was at most forty-five minutes away from them. I also told them that if they needed anything, they should first try to work with the new priest at Chinle, but to come see me if I could help. I was sad to leave them, keeping all the experiences over my first four years in my heart. The Pastor in Chinle said he did not need me to stick around if I wanted to leave a week earlier, so I did. I got rid of most of my personal stuff by giving it to Sr. Bonita's thrift store, but kept two changes of clothes. A friend drove me to Lukachukai, helped me get settled, then left, and there I was: alone.

> *"Bend the bow within your stretch.*
> *Use in your sling rocks which fit your hand…*
> *Follow the Way, and in the moons to come*
> *You will learn its meaning." ISHI*

Lukachukai

We had decided that in the lifestyle that was new to us we did not want a car or truck, we would not use any money, we would not buy food or anything, and that we would put ourselves completely in the hands of the Lord, depending on Him for all we needed. Similar to St. Francis, we renounced everything the world saw as valuable. We would not accept anything from the people unless they allowed us to work for it. So as not to become a burden on them, we did not want to beg. Shamefully, I was never able to stop smoking, and each cigarette became a hammer used to hit myself.

Previously at the mission, St. Isabel's, the Sisters ran the medical clinic, the priests would lend money and hold pawn, and give rides to Farmington and Gallup. None of that had taken place over the last two years, and would not begin again when we moved there, and it took a while for the Navajos to understand that we were not there for that, if they ever fully did. They could see we didn't have a vehicle and that the

Sister's house was gone and the clinic was closed, but a few would still knock on the cabin door and ask for money or ask to pawn their silver and turquoise jewelry. Even that ended fairly quickly when they found out we didn't and wouldn't have any money.

Initially, and fortunately, Sisters Quinta and Bonita helped us out by bringing canned food. Sr. Quinta could can anything, including beans, squash, turkey in broth, potatoes, all in pint and quart glass jars, and would bring us #10 cans of peanut butter. They came often to check on us. Someone dropped off a 50 lb. sack of rolled oats horse feed on our doorstep. Another brought a 50 lb. sack of pinto beans and left it at the door while we were away visiting. Another time someone left a 50 lb. burlap sack of potatoes. We never knew who did this. I went up to the mountain with a family to get firewood. The agreement was we would fill the truck with wood if they would leave some at the cabin. One of the parishioners worked at the coal mines in northern New Mexico, and he brought us a truckload of coal the operation did not want. If a family picked us up to bless their home, it was customary in their culture to give something in return. We would tell them that the next time they butchered a sheep or shot a deer or elk to drop off some meat at the cabin if they wished to. And they did.

"Commit your life to the Lord, trust in him and he will act."
Psalm 37

"Do not be concerned for your life, what you are to eat...what you are to wear... Seek first the kingdom of God and all things will be given to you."
Luke 12:22-31

There were plenty of lean times when all we had was water. We had discovered a spring on the property. It was the same one that fed the well there that supplied the Big House, the hall, Dr. Nancy's trailer, and another vacant small house on the property. Our spring was the runoff from the well pump house that emptied into a small pond, but it supplied us with the clearest, sweetest, coldest, and best-tasting water ever. The added bonus was a large patch of bright green vegetation at the runoff all year long. I tasted it, thinking it would be a good source of veggies for us, and it was really good – I found out later that it was called watercress. We would take turns filling the galvanized water buckets down at the spring and hauling them and a handful of watercress back to the cabin.

"God, Water, and Each Other" -- Tom as quoted in the <u>Padres</u> <u>Trail</u>
Dec. 1981

Larry and I would spend our days praying the Office of the Hours, celebrating Eucharist, reading, walking around the village visiting people with a focus on the sick and elderly, having religious instruction for the boarding school children after their classes in the afternoons, hanging out at the Post Office and visiting with those who came for their mail, planting and tending a sizeable garden of corn, tomatoes and squash, and hitchhiking to Round Rock to repair the small mission church there with the hopes of someday being able to reopen it and have services there. The small TOTSO trading post was attached to the Post Office, and the owners offered us all the goods that went beyond the expiration date. If the goods were too heavy for us to carry, they even delivered them to us at our cabin. On Sundays, we would take turns having the Mass at Lukachukai, while the other would hitchhike down to Tsaile for Mass at the very small chapel of St. Anne's. If there was a friars' meeting at St. Michael's or in Gallup with the Bishop, we would hitchhike there, carrying boiled potatoes for lunch along the way.

I even hitchhiked the four and a half hours to Albuquerque to have a 25th Wedding Celebration for very close friends and their family. After leaving early in the morning from Lukachukai, walking long distances and nabbing a couple rides, I arrived at Gallup's east entrance to Interstate 40 around 4:30pm. Exhausted, I began wondering whether I should be looking for someplace to camp out for the night: Underneath an overpass? Near that large clump of wild sage over there? At one of the two Franciscan parishes about three miles away? Try again tomorrow or head back to Lukachukai? After all, who was going to pick up a crazy man in a dusty brown gown (habit) with a red sunburned face this time of day? It helped to laugh along with the drivers zooming past.

At about 5:30pm, just as I was about to give up, a truck pulled over, and the man, about 60 years old asked, "What are you doing out here Father? You know it's dangerous to be hitchhiking on the freeway!" After telling him I was on my way to Albuquerque, he told me to hop in because he was on his way home there. We had a great talk for the next two hours, and it turned out he was from the same parish as the celebrating couple and knew them quite well. He took me to his house, introduced me to his wife, who was a wonderful cook, and we prayed together. I blessed them and the food, and probably ate too much because I was very hungry. Then he drove me over to my destination.

The next day, we had a wonderful 25th Anniversary Mass at my friends' home, with lots of family, friends, relatives, and food. The day after, they told their son to give me a ride all the way back to Lukachukai in his Jeep, along with two large sacks of groceries.

++++

At times, when Larry and I were out walking, we would play a game and talk about the foods we missed the most. Once, it was eggs, and when we got back to the cabin, there was a dozen eggs at the door. Then it was ice cold milk in the summer heat, and there was a gallon of ice cold milk at the door upon our return. Then, again, we were talking about Esther Price chocolates (which could only be purchased in Dayton and Cincinnati, Ohio). We stopped at the Post Office on the way home and picked up a package with the mail. Back at the cabin we unwrapped the package and found two 5 lb. boxes of Esther Price chocolates, and not a single chocolate piece was melted. No return address, no note. But we both knew Who we needed to thank.

++++

Our ministry would be a ministry of presence, of being one with the people, of God with us and through us to the people, of God with the people and through them to us. "This treasure we possess in earthen vessels, to make it clear that the surpassing power comes from God and not from us." (ll Corinthians 4:7)

While neither of us were promoting our lifestyle for the other Franciscans on the reservation, the Navajo people would ask them why they were not living the same way we were. More than a few of the well-seasoned friars felt threatened and became very angry with us, but more so with me as the "young upstart shitass." One of them angrily told me to my face that if he ever saw me walking alongside the road hitchhiking, he would aim to hit me and run me down with his car. So much for brotherly love and support. I suppose some of them complained to the Provincial and his Council, because soon after that we received a rather scathing letter from one of the Councilors in Cincinnati, (he was not even responsible for our region), berating us for not asking for their permission to live the "new" way we were living and not getting their approval before we did it.

I responded that beforehand we did discuss it with our Councilor, Fr. Kevin, and gotten his support. Both of us presumed that he would be discussing it with the whole Council at their meeting. I also stated that we were not aware that we needed their permission or approval to live according to the Gospels and the Rule of St. Francis, which we had both solemnly vowed to live by. We were fulfilling our vows.

The next week, we received another hastily typewritten letter from him telling us that the issue was never brought up before the Council, that we were being insolent, arrogant, and subversive, and we should cease and desist and live like the other friars on the reservation. Fr. Larry shied away from any kind of conflict and wanted to drop our attempt right there and move into the Big House, but I could not allow a severe judgement and injustice like this to continue. It was counter to the very fabric of my being.

So, I responded to his letter begging this Councilor to please detail for us how we were not living the Gospel life and the Rule of St. Francis, and to explain how we could live it more genuinely and strictly. Also, I sent carbon copies to Fr. Kevin and the Provincial. We never received another letter from him, and when I saw him later he refused to talk to me.

++++

The Coyotes, The Badgers, and the Sheepdogs

Some days, not so long ago, and not so very far away, and even today, no one knows just why there was trouble at this sheep camp. Some say it was the Witch People who did it, others say a Crazed Lizard is the one who burned one of the dog houses (the one for ladies), and the vet hospital, and shot one of the Sheepdogs. But, no one really knows. Anyhow, all the Sheepdogs were then taken away by the Coyotes and put up at other Sheep camps, and no other one in the area really wanted to go back. One Sheepdog (who was really a rattlesnake in Sheepdog's clothing) would go and check on the Sheep now and then, but would never stay there.

The Coyotes were worried and thought that if the Badgers would come and make the old dog house just like new, then some Sheepdog might eventually go and stay there to herd the Sheep. The Badgers agreed, and worked and worked at the sheep camp, but never stayed there. After two years, they had fixed up the old dog house just like new and better, and even put up a tall fence without a sheep gate (to keep the Witch People and Crazed Lizards out? Or to keep the Sheepdogs in? Or the Sheep out? – no one really knows). But still, the Coyotes were not happy, because no Sheepdog would go back to that camp.

During this time though, two Sheepdogs in the area were having the same dreams about their one main ancestor. He used to be called "Little Poor Dog" and would always sleep out in the open or in some abandoned dog-shack. He would not stay at one sheep camp, but would always go around where there were hurting sheep who needed someone to be with them. He was strange from other Sheepdogs of his time, because he would never take anything with him, or use money, or accept special places to stay. All he asked for was enough to eat for that day, and he would make sure to work for it. He would spend days and nights talking to the Shepherd, so he could always stay close to Him, and nothing else would come in the way.

The sheep loved "Little Poor Dog", the Coyotes of his day were terribly worried when many other Dogs went to follow him, and some of them became Sheepdogs. In fact, the way he lived is what made the two Sheepdogs of this story want to be Sheepdogs in the first place. It was because of their dreams of this ancestor that they got together four times (the sacred number for the Navajos) and then decided to go to the abandoned sheep camp to live the way "Little Poor Dog" would today. The Coyotes were happy they went there.

When they got there, the Sheepdogs were sad. The old house was so much like the dog houses they had come from, only it was far better. "Why did the Badgers not fix up the sheep corral instead?" So they decided to use an old abandoned dog-shack in the back. And the two Sheepdogs agreed four times. They agreed they would only use the nice house if any of the Sheep wanted to talk in secret. They also agreed that they must work for what they would eat, and not use any money, and would walk where they must go. The Sheepdogs were very happy and really believed this is what their dreams called them to. And they knew they could talk to the Shepherd better this way and stay close to Him better. Above all, their way of living would determine how they herded the Sheep.

As soon as the Coyotes, and the Badgers, and other Sheepdogs of the area got word of what these two were doing, some would not understand, and others were furious with them. "It is so very different from the way Sheep have been herded for many years now," said Old Sheepdog. "Our Sheepherding is our work," said his brother. "They must be right there to answer when the Coyotes call," thought another. "You can certainly herd sheep faster driving a pickup," laughed Young Sheepdog. "They must stay in the house we fixed up for them!!" screamed the Badgers. Old Wise Sheepdog said, "If this is from God, it will last. And there is nothing we can do about that."

One day a Head Coyote, very concerned but too busy and far away to visit, wrote them a letter. He tried to be encouraging, but said they must obey Articles 29-34 of the Sheepherders handbook. "You have to ask for permission to live and herd this 'new' way." He wondered who would guard the doghouse the badgers fixed? "Would the Witch People and Lizards think that you Sheepdogs are afraid of them?" "Aren't you wasting your time trying to herd the Sheep on foot?" "What do the Sheep think about all this?" "Will the Sheep expect this kind of nonsense from all the other Sheepdogs in the area?" And finally, at least the last question he asked in his letter, "Wasn't it really only just one of the Sheepdogs that had the dream, and then made the other one believe he did also? After all, we know what the Shepherd wants you to do better than you do." He ended by saying, "Help us to understand what we Coyotes can do to you."

The talk and the letter disturbed the two Sheepdogs greatly, because these things did not seem concerned about the Sheepdogs personally or the Sheep at all. And what the Coyotes and Badgers were concerned about was not the main concern of "Little Poor Dog" according to the ancient writings and their early ancestor Sheepdogs. The two said, "Everyone knows that we are not meant to live in palaces, and the Shepherd gave us strong legs to walk with, and asked us to live with our Sheep, and to be with our Sheep in all the various aspects." They said this four times. They agreed four times that their special dream must be lived. And so they did. —Tom 1982

++++

A black and white dog looking like a Border Collie showed up at our doorstep. We had seen him herding sheep on the outside of the chain link fence a number of times, and he would come over to the fence to be touched and petted. Then, he just came into the property and stood at our cabin door. We called him Starving Dog because he was so thin, and had those eyes that grabbed our hearts.

A Lesson from Starving Dog

Not wanted
  (it was explained to him)
Would not be fed
  (it was explained to him, also)
Thought to be a lady
  (he explained it to us)
Found a friend in Odie the Cat
  (who thought he was also a dog)
Told to go home and herd the sheep,
Not to bark at night,
Not to bark at people,
Given away,
Yet he returned,
Yet he stays,
Dancing at the opened door,
Foraging at the school dump,
Back-seated to Cripple Dog,
And yet he stays...
  (with no explanation to that). — Tom 1982

When we made oatmeal or beans, we would make a lot more and give Starving Dog and Cripple Dog (blind in one eye) hefty portions, especially after Cripple Dog had a litter of fifteen puppies, obviously from Starving Dog. The puppies grew fast and found extra nourishment in eating from the three-week plague of locust grasshoppers covering the ground. What fun to watch them run and hop trying to catch those insects. Eventually, we were able to give all the puppies away to parishioners.

Larry and I were told by the people that there used to be a cold cellar in the ground behind the church, but it had been bulldozed and filled in when the remodelling Brothers were there. We looked for it like Egyptian archaeologists searching for a long lost pharaoh's tomb. By probing the ground where it should be we found the stone steps first. As the excavation slowly continued the top wall stones of a 6'x8' room were gradually revealed. We dug out all the dirt and debris and discovered hand-tooled stones all around and up the walls from the dirt floor for six feet. A few people helped us bring over some logs from the large hogan the Brothers had pulled down. (I had already taken most of the logs to build the hogan at Many Farms). The logs formed the pitched roof resting on a center log beam, then they were covered with an old tarp and dirt about two feet thick. That cold cellar was surely helpful in storing our harvest of winter squash in the Fall.

In the summer of 1982, Larry contracted hepatitis. Washing dishes assiduously with strong soap or boiling them on FATSO if we had no soap, we still couldn't figure how he could have gotten hepatitis. He hadn't been feeling well for a couple weeks when Dr. Nancy took some blood samples and handed him the diagnosis. She tested me also, but I was negative. Larry had to be quarantined and was sent to the main mission at St. Michael's, AZ for two months, and I had to have a series of three injections for hepatitis since I was exposed to it. Those two months were very difficult and lonely for me.

++++

Each year a "sheep-dip" was held in the mountains where the sheep had been taken for grazing in the summer. The owners of the sheep paid to have their sheep dipped in a vat which contained some pesticides, harmless to the sheep, to protect their flocks from insect pests which would make the sheep sick and which lived in their thick coats of wool. I was invited by a family to join them overnight on the mountain the night before the dipping, so I hopped into the back of their pickup. It was held in a broad and long valley, and there must have been 40-50 flocks which had been brought there to be dipped.

We camped a little way up the mountain, and after dusk, campfires could be seen dotting the whole valley at the other camps. The family had rigged a large tarp-covered lean-to to some ponderosa pine trees where, after some mutton stew and fry-bread for supper, we all slept side-by-side each with our own light blanket. As luck would not have it a thunderstorm boomed and flashed through the valley part of the night. Me being a storm lover, I really soaked in the thunder echoing back and forth in the mountains and the fantastic many-branched lightning blinding for a moment then giving way to absolute darkness again. On the other hand, each of us tried to find a spot under the tarp that was still dry. The rain made the cold crisp mountain air even colder, and we were all shivering until we could warm up around a newly stoked roaring fire.

As the sun was rising there was a flurry of activity in the now slightly muddy valley to get the scattered flocks together and to the dipping vats before anyone else as the chemicals were more effective before they were diluted with more water and less chemicals during the day. Amazingly, the sheepdogs knew their sheep, the excited teenagers on horseback knew their sheepdogs, and the shepherds called and somehow separated their flock from all the other flocks. I saw with my own eyes that the "Shepherd knows His sheep, and they know Him."

As everything got more organized, the waiting began. My family, and it seemed all the others, gathered at their camp to eat fried potatoes and fresh fry bread for breakfast, everyone digging into the large common skillet, sipping hot coffee from the large coffee pot boiling over the fire -- and then waited, and waited.

That morning I wandered around the valley, going from camp to camp, meeting lots of new people and their families. After being asked to bless their flock, I borrowed a small bucket from one family, filled it with water, prayed over it with the family, blessed it with salt, asked one of the teenagers to fetch me a cedar branch, and I sprinkled the family and as many sheep as I could with the Holy Water. Word got around quickly, and every camp I went to after that asked that their families and flocks be blessed also. While I was doing that each flock was being herded into a corral as their time came for being dipped. The sheep were being shoved one by one through a chute and then pushed into a large deep trough for the dipping. They screamed and scrambled and splashed as they made their way to the other side of the trough and out of the water -- dripping wet with muddy chemical-laced water.

At one of the camps a teenage boy came up to me and pulled me off to the side. He said to me, "Father, my horse hasn't been able to have any babies. I was wondering if you would bless my horse's balls so he could make babies for me?" At first I thought he was making a joke on me, but I could see he was serious when he lifted his stallion's tail. So, with bucket still in hand, and the stallion's tail still raised, I prayed with the boy that his horse would be fruitful and have many colts in the years to come. Then I sprinkled holy water on his horse's scrotum with the cedar branch. The boy smiled and told me he would let me know if it worked.

At the end of the day everyone was exhausted as I helped the family break camp and load up the pickup, and we headed back down the mountain. They dropped me off at the mission in the dark, and I went to bed on the floor right away thinking what a day that was.

About a year and a half later, that teenage boy rode up to our cabin on his horse with two ropes leading from his saddle horn to two beautiful foals trotting up from behind. The boy just beamed with pride as any new father would, as he told me his mare had twins. We said a prayer of thanks, gave the horses some water, blessed his stallion's "balls" once again, and he sat tall and proud in his saddle as he slowly lead the foals away.

++++

Along with everything else we were involved in, I began to teach Navajo reading and writing to a group of about ten parishioners at Lukachukai focusing totally on the Scriptures. We used the three Scriptural readings for the next weekend's Masses for a very rewarding Scripture Study, and the participants were so grateful they could read their own language along with understanding the meaning of the Bible better. I also took two of the Eucharistic Prayers and wrote music for them to be sung in something that might mirror native Navajo chant. Additionally, I took the longer version of the Navajo Holy Prayer and resurrected and perfected the music which had been written for it about fifty years earlier. After teaching it to the parishioners, we sang it together in Navajo after the Communion at every Mass. They loved to sing it. I had to be careful, though, about how much Navajo culture I included in the Mass, because our parishioners did not particularly appreciate it. For example, I wanted to start using native incense, a mixture of dried cedar fronds and sap from a pine tree, but was told they came to the Catholic Church because of the difference of it and not to have their culture included. Besides, they liked the smell of our incense better. Each time I thought of including something, I would discuss it with them first.

"The Christian life will be adapted to the mentality and character of each culture, and local traditions, together with the special qualities of each national family, illumined by the light of the Gospel."
                              -- Vatican II Decree on the Missionary
                    Activity of the Church par.22

"We friars want to make a lifetime effort in becoming one with our people in their way of feeling and thinking and in their manner of life."
                    -- Medellin Document, "We are Sent" No.8

++++

After an early snowfall and bitter cold, my adoptive Navajo family from Chinle came up to Lukachukai to visit. My Grandmother, her daughter (my Aunt), and my Aunt's children (my Navajo sisters and brothers) all came along. I sensed something was not right with them, and they gradually got around to telling me that Grandma's son was missing. He was mentally challenged, helped Grandma herd her flock of sheep, and had not returned for four days. They were worried and distraught and cried at losing him. While praying for his safe return, I instantly got an image of him in my mind. He was laying in a snowbank about seven miles up the south rim road of Canyon de Chelly, off the dirt road, at the turnoff to Nazlini. I knew he had frozen to death there, and there was snow on top of him. After the prayer, and each of the family offering their own prayer in Navajo, I called my Aunt's two sons, my brothers, to go outside with me. Knowing I couldn't tell my Grandma what I saw about her son, or my Aunt about her brother, I told the two sons what I saw and where to find him, and left it up to them to tell the rest of the family. When we went back into our cabin, the sons shared my vision with their Mom and Grandmother. We all cried together and prayed some more, hoping the police would be able to find out how he had gotten that far out of town and what the cause of death was. As they left to go looking for him, Grandma touched my arm and called me the Navajo name for a "Crystal Gazer."

My Aunt called me two days later to tell me they found him in exactly the same place I had told them he would be.

++++

Christmas 1982 was very memorable. Christmas Eve Mass was forwarded with a huge bonfire in front of the church where we gathered around for warmth and to sing carols. Then we all processed into the brightly lit church still singing while the bell rang wildly. Everyone seemed so happy and joyful. There must have been some impact upon the village over the past year since every seat was filled with parishioners, more stood in back, and some preferred the fire outside. Both Larry and I reflected to ourselves on the difference from the previous Christmas when so many were still afraid to come near the place.

The next day, it was my turn to go to Tsaile for Mass, and when I woke up that morning I was awed that it had snowed over a foot during the night and was still snowing heavily. I dressed as warmly as I could, put on some oversized rubber boots we had found in the clinic, and started hitchhiking the ten miles to the church at about 7am thinking I would surely have to walk the whole way. Along the mile road out to the main highway, it seemed no one else was awake in the village, but there was that distinctly Southwestern fragrance of burning pinon and cedar wood rising from the smokestacks of the houses. There were no vehicles on the road to break the white blanket, and there was only the absolute silence that only the muffling effect of falling snow could bring.

This was true also of the number of miles I walked along the main two-lane highway, until the only truck in either direction pulled up and stopped behind me and honked the horn. The passenger door opened, and I got in with the other four in the front seat providing my lap as a seat for one of the children. These people were not known to me and spoke very little English, so for the most part we struggled to communicate, but each one knew how to say Merry Christmas or Ya'at'teeh Keshmish. The driver was very cautious even with chains on the tires and took the road slowly – we were still the only vehicle in either direction. He dropped me off down the hill from the church after I wished them the blessings of Christmas with many thanks in Navajo.

There was easily two feet of snow at the church with the same absolute peace and silence that comes with it. The padlock was frozen, so I had to breathe on it, warm it with my cigarette lighter, and rub it for a while before the key could release. Inside the church seemed colder than outside as I began to get a fire started in the large barrel fire stove to heat up the place. I started to ring the old small school bell on the roof an hour before Mass to let those around know I was there. I set up the altar and got everything prepared for Christmas Mass, rang the bell again at half an hour before and again at fifteen minutes before and at five minutes before. The church was nice and toasty by then, but no one showed up. In the meantime, I shoveled snow away from the front door and dirt for about twenty feet then stood at the open door in awe of the white beauty and the contrast with the green cedar, pinon, and spruce. One break in the falling snow and I could see the mountains and the huge volcanic plug called Tsaile peak. After hanging around for an hour meditating on my own private Christmas celebration, I shoveled snow in the old stove to put the fire out, put everything away, locked up, and thought how extremely blessed I was to have had this experience. I could have been the only person on earth, or certainly the happiest and most joyful one.

There were still no vehicles on the highway as I began the long trek back home. Again, after several miles of exertion while walking in the deep snow, a truck pulled up behind me, and they offered me a ride all the way home. After Christmas blessings and many thank-yous for the young couple, I walked into the cabin, and Larry and I shared our experiences of the best Christmas both of us had ever had as we ate our oatmeal and beans Christmas lunch.

++++

Larry and I slept on the floor in the other room of the cabin on blankets we had foraged from the Big House and the other vacant house. After stoking FATSO with coal in the winter, we would go into the other room to sleep, but on freezing nights we would pick up everything and move to the floor in front of FATSO, who didn't do a great job of getting heat to the bedroom. FATSO was kind of like a god who heated up hot water in the morning, allowed us to make coffee or tea when we had them, allowed us to make our food, and heated our bodies. All we had to do was present a sacrificial offering of wood or coal to feed the god or he would get cranky with us and give us the cold shoulder. If that happened, it took longer to satisfy him and cajole him back into turning hot.

Every morning, every season, warm or freezing, I would wake up at 5 or 6am, feed FATSO to heat some water, and meditate outside facing east for over an hour, waiting for the sunrise. A Navajo medicine man told me he was taught that if you did not get up before the sun and pray to the sun god, he would not rise for you that day. When I thought about it, it made sense to me. I would be there to pray and be with the Lord in the silence with no distractions. In our life, we did not have the distractions of televisions or radio, magazines or newspapers, and gratefully, computers or cellphones were not available yet. This enabled me to enter into prayer and meditation more easily. Another benefit was that it forced me to look more deeply into my being to see who I truly was, to enter the cave willingly to find myself.

"Before Dawn" by Brian Andreas

I've always liked the time before dawn,
Because there is no one around
To remind me
Who I'm supposed to be.

So it's easier to remember
Who I am.

However, in doing so, I had to face all the issues of my life not dealt with properly or not settled constructively. I began wondering why there was so little joy in me, why I was down on myself because of my past, why I was afraid of being found out for who I really am. I wondered if I was well-received, wanting to and yet being afraid of getting too close to others. Why did I kill Tom so long ago? Could he ever be found again? Why the not-so-extreme ups and the extreme downs? Why did the ceiling seem to be gradually getting lower, and will it crush the only part of me that was left? I felt a new security in me, a new confidence in my ability to look at all the issues in total honesty and truthfulness. And I also felt a need for professional help to do that.

Chapter Four
Transitions

In February of 1983, I had a talk with Kevin and Larry about taking some time off and away, perhaps six months in the Jemez Springs Recovery Program run by the Servants of the Paraclete and six months on my own. Why? I felt cramped inside myself, could not be loose or free, as if there was a door I just could not budge to open since it had been closed and locked so long ago. I felt fake as a Franciscan, a priest, a person, as if I was just acting a part that was not the real me. I found it hard to believe Jesus is God any more than any of us are. Was he just acting a part also? I felt I was in the process of choosing life, my life, having too long wanting to be someone else. I never really accepted or chose myself. I felt a need to do this in the open, away from religious life and priestly ministry, while talking regularly with a professional.

Are my strengths and abilities real, or are they just dreams of who I would like to be? If they are real, why don't I use them better without questioning all the time? If a dream, why do I hold onto them? Is what I'm feeling a deeper call by the Father out to the stormy sea to ride out another storm in trust? I knew I had never really come to terms with my sexuality. I just wanted to be somebody normal, nobody special, nobody different from others. I wanted to know and feel what others experienced. I wanted to be part of a family. Perhaps that is where wanting to be out with and live among the Navajo people came from. I never had the experience of just being a person and nobody else. I had always felt set aside, always caged up, used when needed, performing for affirmation, never really belonging, always on the inside looking out, as if in a prison for a crime I didn't commit. My whole life I had been living other people's expectations of me and who I should be from parents and family, friends and the Church, following the rules as best

I could, and as a result living the heavy expectations I placed on myself. I chose it, but I did not ever choose it completely freely without pressure. Kevin and Larry were both very understanding and supportive, and thought it best if I first started by going into Albuquerque once every two weeks for counseling to see how that went. This would change our lifestyle drastically because we would have to get a vehicle for me to make the regular trips. We bought a used truck from a Navajo friend in Chinle, and the province paid for it. Getting money to pay for the gas was a challenge. I was referred to the director of the Servants of the Paraclete at their house in Albuquerque. He was a priest psychologist and seemed fine at first. Then he started to put the moves on me, actually asking me if I wanted to have sex with him. I laughed it off and told him I was not interested; besides, that was not what I was there for, and if he couldn't separate his professionalism from his need for sex, I would not be back. After a couple months of his listening to me, but not really helping me resolve issues, he broached the sex subject again. I stood up, told him he had more problems than I did, walked out, and never returned.

I was then referred to a Jungian psychologist who was a priest in Santa Fe, and drove to the bi-weekly meetings even farther away. He did help me deeply understand the power and impact of expectations and the fear of rejection on my whole life. He also helped me to connect these to why I needed to be so severe on myself, denying myself joy, setting myself apart, wanting very strict poverty, denying love, living for others rather than myself, etc. After a year I would have continued with him, but he was moving to Switzerland to broaden his studies and training.

++++

In June, after a year and a half together, I was informed that Fr. Larry was being transferred to another mission that needed a priest, and he agreed to go. My heart sunk. I felt very sad and angry. Why didn't he just tell the Provincial "NO"?! Larry explained that he couldn't do that, he needed to be needed, he felt he ministered as much as he could at Lukachukai, he thought I could handle being the new Pastor, and so on. "But what about our way of life? Our sharing? Our togetherness here in this journey? Why did we not discuss this beforehand? What happened to our call to live in poverty and closely living the way of Francis? What about total dependence on the Lord?", I asked almost crying. "Tom, it's something I have to do. I'm sorry. You will carry on just fine," was his response. And he left a week later.

It's hard to describe the feelings of hurt I had after that. We were so close. My heart was screaming with feelings of abandonment, rejection, total aloneness, anger, instability, my life falling apart, our way of life falling apart, failure. I knew I would carry on just fine. That was never the question. The future was in doubt both inside of myself and of what we had worked so hard to live. I went to the chapel and screamed at the Lord late into the night like a child needing help, and slept on the floor of the sanctuary exhausted.

++++

There was talk about who the Provincial would assign to Lukachukai, but he assured me I would be consulted before someone was sent there. The thing was, no one wanted to come, either because they didn't want to work with the Navajos, or because they didn't want to live with me, or because they didn't want to live the Franciscan life so strictly. Finally, a young newly ordained priest volunteered. I had heard of him, but really didn't know much about him. We spoke over the phone, and he was excited about the way of life we would be living. He seemed alright, so I agreed. Shortly after his arrival, the tension between us started to build, not about our ministry or way of life, but because our personalities just should not have been near each other. One of his first questions to me was whether I was gay since he had heard rumors. I asked him what that had to do about anything, and he said he didn't like gays. We had a very angry discussion about that. I knew I couldn't trust him or live with him, so we just co-existed there. The feeling of happiness and peace at the cabin was gone; the comfort, the spirit was gone.

I wondered that perhaps I could have handled the loneliness better if I had decided to live alone and run the mission by myself. Yes, this was my fault. We were living separate lives so closely together and dependent on each other. The mental, emotional, and spiritual support I so desperately needed in my life at this time was not there. I was on my own, living in unbearable loneliness again. Yes, the bi-weekly counseling sessions with the shrink did help me hold it together inside. But, the image of a ship, having sailed on quiet seas, encountering a hurricane, and the conviction of the crew and captain that they would surely be smashed on the rocks with few survivors, was deepening my depression. The emotional stress was boiling. I was afraid the seizures would return. I was afraid a breakdown would happen again, but the darkness and unknowing of college was not here this time.

It didn't take long for the boiling pressure cooker to give off steam. Trying to contain the pressure, I knew what was coming next if I couldn't relieve some of the pressure. I had to be presentable to the parishioners and everyone, but other things began to shut down on their own. After a call to the Provincial, and a talk with Kevin, I was asked to stick with it for two months until they could find someone else to take my place at the mission. I said ok, I would try, but when I absolutely had to go, they would only have one day's notice.

First, my preaching was affected. I noticed I was just saying the same thing over and over again day to day, week to week. Then, I just couldn't preach at all. I couldn't think of anything to say that I truly believed. I tried instead to have a ten minute Bible Study and have the people ask questions about the readings they had just heard, but that was a flop. My ability to have Mass suffered next, and at times I would have to sit down until the anxiety and shaking eased some. But it really got bad when I admitted to myself that I no longer believed what I was reading and saying, that I couldn't even just say the words "This is My Body, This is My blood." To think that perhaps the bread wafer had become my body, Tom's body, and the wine had become my blood, Tom's blood, as a sacrifice for the people before me, a sacrament of salvation to set them free, to be willing to suffer as I was for them and with them, as all those who love each other would do for each other, lifted my spirit up some but was not the theology I was taught. I told the other priest he would have to have all the Masses as the anxiety was too much.

Journal entry August 24, 1983
It struck me yesterday at 5:30am prayer: to have difficulty believing Jesus is God is therefore to have difficulty believing God could be man, to reject the incarnation. I can only say, yes it is true. I cannot say the Father fully revealed himself in one man. He is so much revealed in everything, everyone. – Tom

Will the real Jesus, Please
Stand Up!!
Come on, if you are there,
Show Yourself!!
Not in miracles or legend or myth,
But from the center of your being
To the center of my being
In a way I can uniquely
Understand who you are,
If you are. -- Tom 8/27/83

"It was more than I could believe that Jesus was the only incarnate son of God, and that only he who believed in him would have everlasting life. If God could have sons, then all of us were his sons. If Jesus was like God, or God himself, then all men were like God and could be God himself. My reason was not ready to believe literally that Jesus redeemed the sins of the world... I could accept Jesus as a martyr, but not as the most perfect man ever born. His death on the cross was a great example to the world, but that there was anything like a mysterious or miraculous virtue in it my heart could not accept..." – Gandhi - William Mier

What if the Lord (Father, Son, Spirit) and my acknowledgement of them is only a projection of my need for security and answers and to believe there is someone or something greater than me holding it all together, giving it all meaning? What if he only exists in my need to believe he exists and does not exist outside of myself? Am I, then, the one responsible for what happens and how things happen, and the one who gives meaning to it all? My prayers for the sick are then meaningless if I am not willing, and do not actually go and visit them, write to them, heal them with my presence. I will never again say "I will pray for you." Rather, I will say "I am with you", and show that I am.

For me to pray for world peace and to do nothing is meaningless, is fake, is a joke, a cop-out, a placing of responsibility for change on others, on the god. I am the one responsible. I must at least make peace within myself and between those near me, and justice too, and believe that in our oneness as humanity world peace and justice will ripple out and somehow affect everyone. If anything is to be bettered, I must do it.

I've admitted that some of my questioning of Jesus now is because the power and the magic has gone out of the stories, scriptures, and faith in him. When the power is gone, what is left? A man no different from myself.

Now where the power?
Where the magic?
Where the healing?
The stories said so,
But I don't see it.
It's not here now,
(And maybe never was). – *Tom 11/83*

The biggest and best therapy for me at this time was to work as hard as I could in the garden every day hoeing weeds, setting water channels, collecting corn pollen, picking tomatoes, harvesting hubbard, acorn, pumpkin, and butternut squash. Some of the squash got quite large, but the wheelbarrow helped me get them all to the cold cellar before the killer frost. I wondered why I was doing all this since I would be leaving soon, but I just could not leave it in the field to be wasted, and I did put a lot of it outside the front door of the church for all to take.

On October 21, 1983, I decided, after consulting with my shrink, and my Counselor, and listening deeply to myself, that I would take at a least a year away from the Franciscans, the priesthood, and the Church beginning the end of November. To distance myself from expectations, to rediscover or decide against faith, to express my sexuality, to step into the stream of lay life and find myself there – without the colored Trinitarian tri-focaled glasses I had always worn and to find out whether I needed to wear the glasses at all, whether they truly fit who I was, whether I could find my truth better without them – this was my goal.

++++

Initially, my intention was to return to the Navajo reservation and Lukachukai after the year, and this helped to lessen the impact of saying good-bye to the parishioners and other people and friends on the reservation. Most could not understand a mental and emotional illness, more could understand a sickness in my head and heart, others suggested I go to a medicine man to have an Evil Way ceremony done on me to heal me of the bad spirits. Actually, I did go to a medicine man friend of mine about what was going on and about leaving, asking for a ceremony. He said, "Go away. I don't want to see you. That's the way it is with you white people. You come and take and don't leave anything when you go away. Then you leave us alone again." Sadly, I left his hogan without having a ceremony done for me.

Having loved living with and working for the Navajo with their culture, way of life, language, their way of doing things and describing things, the long time it takes for them to trust because they have been hurt so much, not wanting to hurt anyone, forgiving somewhat and remembering always, how I would have to turn my head around 180 degrees to understand many things, the kidding, the just saying it, the nicknames, their connection with the earth and the sky, all this and more that I could write a separate book about, made it very difficult to leave and distance myself from them.

Quickly, a crushing guilt set in: the shame, the embarrassment, the guilt of leaving the reservation and Lukachukai and my way of life there; of having the nay-saying Franciscans laugh at me, of admitting perhaps my work and life there was not God's will and that's why it didn't last, and an extreme anger at myself for letting them all down, myself down, the friars down, my family down, the way of life down, feeling like a total failure in everything. Yes, I had failed. Yes, I was a failure. My Dad had told us kids that we could be whoever we wanted to be, we could have whatever we wanted, if we wanted it bad enough and worked hard enough to get it. I felt I <u>had</u> wanted it bad enough and <u>had</u> worked hard enough, but still couldn't be the person I wanted to be or have what I wanted. I had failed.

++++

A friend of mine from Chinle suggested I contact her Grandparents who owned a duplex in Albuquerque to see if I could rent the apartment they were not living in. I did, and fortunately the apartment was empty and available. So, the day after Thanksgiving, I packed what few things I had in two paper bags and loaded them up in the mission truck. I asked the other priest if I could take some of the squash with me, and he told me take it all, to clear out the cold cellar since he would never use any of it. I did and loaded it all in the truck bed. Then he drove me to Albuquerque. My heart broke as we pulled away from Lukachukai, and I cried.

For the most part, the four and a half hour trip to Albuquerque was spent with him asking questions about where things were that he should know about at the mission, telling me how he disliked being with me for the five months, revealing that he would not live in the cabin and that he would move into the Big House. There was also silence. He had no understanding of what I was going through. It was a long trip.

The Leave of Absence and Meeting Joe

The Grandparents were nice and welcoming, especially the Grandmother. The front apartment was unfurnished, not clean enough for me, and cold, but I was so grateful to have a place I could stay. We unloaded the truck, and he left. I had no money, but they were willing to wait until I could get some to pay the rent.

There was a phone in the apartment for local calls only, but I did have use of the couple's phone in their apartment for long distance if I paid for the bill and wasn't concerned about them listening in. The next day, I called the Provincial in Cincinnati to see if the friars could give me $1,000.00 to get started and loan me a car to get around town and to look for a job. He said he would see to it, and we spoke a while. He understood why I needed to do what I was doing, he was very supportive, and said he was hurting with me. While he knew I had to do this on my own, he told me to let him know if there was anything I needed. I so appreciated hearing what he said.

The next week a check arrived in the mail, and one of the Franciscans in town dropped off an old Ford LTD that exhausted a little white smoke and dripped oil. After opening a bank account, I had to wait a week before I could withdraw money from it to pay the $300.00 for the rent and another $200.00 for gas and food and kitchen items. The first thing I bought at the flea market was a pressure cooker I used for everything. Cutting up the big squash into 4"x4" chunks, letting the unused ones dry until I did use them, pressure cooking them with a chicken leg quarter I bought for $.19lb in a 10lb frozen bag, was what I ate for weeks.

Having decided I was not going to look for other gay men friends at the gay bars or bookstores, someone referred me to a gay priest chaplain who was also a great listener and became a good friend. He told me about a gay organization called Common Bond which met once a month. Fearing rejection, I found I was very shy about meeting others, and it was very hard for me to even think about going to the meetings.

I did go to Mass every Sunday at the local Catholic Church, but found myself critiquing how the priests preached and celebrated the Mass. It all seemed very perfunctory: get it over soon so the parking lot can clear out for the next Mass. The preaching was terrible, asking for money for this or that, not homilizing on the readings, nothing that could touch the congregation's hearts and certainly not mine. The other Catholic churches were the same except for the University of New Mexico students' Newman Center run by the Dominicans, who made the Eucharist and homily something deep and meaningful.

After talking myself out of going a couple times, I did decide to go to a Common Bond Christmas Party and Gay Men's Chorus Concert at the Unitarian Church on the freezing evening of Saturday, December 11th. The church was fairly full, with lots of guys and some women who stood around in groups of five to ten talking and laughing before the concert began. I swallowed my fear and shyness and tried a couple times to join in the conversations and fun, but each time I was brushed off and discarded. I finally realized each group was an exclusive clique, and I gave up trying to meet people, and no one tried to meet me. I decided to leave, but the concert was beginning, so I thought I might as well stay for it and see what it was like. Actually, it was pretty good with the traditional Christmas songs and some funny deprecatory jokes and plenty of "camping around."

After the show, I grabbed a chocolate chip cookie and headed for the door to make a quick getaway, not that anyone would have noticed anyway. On my way to the door I noticed a good looking man standing there by himself. I thought, "Is he waiting for someone?" "Maybe a friend?" "Should I just keep walking by him?" I decided to swallow my anxiety and shyness and try one last time to meet someone. He glanced at me, and I walked right up to him and said with my hand out, "Hi. I'm Tom." He shook my hand and said, "Hi. I'm Joe." After a pause, he said "Are you a teetotaller? This whole group doesn't smoke or drink, and I really need a drink. Say, I just put up my Christmas tree, and decorated the house, and fixed the fireplace for a fire. You want to come home with me, and we'll have a drink in front of the fire?"

Following Joe in his tan Ford Fairlane, I must say that twice I had second thoughts and almost called it off in my mind and almost took off down another street back to my apartment. Then I thought, "Hey, I met a potential friend, and it's only for a drink, and I can leave if it doesn't turn out. Just go ahead and do it." So, I continued to follow him.

> {*I find it fascinating that I am writing this on the exact same date when we are celebrating our anniversary of having completed 34 full years of being together.*}
>
> -- Tom 12/11/2017

At his house it was obvious from the way it was decorated that this guy was really into Christmas! He even had a real pinon tree well decorated with all sorts of ornaments. As he went to the kitchen to pour us some Paul Masson Rose wine from a clear glass gallon jug, I started the fire in the fireplace. He came in and put on an LP recording of Bach's Violin Concerto in A minor. He had me with Bach. I decided to stay for a while, and am sure glad I did. We talked late into the night, sharing a lot about ourselves and our life. It was so easy to talk with him. However, I wasn't at the point to where I wanted to share with anyone that I was a priest, so I told him I was a teacher on the Navajo reservation, which really wasn't a lie. He told me he was a teacher at one of the local high schools, had been married to his wife for ten years and divorced for two years now, and had two kids, a boy and a girl. We both had Master's degrees, both loved classical music, and we could both carry on a decent conversation on all kinds of topics, except sports.

He was broke from paying off the debts from the divorce settlement and paying child support, and had no credit; but he had a steady job and was working another in the evenings teaching at a technical college. I was just plain broke, had no job or debts, and knew nothing about what credit was. I felt so comfortable being with him, and the wine was helping too. We kissed and talked some more. Not wanting to drive after I had been drinking, I took him up on the offer to stay overnight, in his bed, and we kissed some more and took it from there. I left about 4am after resting a bit, and sharing phone numbers, and then drove back to the apartment, still on a high and wondering what all had just happened. I was really impressed with this guy. It felt so good that we could just be so natural together. I wondered also if we would ever see each other again, and if he would ever call me. At the apartment, I crashed on the floor I called a bed and slept late into Sunday morning.

Joe didn't call on Sunday as I had hoped, but he had said he would have the kids that day. He and his ex-wife, Rose, had an amicable divorce, were still friends, and had joint custody of the children during the week and every other weekend. On Monday, when I figured he might be home from teaching, I called him wanting to tell him what a great time I had on Saturday evening and wanting to talk to him about what I was afraid to tell him before – that I was a priest. I felt he was a mature and trustworthy man, and I wanted to start a friendship being honest about that and about the emotional problems I had. Once he heard what a weirdo I was, if he didn't want to carry the friendship any further I would understand, and if he did still want to be friends he would have some better idea what he was getting into. Fortunately, we set up a time for him to come to the apartment on Wednesday on his way to his evening teaching job. I invited him to a dinner of steamed acorn squash and chicken. He was so easy to talk with and trust, and I felt he was as genuinely interested in me as I was in him. Actually, I was surprised when my revelations didn't seem like such a big deal for him, perhaps because he knew the pain of breaking away from his previous life. Surely, he was concerned that his baggage of being divorced with children could be a relationship deal-breaker for me.

For Friday, he invited me over to his house for a meat-sauce spaghetti dinner with salad and garlic bread so I could meet his son and daughter, Joey age 11 and Margaret age 8. I felt kind of awkward meeting them, because I didn't feel I related well with children in general, and because I was concerned about what they would think of me. But, after I accepted I was just a friend of their Dad's coming over for dinner, I eased up a lot. Both Joey and Maggie were polite, funny, well-behaved, and well-mannered, but not in a stiff way at all, quite a testament of their upbringing from their cultured Mom and Dad. Shortly after dinner, I left with a wonderful feeling of having met the two most important people in Joe's life.

Joe and I got together at least twice a week either at my place or his place for something to eat, sharing and overnight. During the day, I was trying to write a resume, which I had never done before. Joe got some books on the subject from the high school library for me so I could study what should be included or not, and what the format should be. Wanting to be honest, I had to be very careful about how to word my "work" experiences of the past. It was okay to say I was a minister on the reservation, and try to re-code my qualities and skills from there into something which would benefit a company. Each Monday, I searched the Classified Ads from the used Sunday newspaper Grandma would pass onto to me.

I knew I wanted to work with people in some kind of social situation, but there weren't that many ads which piqued my interest. Mostly, managerial or manager trainee positions that were advertised required five plus years of specific experience. Social work ads of course required a degree plus experience. If I had the money, I would have gone to the University for a degree in social work. There was no market for someone with a Masters degree in Divinity. Even after continually sending out and dropping off a lot of resumes, the only responses I got back, which were very few, said I was overqualified. For some reason, I thought finding a job would be a lot easier, and I was getting very discouraged. Gradually, because my funds were getting severely low, I decided I would do anything to make some money at least for food and gas. I didn't know how I could be overqualified to waiter in a restaurant, or flip burgers at some fast food place, but I was. I tried carpet cleaning with a small crew, but my back couldn't take it. I now have great respect for what those guys do.

The Letter

Letter to Mom and sisters and brothers 1/3/84
  There are a few things I must talk about, and I hope I can address your concerns and worries directly. You ask if I miss my duties as a priest. Actually and honestly, the only ones I miss are preaching, counseling, and being with the Navajo People. I do not miss celebrating Mass — in fact, it was becoming too much of a burden for me. Why? That leads to something I have not shared with you: in my meditation thru the years, I prayed to Jesus as the focal point, then gradually my spirituality was directed to the Father, and then more recently to the Spirit — but not the Holy Spirit in the sense we are so used to thinking of him — but God as pure Spirit who is in every<u>one</u> and every<u>thing</u> — even the ground I walk on, the rock I pick up, the air I breathe — everything that is living and everything that just is (perhaps not all to the same degree, but with Spirit there is no degree, only a person's or object's ability to be open, trusting, receptive)... I cannot believe that God/Spirit is completely contained in anything or anyone. There is something about God in a tree which I can only learn from a tree and never find in a person. That is one reason why I cannot believe that Spirit is completely revealed even in Jesus. If God has children, then we are all Sons of God and Daughters of God all in the same way as is all of creation. Granted, perhaps Jesus was very aware of himself as Son of God in a way that most of us never will be, for that I respect him as a great example and teacher, not for what legend and the Church has made him to be.
  That's why it was so hard for me to stay in the ministry. I could no longer say things, in sermons or Mass or to the people, that I didn't completely believe in anymore. I could no longer go thru the actions, be someone to others that I was not.
  I know I was a fine priest and have helped many people in that capacity, and I am grateful for the experience. I have learned so much. But why did I become one in the first place? As I look back at my motives when I was 14 and even up to the day of ordination I see many expectations from others that I would be a priest. Yes, I accepted these, made them my own. I blame no one because there were many opportunities when I could have left and didn't, and some when I almost did leave and didn't. So, why did I stay? — because I was working under the false but very real presumption that I had to BE someone to be worthwhile, I had to <u>do</u> something good with my life in order to be accepted or loved, I had to prove to others and to myself that I was <u>worth</u> loving. What better way to do that then to fulfill expectations and enter a profession where I would constantly be needed and supposedly loved —

despite the feelings of loneliness that used to crush me to the ground, and the feelings of being used that would make me so angry.

Once in my own trap, I couldn't quit until I finally realized what I had been doing, which made me see my profession as a ploy, an act to hook others. Yes, for sure there was more to it (a deep desire to help and be of service to others, which will always be there)(that in itself another ploy?), but I really feel that was the root. I am taking this time out because I need to be free to love myself, to be as authentic and true to others as I have been with myself, to find out what it is like to be loved just for who I am and not because of a robe or title.

One aspect that has led me to the present moment has led me thru the closest thing I can think of to hell on earth: thru twenty years of guilt because others have said I was no good and fear that I would be found out, thru ten years of being clammed up inside because someone misunderstood, thru nights beyond counting of crying until I couldn't feel anything anymore, thru the shame of using others to meet my needs, thru the pain and loneliness of most of my life, thru the "sickness" of the not too distant past, to the healthiness and wholeness of the present when I am no longer ashamed to admit that I am homosexual. I would not be around today if some have not continued to love me unconditionally.

When I came to Albuquerque, I decided I would not go to the bars or porno shops, and I have not. If I were to find other gay men to relationship with, we would have to meet otherwise. I have met some I care to continue relationship with: one after Mass at church, another after a gay Christmas program at another church.

You have worried about me, but I am more happy now than I have ever been, perhaps because I have made a decision to be completely open and honest with myself in all my various aspects and to be able to be honest with others, and because I know now I no longer need to look in "sick" ways for other men my own age to form relationship with - a freeing experience.

I have wanted to share these things with you for years, but was either discouraged in doing so, or felt it would hurt you too much. I can only now trust in your complete love of me and wish that I be happy. Maybe you have known some of these things already, perhaps thru the closeness of our co-psychic powers. Whatever the case, I have nothing more to hide as I present all of me for your love.

Where this year will lead, I do not know. I will not read the end of the novel until I have lived the rest. But, some inklings I have are that I can no longer allow my spirit to be dictated to by any religious institution. I will look for truth and guidance wherever and however I can find it.

Perhaps what I have shared causes you to worry even more for me. I only ask that you trust in my own integrity and authenticity and common sense. I am not promiscuous, nor could I emotionally handle multiple relationships. Also, I have found the only way to true growth, realistic love and acceptance is thru the joy, and at times pain, of living with one relationship. Your relationship with Dad and your sticking by us has exampled me of that.

My spiritual orientation, I hope, does not say anything about your religious tradition or that of any of my bros. & srs.. I know it is deeply meaningful for you, and I will always respect that with the utmost charity. After all, I am immensely grateful for being part of that tradition and spirituality – it has led me to where I am now.

I can think of nothing more to share. Undoubtedly, you have many specific questions and concerns. I would be glad to discuss anything with you in depth.

After thinking about it, I will xerox this letter and send copies to all in the family. Rather than speculate among yourselves, kindly communicate with me, is all I ask.

Again, for your worry and support, signs of your love for me, I thank you more than I ever have in the past. And I love you now, all of you, with everything I am in the present.

- Tom

Some responses from my brothers and sisters regarding the letter:

"I thought I would be more disappointed when you sent 'the letter' to everyone saying you were gay, and instead I feel proud of you for opening up to the whole family and relieving yourself of what you feel instead of what everyone else feels you should be."

"I knew you were unhappy in the priesthood but didn't know why. Basically, I feel that you are in charge of your happiness and I love you no matter what decision you make. Mom is really struggling with your decision. Wondering why. Thinking that maybe the seminary influenced you. She said that she would try to get to the bottom of it and maybe understand more after she speaks with you."

"Regarding you leaving the priesthood and subsequent coming out: I received your letter, and after reading it, I feel like I have been hit by a stun gun. It took me by surprise. I won't discuss it with the siblings as I feel it is your personal life, and I don't want to get involved in their bible quotes and passing judgements on you."

"We never chose to share it with our children like some in the family did to shame you. It was so personal it wasn't any of the children's business."

"I honestly feel your means of telling us you are gay is very cowardly -- addressing it by letter form. I am also very aware that it is a VERY difficult task to come up with the courage to make the announcement, because gays are not accepted in society. But, I feel mom is more deserving of hearing it from you, than her mail carrier."

"I feel that if you had delivered 'the message' in person you could have made the acceptance of some a little easier."

"I hurt for you….I wonder how you managed to keep your sexuality hidden. I wonder how you dealt with it? Being trapped inside of a body and not being able to express it. True struggles and no one to talk to or turn to about it on a true personal level. This is what families are for when someone is in crisis."

> *"I knew you were depressed, and I thought you had a girlfriend. I told you that Mom says she would rather you be happy than miserable as a priest. Mom is having a really tough time with your decision and cries a lot. She thinks you will go back to being a priest."*

> *"The family is split because of you, the letter, and your coming out. Some say that if you are gay, they do not agree with it. Others feel that it is wrong, they do not like it and cannot accept you!"*

> *"We all have our own stories, but we keep them to ourselves and don't talk about them. I could be more accepting because I have worked with gays and would hear their stories of how their families basically disowned them."*

> *"I am shocked by the letter and how graphic it is. The letter makes your life seem so seedy and shameful. Always in the shadows hiding. Terrified of what the family would think, particularly what Mom might think of her priest being gay. It sounds so much like a cry for help, but I understand it is a cry for acceptance and understanding. It is so painful as you poured out your heart. Most of the family just can not believe it or tune into it. It doesn't cause me to stop loving you. LOVE is the first thing. That's enough."*

A Different Dose of Reality

A friend of Joe's worked for the main mortuary in town which also owned two cemeteries. He said they were looking for a cemetery superintendent for this twenty acre cemetery at the edge of town, which had really gone down because the previous workers didn't care for it at all. The well didn't work. Vagrants were living in the very small caretaker's trailer. There were heaps of trash everywhere since the locals used it as a fenceless dump. They needed someone to clean the place up, including removing the vagrants and the trailer, repairing the well and irrigation system, installing headstones which were piled behind the maintenance building, raising some headstones which were covered by the blowing sand over the years, using the small backhoe to dig new graves and shovel-trimming the sides, probing the ground first to find out if someone was already buried there since the records were not accurate, cutting the grass, raking the leaves, etc. I agreed to take the position since I had a knack for cleaning things up, making them right, managing things and working hard. And, I had heard that working at a cemetery was the only job where I could start out on top.

Not only was I to be the manager there, but also the only person actually doing the work. Even the owners didn't seem to care how, what, when things got done, so long as there was visible improvement enough to keep the deceased's relatives from constantly complaining. Monday through Friday, March thru December of 1984, I drove to the funeral home by 8am, picked up the old Ford truck, and drove it through morning rush hour traffic one half hour North of town. The first day at the cemetery, I raised the flag on the flagpole at the main entrance, opened the workshop doors, started a fire in the rigged 50 gallon heater, did an inventory of the tools that were not stolen by previous workers, started the tractor to warm it up, and began cleaning out the shop of the trash and rat nests. The drunk and drugged vagrants gave me a problem about leaving the trailer until I gave them an hour to leave or I would call the police to remove them. They left amid much cursing and threats. Having stuffed it with more trash, I hitched it to the tractor and dragged it further into the desert and set it on fire.

Within the first week, a well company came and replaced the submersible pump, and another company dropped off their largest roll-off dumpster for the trash. I even worked out a deal with the three men who dropped it off for them to come after hours and on the weekend to clean up the trash and fill the dumpster, including the chassis of the burned trailer. It took four overflowing dumpsters to finish. Having cleared it with the main mortuary downtown, and picking up the money, I paid the men with cash.

We Begin to Live Together

Joe moved into the apartment with me in July. To do this, he had to leave his home and allow his ex-wife to use it so the kids would have a stable living situation. She had joint ownership of the house anyhow. I am sure that was a tough decision for him to make, and it was a huge step in our relationship. We had some furniture finally as he brought some with him. We were seeing each other mostly everyday anyhow, but it sure was nice having him with me all the time and every night. Quite a commitment on both our parts! I was very happy. Also, I got to know Joey and Margaret much better since they would be with us on the days Joe had them, and we took trips together to Carlsbad Caverns and Jemez Pueblo Feast days.

But, the situation with the Grandpa who owned the apartment got to be very stressful. He told me he rented the apartment to me only and no one else, and if I had someone else living there he was going to double the rent. He also took to looking in the windows and spying on us. A couple times we heard him on the roof, taking off the panels of the cooler to listen in on us through the ceiling vent. I heard him breathing heavily through it. He snooped in other ways as well: on the other side of our bedroom wall was a closet in their bedroom, and I heard him move stuff away from the thin closet wall so he could listen to our conversations. None of this happened before Joe moved in. I told Joe we couldn't live there with this going on, and even though Joe had just moved in, he agreed we had to find someplace else and move to where we could be ourselves.

It didn't take long, and Joe found another apartment, a little smaller, but very Southwestern, with red brick floors and a kiva fireplace, vigas holding up the ceiling, and a small patio in front – it was nice and comfortable. We got our friends together to help us move out of the other apartment in August. Grandpa was furious and threw a fit of threats when we were loading up – another indication it was better for us to get out of there.

Turns out the position at the cemetery was the best place for me at the time. Working with my hands, being creative, fixing things, making things happen, being outside in the sun, working hard, sweating and getting dirty, being in tune with the healing power of nature, and focusing on something outside of me were all good therapy; and there was no one breathing down my neck. In fact, there were days when no one came to the cemetery except a roadrunner that used to show up at lunchtime for the bits of my sandwich I used to feed him. Sometimes, he would cautiously approach, grab it from my hand and run – beep, beep. Of course, I called him "Beep Beep" from the roadrunner and the coyote cartoons. And, yes, I hurt my back a couple times and had to go to a doctor for help, a friend of a friend, until he propositioned me and I dropped him, preferring to live with the pain and ibuprofen. Overall, the job worked for me until the weather started to get cold in the Fall. There was less and less to do, and I couldn't make a friend of the cold. It seemed I was sitting in the maintenance shed freezing, even with the wood heater, waiting for someone to die to have something to do. So, I gave notice and quit the second week of December 1984.

Letter to Fr. Jeremy 11/25/84

  *Last Tuesday it had been one year since I left Lukachukai.
On that day, I thanked you for suggesting that one year would be better
than six months (my original request to be away from the friars). One
year is so short. When I think that I have experienced so much and
learned so much, I realize how little it really has been. Actually, it took
me until August or September to get over thinking everyday about when
I would return, or what it would be like, or whether I even could return
to more active friar-life and ministry. I think about it much less often
now, trying to attend to each day and each new experience; believing if I
am to return, I will, when it is right. If I am not to return, then I will be
fine.*

  *I have met so many new friends this year. Most of them other
gay men, all of them very supportive and encouraging. None of them have
meant more to me than Joe. We met at a Christmas party last Dec.
11th. He invited me over for a drink that evening, and we have seen
each other most every day since. Especially since we moved in together in
July. It is difficult for me to explain what a difference Joe has made in
my life. It has been so good to have such a close friend. We share many of
the same interests, we share our moods, our thoughts, our life, our love.*

  *Love – I always had a problem with receiving it, with
believing that I was lovable. I am receiving it now, and believing that I
am worth loving. Joe has touched every part of my life with his gentleness,
has helped heal the scars, given me hope, and made Love incarnate once
again.*

  *Through each of the people I've met I've come to see more what
life is really like. What most people go thru! What pulls them down,
what worries them constantly – job, money, house, car, family, getting a
little ahead – and what pulls them up, someone who cares, their families,
the warmth of another person. I have experienced these things, and I
could never preach again the way I used to. I could never place the
challenges, demands, and expectations on them again.*

  *I've learned a lot about myself also. Talking with my counselor in
Santa Fe helped a lot. We centered on healing the underlying anger
within me, on the feelings of being caged and used and misunderstood as
a friar/priest, the deep loneliness and boredom. Being an avid and vivid
dreamer helped me to see many connections and verify my feelings. He left
in September. I miss talking with him.*

  *I'm still working at the cemetery. It was the right place for me
from March thru the summer. The lack of pressure, the physical labor,
the sun, heat, all of nature around was so <u>good</u>. Now, I'm looking for*

work with people – PR, social, or whatever. I've got my friends looking, too.

From reading this letter so far, I suppose you can see that I'm planning on taking more time, and I don't know how long. I do know that now is not the right time for returning. Honestly, Jeremy, I do not know that I ever will, and I do not know that I will not. I will not do myself and others the injustice of pressing the issue.

I am planning on being back East for Christmas, weather permitting, between December 23rd and 28th. Perhaps we could get together then if you will be available. Well, I blew it for letter writing for the rest of the year with this one. Thank you for listening, thank you for everything.

Tom

++++

Just when I met Joe's parents I can't remember. They lived about forty-five minutes south of Albuquerque right on Highway 48 in Peralta, NM. Joe's Mom worked at a government office in Albuquerque, while his Dad ran the Senior Center in Los Lunas and farmed land around their house and a lot of acreage all around the town. Basically, he grew alfalfa for extra income and for a couple dozen head of cattle he had in the barn and corrals out back. They both worked hard and had that special New Mexican way of making me feel at home and welcomed. I was ashamed to have them know I was a priest on a leave of absence so I didn't share that, not knowing what they would think of me and how that would be talked about around town and at the Catholic parish they belonged to. We got along great. I felt they were my parents out West, and I offered to help them both in any way I could. They even invited me to Thanksgiving dinner with the family and to the Christmas Eve family celebration. After that, Joe and I would visit them at least twice a month bringing the kids down to visit with their Grandparents, and we all went there for every Thanksgiving and Christmas Eve.

++++

In January 1985, I found Betty, a Jungian therapist who told me at our initial meeting that she would take me on, but also warned me that her style is "to go after the jugular vein." Figuring that might be just what I needed to deal with everything inside of me, and what to do with my obligations to the Franciscans and the priesthood, and my relationship with Joe, and finding myself, I agreed to her intensive therapy. At first, we met once a week, then soon enough twice a week. It is hard to explain the intellectual, spiritual, and emotional connection we had, but early on I found I trusted her implicitly, her ability, her helping me understand my prolific dreams, her helping me find what was best for me. She was truly a very gifted lady. Lancing all the old wounds to let the poison drain out was particularly difficult and exhausting. No issue or topic was left unperceived, untouched, uninvestigated, unanalyzed, unconnected to the others, unenlightened, or unattempted to be forgiven or resolved.

All of this introspection and analysis came together for the BIG AHA! moment on March 15th – Beware the Ides of March! Apparently, a couple times during our sessions I quoted to Betty Dad's prescription for success: you can be whoever you want to be, and have whatever you want, so long as you want it bad enough and work hard enough for it. She stopped me this time and asked, "What if you did want it bad enough, and you worked very hard for it, but you still weren't able to be the person you wanted to be, or have what you had worked so very hard for, no matter how much you wanted it or worked for it?" Instantly an image entered my mind. I was in a dark, cold, filthy, inner-city alleyway all by myself, sitting on the dirty ground next to an old large metal trash can which was vomiting all the stinking and rotting trash out the top and then right on top of me. I told Betty I would feel like trash, like I was no good, like I wasn't worth anything, and I began to sob deeply. She told me to take my time and let it out, but I couldn't stop. My session went overtime, and she didn't want to let me drive home in the state I was in, but I had to get out of there and believed I would be fine and left.

Taking the side streets, I cried all the way home, and started to sob again when I went in. Joe didn't know what the hell was going on until I tried to share the session with him, and he respected my need to spend time to myself. The next day I called Betty, and she took me right in. There was so much to share since the day before, and when I left her house that day I remember taking a big deep breath of the freshest air I had ever taken in, and the sun was so bright and clear, and the sky was the bluest I had ever seen. Ever since then, I have celebrated March 15th as my second birthday.

++++

The puzzle that was the picture of me I had painted throughout my life had mostly been successfully taken apart piece by piece. In the weeks that followed, we put a new puzzle back together again, not something which would be permanent, but which would be ever-changing. One big piece to this puzzle would be my responsibility to the Franciscans, particularly whether I could ever return to that life and the priestly ministry again. Joe and I spoke about it a lot, and I am sure he didn't want to talk about it much since he always knew that my returning to them was something I was struggling with, and it was always a possibility. Having a much better understanding and acceptance of myself, I felt I owed it to the Franciscans, the ministry, and to myself to give it another try; not to see if I could fit into it again, but to see if it could fit into the puzzle that was now me. It was something I had to do for me, and to see if it would help dissolve the heavy guilt of leaving that was left unforgiven inside. If I did, I would want a balance between solitude and being with people, would not want to live in a community of more than two, would not want to be in parish or school ministry, would want to live poorly, and would need to be free. It would be similar to a Robinson Crusoe deciding if he really wanted to commit himself to leaving his island and return to "civilization" after the relief of being away from it.

The two journal volumes I kept during my therapy with Betty record in much detail the talks we had, the insights and thoughts arrived at, the overnight dreams during and the daylight analysis after, the decisions made and why, and so on.

Chapter Five
The Return

I called Fr. Jeremy and told him where I was with myself and with coming back at the end of the six month extension of the leave of absence in June, and asked if there was a ministry that would fit with me. He was happy to hear of the decision, hoping it was the best one for me, and said he would consider it and get back with me. He also wanted me to consider getting some instruction and counseling regarding theology and my approach to God.

"Purity of heart is to will one thing." (Kierkegaard)

To return, or not, would mean committing myself totally to one thing or the other, but not to both. I would want to achieve integration of my personality. I could not live as a split person, trying to integrate both lives into who I was. I realized I could not live as a full Franciscan and Catholic priest and also incorporate a full gay relationship, or have a full relationship on the side as many had done and were doing. A couple priests and friars told me of their lives and how they were incorporating the "both/and" into their lives. I knew my integrity couldn't handle that. With my decision, I would have to take the puzzle pieces of the ministry, organizational religious life, priesthood, sacraments, service to the people, option for and with the poor, etc.; and see if my interpretation and understanding of that would, could, or whether I would even really want it to, fit into the larger puzzle that was now me. I also knew that to choose that would mean to lose, to remove, the puzzle pieces of my life with Joe, my life as a lay man with no ties to any organization, the freedom I had experienced, etc.; and, whether

I could or even really wanted to do that, and whether the whole puzzle of me would sustain too much damage by doing that.

Leaving Joe

Of course, naturally, the most extremely difficult part of this decision was leaving Joe and hurting him so deeply, doing violence to both of us, and also dealing with the intense guilt and sorrow of that. It struck at the very depth of my being, and I am sure his. I know he had a lot of anger about my leaving, a lot of feeling that he had put so much into our relationship, had given up so much, and now I was tossing it away. Wasn't there more meaning to our being together than returning to something which had lost its meaning? Did I even have any idea what this was doing to his own life and his own self-image? He didn't express most of this to me. He held it in, but I knew it was there. He did what he had to do to cut the ties with me, to push me away, to make it more bearable for him to say goodbye with no real hope of our meeting again. He made it very clear that if things did not work out for me back in Ohio, that I should not expect him to be waiting around for me to return. It seemed that it would be easier for him for me to leave not as a friend, but as an enemy, a traitor, as one who had given up on him. The guilt of leaving him, of failing him, weighed deeply in me and was very emotional. I knew he would always be a great friend of mine and would remain a tremendous influence in my life.

We were together for a year and a half before I decided I needed to give the priesthood another try. I would share with Joe everything I spoke about in my counseling sessions. While he wanted to blame my counselor, he knew it really wasn't her fault. He understood, but he didn't like it one bit. It was tough for both of us.

I really wondered if the price of leaving Joe and entering the next stage of my life would be too much for me. And, I was really scared. I knew I would have to get into it slowly and take my time to find out if the religious side meant anything anymore. If not, could I honestly stick with it? If not, how could I preach or accept myself as others would see me, as a religious person? I was really scared of the loneliness I knew would be part of all this, and scared that I would be looking for someone all the time, and the possibility of scandal. It would be very rough for a while. The future would be so uncertain, and I was afraid that if it didn't work out, I may lose absolutely everything, including my wanting to live.

Returning to the Franciscans and the Priesthood

My departure date was set for Memorial Day, May 27, 1985. We said our goodbyes and thought, "Goodbye, forever." When I walked out of the door for the last time, Joe was so angry and hurt. He was crying. I was crying. It was the final thing. I wanted to hug him and kiss him, which we did briefly, but it was hands off after that -- "Just leave" -- and he slammed the door. That was kind of appropriate, in a sense, just slamming the door shut on our relationship.

Fr. Jeremy had gotten back to me about a month earlier with an assignment to St. Leonard, where I had spent four years in theology seminary eight years before, but which had since been sold to the Sisters of Mercy, who renovated it into a retirement and extended care facility. They needed another chaplain to minister there. I would be living in the old brick farmhouse with another friar. I felt that assignment would fit me well.

When I shared my return with my family, Mom was overjoyed with the answer to her prayers -- that I was returning to the priesthood. While my brothers and sisters were glad for me, if this was what I really wanted to do, the letter I sent to them all in January 1984 was still fresh in their minds, and most were quite confused. They didn't know what to make of it, and some thought that I was being a hypocrite. One of my brothers said, "How can you do that? How can you live the way you did and return to being a priest and offering Mass?" I don't remember which brother said that, but I responded, "That's what confession is for. It's to be honest, ask for forgiveness, and move on." My youngest brother, Ted, asked if I would officiate at his wedding to be held at St. Peter in Chains Cathedral in Cincinnati. My brother Ed asked if I would baptize his newborn son when I got back. Since I would be home for vacation, I agreed.

I went back with every intention of staying there and working it out, not returning to Albuquerque. I knew I could be a gay man and a Franciscan friar and a priest, unless I wanted a full relationship with another man.

The Journey Back East

The long drive back to Ohio was good to have at that time as a distraction from thinking about me. To avoid being so depressed and afraid, I tried to focus on hopes for the future and positive expectations and being confident. Before I left, I had made some phone calls ahead to line up places to stay and visit along the way: Wichita, KS. to visit the friars whom I knew; Emporia, KS. to visit a friar-priest friend from St. Leonard college who was ordained a few years after I was; Kansas City, MO. to visit one of my classmates; and Allerton, IA. to visit Ross and Lorena Blount.

When I arrived in Wichita late in the afternoon, I went to the parish the Franciscans staffed. I told the Brother who I was, and that I had called the Pastor about staying there for the night. Irritated, he told me he didn't know anything about that, and that the Pastor wasn't there at the time, and that I should come back in a couple hours, and closed the door. So, I went out to get something to eat and took my time. At about 8pm, I returned to the parish friary, rang the doorbell, and the same Brother answered. He looked at me, said the Pastor still wasn't there, and told me to just go get a hotel room, and closed the door – all without me having a chance to say a word. St. Francis would have called this a "perfect joy" moment of being rejected by your own brothers.

The next day, I arrived in Emporia, KS about 9:30am, went to the Franciscan parish, and my friend answered the door and immediately invited me in. He served coffee and cookies, and began telling me how very rough his life was living with a severe alcoholic and verbally abusive friar who was also the Pastor. As he poured out his pain, he cried for a solid hour. My heart cried with him. He said he had no one to talk to, and I was glad I was there for him. However, I did ask that he find a therapist to share with before he broke, and to report the Pastor to his superiors in Cincinnati. I hated to leave him.

In Kansas City, MO. it was great to see my classmate and get the grand tour of his thriving inner city parish and school. He was also able to sponsor three seminarians for the summer to give them a taste of what this ministry would be like for them. In Kansas City, KS. across the river we had a lip-smacking and finger-licking dinner at one of the best BBQ joints in town. During dinner, I noticed that one of the seminarians kept trying to lock eyes with me, and I knew exactly what was going on. With everyone living in the friary already there was no extra room or bed for me, but I was fine sleeping on the floor of a storage room off the kitchen with a few blankets as a cushion. At about 3am, the burglary or fire alarm sounded at the school, and everyone came down through the kitchen with flashlights heading for the school. I joined them to find no smoke or intruders. As I was trying to get back to sleep, the seminarian from dinner opened the door and laid down on the floor with me. He spoke into the morning of his loneliness, doubts, and fears to someone who could so totally listen, and know, and empathize. My heart ached for him as I encouraged him to make a commitment first to himself, sooner rather than later.

Lorena and Ross in Allerton, IA. had always been a deep breath of fresh air and insight for me. We spoke of the struggle of paradox, of counseling and listening for the good spirit behind what is said, the life struggling to live, of suicide, of questioning as the first hint of looking, of affirming life and accepting death, of affirming good and accepting evil, of either standing in others' shoes or holding others in love, of the devil's food cake coffee mug and the angel food cake coffee mug and which one will take the cake – those are the questions! I loved being on their farm with them. They always challenged and comforted my spirit.

From there, I headed on to Mom's house in Fairfield, OH. about twenty miles north of Cincinnati. I had already made arrangements to stay with the four friars at St. Stephen's Church in Hamilton, OH. during the two week vacation I was taking before moving onto my assignment, but I wanted to stop at Mom's first to assure her that things were going well for me. The experience at the friary was far less than what I had hoped for and much worse than I could have expected. Perhaps naively, I hoped to be accepted as a fellow friar and one of their brothers, and to be welcomed. But, instead, I felt their suspicion and complete lack of support, care, concern, or welcome. I was briskly shown a room in the attic space which had not been dusted or cleaned in forever, the thin mattress on the bed was dirty and not made up until I requested sheets and a pillow so I could put them on, one of the windows would not open, the other window had no air conditioner as did all the other bedrooms, there was no fan in the room, nor one to be had when I requested one, and it was an extremely HOT and humid early June. (I was reminded of a very short midsummer sermon at this same church when I was a kid: "If you think it's hot in here, just think of how hot it is in hell" -- end of sermon.)

After I settled in the room, I went downstairs to the TV room to join the other friars. They were intent on watching some show and sipping their drinks, and no one asked how I was, or how the trip was, or if I needed anything, or if I wanted a drink. When I asked them any question about themselves, they seemed intruded upon and didn't want to have any conversation. I even asked if I could get into the church to pray and was told it was locked and the security system was set for the night. No one budged. So I went downstairs to the kitchen to get something to eat. I sat there at the table eating a lunch meat sandwich, very alone, feeling this was the way it would be in any friary and on into old age. I was thinking of what the hell was I getting myself into, and maybe that I was expecting way too much. Maybe they were trying to make it as tough on me as possible to see if I had what it would take to stick with it and last. Needless to say, I did not sleep at all that night with the heat, the sweat, the feelings, the thoughts.

The church bells rang for 8am Mass, but I was already cleaned up and dressed. I sat in the back of the large gothic church because I really didn't want to be noticed by the parishioners, who would know me from earlier years. During the Mass, I decided I really didn't need to stay here and be this hard on myself. After some coffee and toast for breakfast, I asked the housekeeper who had arrived where the cleaning supplies were, and went to clean the room totally, windows and floor and all. Close to noon, I stopped by the room occupied by my old friend and spiritual director from the Novitiate some fifteen years earlier. He was in retirement there and was bedridden. At least he seemed interested in what my life had been like during those years. But, he ended our conversation abruptly by saying, "Well, Tom, you ought to just go ahead and leave for good. I have never seen anyone come back from a leave of absence and stay." Was this another sign, along with the ones I experienced during my trip back East, that maybe I should do just that?

I decided to leave there and go stay at Mom's where there was air conditioning and where I would be welcomed. Having said goodbye to the friars and explaining why I was going, I drove the few short miles to Mom's. We had many deep conversations, and I kept nothing to myself, and she had so many "why" questions, and I had so many apologies for hurting her unintentionally during my quest. But, I knew she could never fully understand my theology or approach to the priesthood, or why they had changed so drastically, or why I just couldn't fit into the mold anymore. Most of my sisters and a few of my brothers tried to understand and accept me. Two or three of my brothers actually told me they thought I was the Devil Incarnate, "intrinsically evil", and I was going to hell. They refused to understand and could never accept me, but they would love me as a brother but not for who I was. I thought, "Really? What's with that?" "I don't even know what that means -- to love that we came from the same womb, but not who I had become as a whole person." I knew they had changed a lot also and were seeking meaning and security in their lives through extreme fundamental Christianity. So, I tried to understand why they would say what they did, and I knew that as long as the rigidity was inside them, as long as their hearts were hardened against me, we could never be close. Even so, it didn't settle well with me at all then and still doesn't.

++++

Fr. Edwin helped me a great deal in getting the required approval from the Archbishop of Cincinnati to function as a priest in his Diocese, and even went with me to Columbus, OH., the state capitol, to get certified by the State to function as an ordained minister for weddings. He helped me so much in the re-entry process, his prayers that I would come back were answered, and we spent some quality time together. Also, I was able to get around Cincinnati to visit a few other friars. Two of them were at the old St. Francis Seminary where I had gone to High School, but which had since been turned into a retreat and conference center. One was my dear friend and music teacher, Fr. Aubert, from the seminary who was again assigned there. We met up, walked the large property, and shared a lot. He told me he had been assigned to a parish in Louisiana for some years, but had recently been removed from there. The reason? He found the lover he had hoped for his whole life, a black man he dearly loved and also dearly loved him. As he told me of being ripped away from him he sobbed, his heart and spirit totally broken from being so alive and now so alone and lonely once again. I was so one with him as he sobbed, I cried with him and held him for a long time. I felt closer to him than I ever had before.

The other friar I wanted to see was the one who had written those scathing letters to me and Fr. Larry at Lukachukai. I wanted to make amends and ask for his forgiveness for having offended him by my responses to his letters. I went to his room after being assured he was there, knocked four times, and waited. No answer. I identified myself loud enough for him to hear, and knocked four times again. No answer, but I could hear him through the door speaking quietly to someone. I spoke again and told him I was there to make amends and to say I was sorry, and that I would sit outside his door until he would come out and talk to me. Angrily, through the door he told me to go away, that he didn't want to talk with me. I said I would be waiting outside the door. Before I could sit down he flung the door open in a wild fit of rage, stood there in his underwear, and yelled at me, "I SAID GO AWAY! I DON'T WANT TO TALK TO YOU! I DON'T EVER WANT TO SEE YOU AGAIN!" Before he could slam the door in my face I could see beyond him into his room, and saw a naked woman lying on his bed. SLAM! So, here was this moral theology professor, this self-righteous paragon of virtue, who told us how we should live. The shock was too much for me. I went to the chapel and prayed for a while, and then forgave him with an ever so slight smile on my face.

Were these two more signs to include in my decision-making process?

++++

The wedding at the Cathedral was such a wonderful event and celebration of Ted's and his wife's love, and their promises to do whatever they had to do to stay in love forever. My sermon was fairly decent, and Fr. Edwin assisted me at the altar. Actually, it was only the second wedding I officiated at in the eight years since I had been ordained. Another family event and celebration, the baptism of my nephew, went very well on a hot Sunday afternoon. He was baptized in the 100-year-old baptismal gown that all of us were baptized in. A lot of faith history was in that garment.

Journal entry June 13th, 1985:
> *One great need of mine is to have a very close friend I can be with, to love, run around with, do things together, go together, be sexual together – and have the same interests.*
> *-- Question? – can I find someone among the friars? If not, can I find someone outside the friars and would that be okay? Someone I can be for and he can be for me?*
> *-- Question? – how long can I take it before I find someone, or leave this aside and return to Joe, if he would take me back?*
> *-- "Celibacy does not necessarily mean abstinence" -- I have been told. But, does that mean to go ahead and satisfy natural sexual needs and have relationships which can do that for me -- just so long as they are not permanent and distract from the primary committed relationship to the Lord, the Church, and all the people? I'm not really sure.*
> *-- I cannot, nor do I want to take the loneliness without someone special.*
> *-- turmoil-struggle between personal/emotional/physical needs and spirit needing channel for release.*
> *-- religious life affords me – leisure to be with creation, to touch the mystical, contemplative side, time to touch the spirit, availability to touch others deeply*
> *-- difficult to find the friendship I need with the friars (difficult or not possible?)*
> *-- main interest is in "being with" someone*
> *-- less interest in ministering -- helping others*

The Old Farmhouse at St. Leonard

The assignment to St. Leonard Retirement Center began on Monday, June 17th. With much anticipation and anxiety, I pulled up to the back door of the farmhouse about mid-morning, entered the door and met the chaplain with whom I was slightly familiar. He was very welcoming, happy I was there, and freely shared about his ministry to the elderly at the main facility. Though I had lived on the property for four years of college theology, I had never been inside the "farmhouse." It was a very old two-story brick house from the early 1800's. It was painted white outside, had been renovated and updated inside but not extravagantly. It had three bedrooms upstairs, wooden floors that creaked, some original floorboards were wavy and uneven, a bathroom, a downstairs bedroom, a large common area and kitchen, a shower room, and an add-on used for storage. My room was to be the one downstairs. He told me to make myself at home, not to go up to the main facility until he had a chance to introduce me to the staff, that he had to go into town for a bit, and he left.

Some of the boxes I unloaded from the car were very heavy with books which I had stored at Mom's house, and I probably shouldn't have lifted them by myself, but I managed to get everything out and into my room, being very glad it wasn't on the second floor. By lunchtime, I was drenched from the summer humidity and heat and was tired and hungry. Helping myself to a lunchmeat and cheese sandwich from the fridge along with a Coke and peanut butter and crackers from the cabinet, I sat at the table by myself and wondered what was next. Should I wait until the chaplain returned before I did anything? What ministry possibilities were in the Dayton area? The eight years since I had been here seemed so long ago yet very familiar. I felt like a college student again, only this time without a clear picture of the future and no one to paint it with me.

After resting a bit, I took a stroll outside around the house, and the good memories of cutting grass with the tractor and maintaining the large campus came flooding back. I could tell the grounds remembered me also, and wondered where I had been for so long, and welcomed me back. The grass around the house was about a foot high, and the yew bushes next to the house were very overgrown. In the shed out back, I found a gas-powered lawn mower, rakes, loppers, and a manual bush trimmer, and I began giving the large yard a haircut in the late afternoon heat. It was hard work, and it felt so good to sweat profusely and to have increasingly sore muscles. I spoke to the earth about why I was there again and what my hopes were. The ground kept telling me: "Listen to your body. Feel it. It's all you really have. The worries, plans, thoughts, fears, and anxieties are all just fabrications in your mind. Feel your body. Listen to your body. It's the only way you have to hear beautiful music, see wondrous things, taste satisfying food, touch others and be touched by them, smell the sweet earth, and stand firmly anchored on her. And, by the way, the only way the Spirit has a way to manifest itself is through the vehicle of the body. Listen. Feel." And I did. And it was good. And I felt good and happy. After the initial pass, I raked it all up and carried the heavy clippings behind the house to the brush pile. By the time I was finished with that a four-foot snake had come to sun itself on the grass and to inspect what was going on. I spoke to him and coaxed him with the rake into the ditch next to the road. Then I barbered all the grass again a little shorter, raked it all up again, carried the hair clippings to the brush pile, and quit before the sun went down. I felt my body's very sore muscles while having a peanut butter sandwich and a coke, and then I took a hot shower.

Journal Entry Monday, June 17, 1985
Today I moved to St. Leonard. I don't know why I am here, except that for some reason I am to learn and discover something here. I admit that there is nothing of the established religion or faith that interests me, other than the deep spirit and essentials of human kindness. Rather than sitting around doing nothing, I will look into all kinds of possibilities – soup kitchen, Dignity, street people ministry, … – I'll also do yard work here.

Since the chaplain hadn't returned yet, I was alone. I locked the doors, turned off all the lights except one, and crashed on the bed in my room. It felt so good to lie down and be done with the day. But, during the night I woke up as I sensed a heavy darkness filling the room, an evil presence. I got up and went to the kitchen for a drink of water and to make sure it wasn't just a dream, but I didn't sense the darkness elsewhere in the house. I went back to bed, and the darkness returned. I sat on the edge of the bed and extended my hands with palms out in front of me and then walked around the room, sensing the air in the room and around all four corners and walls. Being a sensate and highly perceptive, I felt that the presence was the strongest around and in the small fireplace on the north wall.

The fireplace was being used as a portal, and I was sensing it because I was so open to those things. And then, the darkness grabbed me and enveloped me as the presence manifested itself. Having no control and feeling very weak, I had to lie down. Even making the sign of the cross over myself several times and into the air, trying to expel the demons or whatever it was, with the words of exorcism I remembered from Chinle, did nothing. In fact, the possession seemed to get worse as I was dragged deeper into the cave of severe depression where I had been so often before. The demons chuckled as I re-lived and re-felt all those horrible dark times of the past. "Aren't you just kidding yourself by being here, trying to repress and suppress your real self, trying to hide the true you again? Aren't you killing yourself hoping to be brought back to life again as some different you, the minister you, the religious you, a you you don't believe in anyhow? You won't be a good person, more acceptable, feel less like trash by doing anything or saying anything or being anything to or for others or yourself. It's all a great big JOKE. It's fake. Not real. Just like life. Period! Why didn't you go ahead and kill yourself when you thought about it the first time you were here and had that nervous break? Why not when you were living in Chinle or when you were leaving Lukachukai? Why not now? There would be no more hiding, no more struggle, no more fear, no more trying to prove who you aren't, no more you."

I found it difficult to breathe with the heaviness around me. Fear paralyzed me. Fear of the Darkness. Fear that I might actually end it all. And this went on all night. There was no sleep, no rest. I was the lone defenseless prey the pack of wild dogs chose to attack because they could sense my fear.

When the dawn began to dispel the darkness outside, the darkness in the room also dissipated, concentrating and pushing itself toward the fireplace, gradually lifting and disappearing altogether. I layed there until the sun broke through the eastern window and I could get some will to move my legs and arms. My whole body was sore and drenched in sweat. "Listen to your body. Feel it!" Finally, unsteadily, I got up, got a glass of water, put some coffee on to brew, and sat at the table thinking: What the hell? I didn't have to think what the hell that was all about because I knew all too well, and knew I needed to make a decision that day. I could not be torn apart again like I was last night. The chaplain hadn't return over the night, so there was no one to talk to. Last night was real. It wasn't an hallucination, and I wasn't hearing voices. Anyone I might talk to about it would think I was going crazy or psychotic. But, I knew I wasn't. With a cup of coffee and a cigarette, I strolled around the property for a while feeling the warmth of the sunshine and inspecting the yard work I could do to distract myself. Returning to the house, I wrote in my journal.

Journal Entry Tuesday, June 18th:
Last night I even considered suicide. I accept that too as a part of life. There are ways I am doing it slowly to myself already, and from what I see there are ways that some people and some among the friars are killing themselves — if not their bodies, then their emotional involvement in life, their creativity, their freedom, their self-esteem, their confidence, their

whatever. What pulls me away from the thoughts of physical destruction are the thoughts of what I have physically: a warm and dry place to sleep, the soothing breeze, the green trees, the sun's light and warmth; and to know that if these were not enough here, then there was more elsewhere: with Mom, family, Joe, Betty, and knowing I can make it as long as I have someone to make it with.

Before it got too hot in the day, I went after the overgrown yew bushes out front which were hiding the narrow front porch. With the loppers, a saw, and hedge trimmers, I must have taken off four feet from the tops and all sides around, and then shaped them thinking they looked pretty damn good and a lot better from the road. Again, it felt great to have the sweat melting down my skin and to have my muscles reminding me I was alive. After hauling all the branches and clippings to the back, I needed a break. I'm glad I was in the house when a Franciscan priest from the New York region showed up to visit with the chaplain. Even though the friar had pre-arranged meeting with him that day, he had still not returned, and the friar decided to stay and wait for him. He said not to worry about the chaplain as he had a "special friend" he would often go to stay with – "if you know what I mean." (Another sign?) That friar was so good to talk with: he was bright, interesting, well educated, insightful, a great listener, and interested in what I was going through. I knew I could trust him.

After a quick shower, I made more coffee. Instead of going out for lunch, we each had half a peanut butter sandwich together with our coffee. I was still very hungry, but not for food. I was totally drained from the day before, the night before, and that morning; and the deepest emptiness in me needed to be filled with meaning, understanding, kindness, comfort. We spent hours walking all throughout the extensive property: the tall wild grass, the old farm, the long-abandoned barn and silos, the creek, the lake, and the woods I had spent so much time in cutting and chopping wood for four years. He picked up a green leaf from the moist earth, put it in my hand, and asked me to focus only on it as something real, tangible, physical, concrete, down to earth, something contained in itself, something out there, outside of me, individual, not a fabrication of my mind or what I wanted it to be, no shoulds or oughts, no guilt or shame, or expectations. It was just itself, anchored in itself – like me.

When we returned to the house, his friend hadn't gotten back yet. So, after a big hug, the friar left about 3pm, and he left me with my vision clear and my final decision made. He never suggested or coaxed me toward what the decision should be, but just helped me listen to and be honest about what the deepest parts of me were saying. "Look at the signs all along the way. Do you really see yourself getting old with the friars after what you have seen through the years, and especially the last few weeks? Listen! Feel!"

Chapter Six
Freedom From, Freedom For

My decision was to leave the Franciscans and the priesthood totally, to take charge of my life, to be the real me, and return to Albuquerque. I called Betty to talk it over with her, and she assured me that while it would take time to get used to the change, the final divorce, she would be there for me. I called Fr. Edwin to let him know. That was a tough phone conversation, as he said I was giving up too fast, didn't really give it a chance, making a mistake, and felt I let him down. He tried to talk me out of the decision, and tried to convince me to go to a "rehab" center to see if that would help instead of leaving. When I told him I would not follow through on his suggestion, he said he was so disappointed he couldn't talk with me again. I called the main Franciscan office in Cincinnati to speak with Fr. Jeremy, but he was gone for two weeks, so I talked with the second in charge and informed him of my decision. He also thought I made the decision too hastily and should wait until Fr. Jeremy returned to speak with him. I told him I would call Jeremy from Albuquerque.

After reloading the car with everything I had unloaded the day before, I left a note for the chaplain on the kitchen table, and headed for Mom's house in the early evening to try to explain my decision to her. As I was leaving the St. Leonard property, I felt I was being released from a prison where I had spent the past twenty-one years, a prison I at first felt comfortable in, a prison I had become dependent upon, a prison I kept going back to, a prison where my shackles became unbearable, a prison I was now leaving, unfettered, never to return again, finally free – but not yet. Purposely, I didn't call Mom ahead of time, preferring to tell her everything face to face. As I expected, she was surprised to see me, and we talked late into the evening. She didn't try to talk me out of the decision, said she could tell I was working on a lot of stuff inside and really wasn't happy, hoped no one was influencing me to leave the priesthood, asked what I would do now, how I would handle leaving with the Franciscans, where would I stay, hoped I would stay involved in the Church, and that whatever I did, she just wanted me to be happy. I stayed there that night, sleeping deeply and late into Wednesday morning. Not having eaten much the last two days, the big early lunch with Mom sure was good.

I called Joe as soon as I could and told him I'd made the final decision that it wasn't fitting me, that there was no way I could live that way. I said, "Do you think we could make a life together?" Hesitantly, Joe said, "I think so, but I don't know so. But, we can give it another try." I don't know what I would have done if he had told me he found another boyfriend, or if he had said no. We had a very long talk about how that might work out, how it would be very different now that things had changed in him also, how it wouldn't be the same as a few months ago. But, he said yes! Overjoyed and very happy, a great load of worry lifted from me.

I made plans to leave early the next day, Thursday, June 20th, for Albuquerque. A few of my sisters and brothers came over to Mom's house Wednesday evening to wish me goodbye and a safe trip, but I thought it was more to see how Mom was handling my decision. Early the next morning I was on my way, driving down the same roads I was on four weeks before. I just couldn't stop thinking about how much had happened in that short time away, about all the people I spoke with on the way back East, the experience with the two friars at the Retreat Center, the good times with my family, the deep feelings at St. Leonard and the terror of that night, the definitive decision and freedom, and so much else. Other than that, I don't remember anything else from the journey except arriving in Albuquerque at 11pm on Friday, June 21st, and hugging and kissing Joe.

We Make a Life Together

We had many deep and revealing talks in the weeks and months that followed with the goal of committing to each other and making a life together. We both acknowledged that it wouldn't be easy all the time, and that there would be a lot to work out all along the way. But, so long as we were willing to work on it together, to talk about it, to make it happen, to take a chance on each other, to trust each other, to respect each other as complete individuals with his own needs and interests, not expecting each other to change or even wanting him to change, but accepting each other for who we were as separate persons who loved each other and wanted to help each other get through life together, our relationship would last.

Joe handed this poem to me shortly after I returned:

"When we're rich"

We say "When we're rich…"
And then make plans
Real plans and good
They please my ears and mind,
But when we said,
"Let's build a life together"
I wouldn't have traded places
With Rockefeller, Getty or Onassis.
And the feeling of ourselves –
Warm healthy bodies
Wrapped together in the night
Makes me snub Kublai Khan as a pauper
Because of the riches
Our togetherness
Has bestowed.

- Joe

++++

My relationship with Joey and Margaret would be evolving also. I had to keep reminding myself that they were not young adults. They were kids with their own dependence and independence needs and thoughts and drives. Their Mom and Dad would be the most important persons in their lives, and I would not be. I would help them all as much as I could, but I would always take a back seat in their rearing so as not to interfere in that dynamic. At times, I suspected that the kids saw me as an obstacle to their parents getting back together again, or as someone who would take away some of the attention and care they were used to receiving and needed at this time. No question – Joe loved his children and would do anything for them. For Joe, as it naturally should be, they would always be first in his life, and I would not be. That would be particularly hard for me to accept and adjust to, and my feelings would be hurt many times because of it. I learned to understand and accept through our relationship the discrepancy that he would be primary in my life, but I would not be primary in his. Did I feel he loved me any less? No. I could tell he didn't totally know how to juggle it all either, but we trusted in our ability to work on it together.

Gradually, though, I grew up with Joe, and Joey and Margaret, learning to appreciate their energy and creativity, their drive for independence, their successes, their rough times, their graduating to the next stages in their lives, and too fast becoming teenagers, young adults, and fine adults. If you meet fine adults, you know their parents had a lot to do with their development. I like to think I contributed a lot to that also. In a way, we all raised each other together.

++++

About a week after my return, a friend of ours who owned a small apartment complex of seven units asked if we would be willing to move into one of the units and manage the complex. Doing that would decrease our monthly rent to about one-third of what we were paying. After discussing the change, which would include leaving the nicely cultural place we were living in, and moving into a drab and generic unit separate from the other apartments, and would mean more responsibility managing, maintaining and painting (for which the owner paid us separately), screening tenant applications, collecting rents, etc. We accepted the offer mainly because it would help our financial struggles. We stayed there and managed for one year.

++++

Letter to Fr. Jeremy -- June 29, 1985
Peace! Yes, I am writing to you from Albuquerque. I have returned after being back East for almost a month. I am glad I went back. It helped me to listen to myself more clearly, and to hear myself repeating my story over and again to those I spoke with. It took packing everything, leaving Albuquerque, leaving Joe; the long drive alone; it took speaking with friars along the way, and speaking with friends in Iowa; it took having my brother's wedding on June 8th and a baptism on June 16th; it took speaking with many friars in the Cincy area, me listening to them, me listening to myself; it took hearing what was important to them in their life and how they deal with it; it took being very open and honest to my Mom and brothers and sisters about my searching; it took moving to St. Leonard, repeating my story again; it took all this to realize what I was saying underneath all the words, and to decide to return to Albuquerque, and to leave the Franciscan Order.

161

As you know from our talks, I have been on a long pilgrimage, seeking understanding and direction all along the way. The most important, and the most difficult part of the journey, has been over the last six months. It was during this time in counseling that I discovered what was driving me in life, what had influenced (controlled?) if not everything, then at least the major directions I chose in life. It was during this time that I admitted and owned the fact that I never really wanted to be a Franciscan or a priest. Realizing that, and being freed by my discoveries, I wanted to return to the roots of my original decision, my family, the friars, the places, to see if I wanted to choose the Franciscan community and ministry from where I am now as a 35yr. old adult, to see if it could fit me. Going back East, I discovered that I did not want to choose that direction anymore for two main reasons: 1.) I am no longer interested in Franciscan life or ministry for me; and 2.) What I do want is not possible as a Franciscan. ...It is as if that vehicle of expression for me has lost its fuel and spark, as if there is no more spirit to animate it for me. The psychological magnet that attracted me to that life, and held me there, has lost its force in my life.

The decision to leave is not a "quick" decision. It has been building up along the way. During the minor seminary, novitiate, Scotus, Leonard's, before solemn vows, diaconate, and before priesthood ordination – at sometime at each step I had seriously considered leaving. Each time, I eventually disregarded that possibility because deep down I felt I could not leave, I had to stay. I had to live up to the expectations of others through the years, the expectations I placed on myself. ...It was the only way I could feel acceptable to myself and to others. That no longer holds true. ...There has been much psychological discovery and growing up and healing of the past and the present to where I am more free now than I have ever been to choose, to love myself, to love others, and to be loved. That brings me to my second point.

As far back as I can remember, what I have been looking for is a very close friend – someone my own age who shares the same interests, someone with whom I can be equal and do things together, someone who can accept me for me. More recently, I have been looking for someone to build a loving relationship with, in every aspect of our humanity. I have found that person in Joe. Everywhere I went, I was searching for someone, each time I ministered I was looking, hoping to fulfill that need in my life. I have looked at all the possible combinations of either the Franciscans or that kind of relationship, and of both the relationship and the Franciscans as I have been encouraged to do by some friars and some priests. While back East, I realized that my main interest is in a loving relationship; that it would not be fair to anyone, nor did I want to be divided in a both/and situation. Accepting the fact that the kind of relationship I wanted was not possible as a Franciscan for me, I am deciding to leave.

The next part of my journey will not be easy. It has not been an easy decision to make, but I feel good and peaceful about it. ...Thank you for your willingness to let me find my way. – Tom

When I spoke with Fr. Jeremy the evening of July 2nd on the phone, he had not yet received my letter. I tried to explain that my going back to the friars in June helped me to be released from a lot of personal guilt, that I just didn't see myself in that lifestyle or ministry anymore, and that I wanted a loving relationship with a man. He recommended that I consider dispensations from the Franciscans and the priesthood if that was my final decision. When I asked what a dispensation would really mean, he said it would be like saying my vows of profession and ordination to the priesthood were invalid, and that I should never have been ordained as a priest or accepted in the Franciscans. It would be a very long process, a legal process in the Church, similar to a marriage annulment that says the couple were never actually married. While a dispensation would wipe away any bonds and restrictions, or obligations to the friars or to the institution of the priesthood with the intention of freeing up the individual to live as he wished, it would also be saying in effect that the vows and ordination never actually happened from the start. I was not willing to accept that, but I told him I would think about it.

Letter from Fr. Jeremy -- July 10, 1985
Dear Tom,

Greetings in the Lord and his peace! Thanks for your phone call and for your letter of June 29.

As I mentioned to you on the phone, Tom, your decision leaves me struggling with very mixed feelings. On the one hand, I would really like to have you continue full life and ministry in our brotherhood. I admire you and your Franciscan values and your idealism. I believe that you have much to contribute to the Province and the building up of the Kingdom as a Franciscan. It would make me happy if your thinking and searching and praying would lead you to new motivation and new spirit and renewed commitment to your life as a friar. I think it is possible to choose again, even if there is not at the moment a strong attraction on the feeling level. I don't want all of this to sound judgmental, Tom. I am just trying to tell you how I feel and to say that

*you are a cherished brother and I would be very happy if you would
choose to remain a friar.*

*But, on the other hand, I do respect your honest searching and
I do respect your conscience-decision. I know that you have prayed and
reflected and sought counsel.*

*I thank you for your years of Franciscan life and the great
contribution that you have made. You have touched the lives of many
friars and many others in the Church. You have given witness to
simplicity and poverty and prayer. I know that you will continue to strive
to be open and at one with God and nature and to be a peaceful and
loving person. May the Lord be your guide and show you the way and
lead you to even greater fullness of life.*

*If at another point in your pilgrimage you are led to reconsider
your decision, you know that your brothers are always welcoming. We
want to help and assist you in every way possible.*

*...Since you have made your decision, I am glad that you want
to start the process for a dispensation. We agreed on the phone that you
would contact Fr. Art. I have talked with him and he said he would
happily talk with you and help you begin the process.*

*....May the Good Shepherd continue to guide you Tom.
Know that you are loved by Him and by your brothers.   Fraternally,
Jeremy*

I did call Fr. Art, the head of the Archdiocese of Santa Fe Tribunal
Office, and we met on July 8th. A very nice priest, hospitable and
cordial, he tried to put my mind at ease and said he would be willing to
help me through the process of dispensation from religious life vows
and laicization from clerical life and the priesthood. If the process were
successful, and there was no guarantee that it would be, it would return
me to the secular life and the lay life. For a dispensation from religious
vows there would have to be a grave reason; proof I was working with
counselors, a confessor, and had guidance; a formal petition through
the Provincial to the Minister General of the Franciscans in Rome.

He explained in detail how very lengthy, extensive, and legal the
process of laicization would be. It would involve the legal system of the
Church, Canon Law, Church lawyers, depositions, a Church court,
Church judges, a "trial", a decision by the Pope, and more. I had no idea
it would be so involved. My note taking as Fr. Art explained:

- The process is <u>purely punitive</u>, to punish the guy going through it.
- The two situations for laicization are 1) if the guy has been out for a long time like 30 yrs., or he is dying, or 2) if it could be proven that the guy should never have been ordained, either because a) there was deficient consent, or b) he had an inability to engender and sustain the duties of the priesthood.
- To begin the process:
  o I would have to write to my Provincial, Fr. Jeremy, stating I would want to be returned to the lay state and the reasons why.
  o Jeremy would write back to me asking me to return.
  o I would write back to Jeremy and say I will not, and ask for his help.
  o Jeremy would appoint Fr. Art to handle the process.
  o Art would give an EXTENSIVE recorded interview and questionnaire and send the transcripts to Jeremy. This part would also involve an actual legal brief with statements from the formation team, eyewitnesses, family, professors, classmates, counselors, a specific and exacting history since 1977, changes in behavior, demeanor, or geist – accentuating every weakness, doubt, sin, and fart – with the intention of proving that I should never have been ordained.
  o Jeremy gets it and asks me to return again.
  o I would write a formal letter to the Pope asking to be released from Orders and reduced to the lay state. The letter would go through Jeremy, then to the Minister General in Rome, then to the Sacred Congregation, which would have some sort of trial, then to the Pope who would have the final say.
- However, even after doing everything properly, jumping through all the hoops and putting up with all the ecclesiastical bullshit, there was never any assurance that it would work and the request would be approved.

I wrote to Jeremy that evening, told him about my meeting with Fr. Art, and said I was not sure I wanted to spend the time, energy, and emotional drain needed to work on this at this time, or ever. Also, I was not ready to say that I should never have been ordained, that my becoming a priest was invalid, and I would be talking with Betty and Joe to clarify my feelings about the whole thing. My thoughts were that I would not go through with the laicization. I would not degrade my integrity or have my reputation or life dragged through the mud. I was not a little kid to be punished. It took a lot of courage to do what I was doing. It was the right decision to leave, to stand up for myself, and it felt good.

++++

My main focus at this time was to find a job to support my end of our finances. Joe and I have never argued about money, we each paid half of everything, and kept separate bank accounts, except one we called our "House Account" to pay for rent, groceries, utilities, and anything else we bought together, replenishing that account equally as needed. As a way to make some money, since I wasn't working, we did a lot of painting jobs together for friends and then friends of friends. We always seemed to underjudge how long each job would take, and underestimate what we should charge our clients. It was hard work, and we were exhausted every evening. But each one of our clients was happy, and our schedule was full as word got around.

Finding a career in City, State, and Federal governments was the focus of my job search. Each Sunday's classified job opportunities that appealed to me were evaluated, circled, and flagged to receive a resume or a phone call from me. I felt I was fishing alone from a boat in the middle of a lake, waiting for the float to move, hoping the fish would take the bait and get hooked. When I got a rare response, I felt I had one on the line, hoping I would get a phone call, or an interview, which would be even more rare. Too qualified, no years of experience, no background in the field, no education or degree in the field, didn't meet the minimum listed qualifications, no transferable skills, Native American preferences, wanting to hire me but the Law wouldn't allow it, right now there was a freeze on hiring but I would be put on the list – and the fish all got away. I would row back to the shore, only to go out fishing again the next day and every day getting more and more discouraged. I had no idea it would be so hard to find work, a job, a career – so hard to break into corporate or business America.

Letter from Fr. Jeremy -- *October 25, 1985*
...I thought of you specifically at our recent O.F.M. Conference meeting because two of the provincials reported that they each had received two laicizations from Rome. It is heartening to know that the Vatican is giving some.

...I know in your letter of July 8th, you said you wanted to think about it for awhile. You know also that I expressed some apprehension that your decision last June came rather quickly. You know that I want what is best for you, Tom. I am not opposing your

decision but want to be sure it is a well-considered one that will ultimately be for your benefit.

...With that background, if you are fully satisfied and settled on your decision, I would urge you to apply for secularization or laicization.

...I do not think you need fear that in that process anyone would pressure you to say anything that you do not believe, e.g., that you should not have become a priest. It is my position, Tom, that we should apply and honestly do our part of the of the process. If the Vatican does not grant our petition at least we have the peace of knowing that we have done all that we could do.

...So, let me know what you decide. Blessings always. Peace and joy in the Lord!

> *Fraternally,*
> *Jeremy*

Letter to Fr. Jeremy -- October 31, 1985

Received your letter yesterday, and I thank you for thinking of me and being concerned about my welfare.

...In response to your letter concerning applying for secularization/laicization, I have called Fr. Art and discussed it with him again. He informed me again, and I thought I was correct the first time, that a decree of laicization would only be granted in two instances: if the person has been bound by a civil contract, e.g. marriage (age and length of leave from ministry has something to do with it too), and if the person declares that he should have never been ordained in the first place (tantamount to an annulment). The first does not apply to me, and the second I am not willing to consider. However, I will be meeting with Art on November 8th to make sure my approach to this is sound.

...Even though my decision may have seemed rather sudden, I assure you that it had been building for some years. I am fully satisfied and settled on my decision to enter a different profession and career and life. I have no intention of secularizing, and I have no intention of re-activating with the Order or ministry. My decision has been well-considered and, I trust, ultimately for my benefit.

Jeremy, I have never been much of a legalist, and do not have the patience for it. Though I fail to see how pursuing a laicization would benefit me any, I am willing to show some good will in helping you out on your end. I will investigate it as far as I honestly can and keep you informed.

Never can I thank you enough for your understanding, support, concern, and help. Thank you for ministering to me.　　　　*— Tom*

Joe Meets My Ohio Family

Christmas of '85, Joe and I flew back to Ohio for a week of introducing Joe to my family, parties, gatherings, visiting places of my past, and driving to Detroit to visit my classmate Fr. Dan. I knew it would be a rough visit and was very apprehensive about how the family would accept Joe. We were not disappointed. My sisters seemed to have an easier time accepting Joe. They were kind, hospitable, and tried to include him in everything – even giving him wrapped Christmas gifts! Most of my brothers were more reluctant, at least stand-offish or not comfortable with him, or downright cold and non-accepting. I so wanted to confront them, remind them of their own pasts that I was very understanding and accepting of, but decided it was not the time or occasion or place, realizing nothing would change their attitude or approach to me or Joe. We also decided to focus on those who did accept us with their warmth and generosity of spirit, and this included Mom.

But, using Mom's car, the two day visit to Detroit was a welcome getaway when we could just be with each other and be ourselves. We had a great visit with Dan and the grand tour of Duns Scotus. Joe loved the old-worldness of the place. Unfortunately, we woke up the next morning to nearly a foot of snow on the car and the roads. Mom's car wouldn't start, so we got a battery cable jump from Dan. While driving back to Ohio, I developed a serious migraine headache and was in such pain and visual impairment that poor Joe had to take over driving the four hours back in snow to Mom's house. Surely, the headache was exacerbated by the family stress. After it all, it was nice to fly the distance from it back to Albuquerque.

Reflections of my brothers and sisters:

"I am not sure if you ever perceived mom's acceptance, but at our many talks I truly believe she felt that you and Joe were just good friends sharing a home together. And you know what, that was ok. She couldn't completely grasp what 'being gay' meant, and I wasn't going to explain it to her."

"I think Mom finally made peace with you being gay because you and Joe were just good friends and probably believed it till she died."

"You experienced the horrible treatment from some of the family when you came home with Joe for the first time. My heart broke for both of you."

"I am proud of you coming out and being able to enjoy the life that you were robbed of years ago, and that you are sharing it with someone you love – Joe."

"My joy is that you have found love, happiness and comfort in your life. Mom loved you just as she loved all her children regardless of who they became. She embraced you and your lifestyle and loved you just the same."

"I know Joe feels he is not welcomed by some. However, you and Joe are always welcome at our house."

"There is a lot about you that your family will never know because you are such a hard nut to crack."

"I am not sure who said this: 'If at the end of your life you have 3 or 4 people with whom you could share anything...any secret, indiscretion, failure, disappointment, regret, loss, sin.. someone you can deeply share your heart with...then you are indeed a very lucky man.' If that is true and I believe it is, then I am a most fortunate man because you are one of those people for me."

"You always had your own identity. You are aloof at times, but intriguing. Perhaps pretentious at times. Your trying to understand us comes across as trying to psychoanalyze us."

"There are more than a few things we disagree on."

"I wish I would have had more of a connection with you and gotten to know you better. You have so much to share from the journey you had, your life, the priesthood, the Indian reservation, travels, lifestyle. We could all still learn a lot from you."

Regular Work Found

To fill in the work vacuum throughout the previous year, along with our painting business, I had put a couple ads in the classified section of the Albuquerque Journal looking for yard work and light handyman work. Out of the responses I got, I kept five regular weekly customers for yard work, and a number of customers who would call only when something was needed. During the winter it got to be slim pickins and not much to do.

While at an Allwoods Home Improvement Center in January 1986 to pick something up, I decided to ask if there were any job openings. With my back problems, I knew I couldn't lift much, but there was one opening for the housewares and plumbing department I felt I could do. While filling out the application, I fudged on past work history and wrote about being a self-employed maintenance man and handyman just looking for more steady work. The next day, I got a call to come in for an interview with the manager that afternoon. That went well, and I got a call the next morning that I had been hired, to come in to fill out the necessary paperwork, and to be oriented to the store and the department. I started full-time the day after, and stayed there for one and a half years meeting lots of new people and learning as much about the business as I could. Also, many customers had no idea how or who to call to repair their minor plumbing issues or install a new fixture for them, so I gave them my phone number. My handyman business on the side continued. I got to meet a lot of very nice people, mostly elderly, some young professionals, and I kept these friendships as the years passed. David and Helen, in particular, became such good friends we were more like family.

One of these "customers" was a young professional couple with two fantastic children. They had serious marital problems. The wife called me late one evening asking me to come over right away. They had a fight, and the husband, a doctor at one of the hospitals in town, slammed the kitchen sink faucet in his anger then left the house. The faucet broke off at the base and water was shooting up to the ceiling. I turned off the water underneath, helped her clean up the water, and sat and talked/listened to her for quite a while. How sad for a couple which seemed to have everything going for them. It was too late that night to get a new faucet, so I went back to their house the next day with one when both of them were there, removed the old and installed the new faucet, while each of them apologized profusely for what happened, and for drawing me into their struggles. Surely, the inside of me wanted to help them work things out, but rationally I felt it better to encourage them to get some serious marriage counseling. But, they felt they couldn't, as they were both well known in town and worried how it would affect their careers. I was so sad for them, but left it up to them to work on it the best way they could.

Two weeks later, I got a call from the wife in hysterics. The Dr. had shot himself through the temple an hour before and killed himself in front of her and the kids. When I got there, the police and medical examiners were swarming the place and doing their thing, but they wouldn't let me in until I told them I was her minister. I held her and the young kids, letting them all cry, feeling their deep grief and unknowing, listening to their pain and guilt and shame, just being with them until her family and his family came to be with them. I often wondered how life developed for that small family left behind, and I wondered that if I had gotten more involved in counseling them whether this catastrophe might not have happened.

++++

The old tapes would start playing at any time, that moderately silent noise in my head and being that no one else could hear. They were the feelings of guilt that I left the friars and hurt my friends among them; the feelings of guilt that I left the priesthood and hurt my family and friends among the laity; the feelings that I had let them down and not given them all something I could have given them but didn't want to give them; one of the times that I have not given the best I could to others; one of the first times I thought of doing the best for myself; the tension and incompatibility inside me. As I get older, the noise is there less and less and is more faint. I took to making a friend of it and releasing it to leave on its own.

++++

My life was packed with a loving relationship I worked hard at, an accepting adopted family, lots of friends, a regular job, lots of handyman work, lots of painting work, continued counseling with Betty, and the search for work where I could use my many talents and feed my inner spirit. It was also about this time that Betty thought it would be a good idea for me to start taking antidepressants. She referred me to a psychiatrist who then prescribed Prozac and something else for the depression, anxiety, and constant recurring thoughts. Amazingly, after about three months, they seemed to really work for me, not completely, but they sure took the sharp edges off and restored some balance to my life, and I still take some form of those medications and will continue taking them for the rest of my life.

A Home of Our Own

Also, we were both catching the bug to have our own place after renting various apartments for two years. In our free time, we both looked around for a house that would suit us and be within our means. Joe found one on Grove St. on his way back from his evening teaching job. The house was built in 1948, with two bedrooms, two bathrooms, and almost 1,100sq.ft.. It was built on a lot with an area of 50x150ft., and was owned by a young couple who wanted to move. It would take some work, especially the yard, but it had a beautiful 40 year-old honey locust tree in the front, and the house was back from the street about 50ft.. We gave them a reasonable offer for it, and they accepted it. My introduction to real estate and mortgages and amortization schedules began. Closing and moving in was set for the end of May 1986. It was a big step for us in our relationship and commitment to each other, and it was good.

Joe's expertise was the interior arrangement and decorating, mine was the exterior and the yard and doing any repairs inside. We could finally do what we wanted to do for our home and our yard and not have to answer to anyone. It was ours, and it suited us. In the seventeen years we lived there, we did a lot of upgrading and repairs, paid it off in five years to get out of debt, had lots of visitors and parties, and provided a stable home for Joey and Margaret when they were with us. Working at Allwoods Home Improvement, I got a nice discount on what we needed. We replaced the window coverings with mini-blinds and sheer drapes to let in more light, replaced the vanity in the small main bathroom, removed the wall-hung sink in the back bathroom and replaced it with a pedestal sink, and planted lots of trees and flowers and tomatoes in the backyard. Over the years, we gutted both bathrooms and upgraded them, repainted the whole house a couple times, and ripped everything out of the kitchen (including the five layers of linoleum on the floor). In the wood-burning fireplace we had installed a gas fireplace insert with a blower (which ended up heating the whole house), took out all the carpets to enjoy the beautiful oak hardwood floors, re-roofed the pitched part of the roof and the flat part, installed security doors on the front and back and replaced all the windows with energy efficient ones, added a nice back patio roof, and watched everything grow.

The house came with a resident spirit. Shortly after we moved in, one night as we were sleeping, I smelled smoke and woke up Joe. We checked around the inside of the house but didn't see any fire or even smell smoke except by the windows in our bedroom. After checking outside, there was nothing and no one there, either. The smell was strange in that it smelled like heavy cigarette smoke. Also, a few times before, we found the Kentucky bentwood hickory rocker in the living room rocking gently on its own, and I would catch glimpses of someone out the side of my eye.

In her yard the next day, I saw the lady who lived behind us. During our conversation, I asked her about the past owners and residents in our house. She told me about the original owners, the Kings, of some forty years ago. The husband loved the place and took great care of it. He converted the one car garage into a livable den with a fireplace and made other improvements for his family. Sadly, as his children grew older, his oldest son got a motorcycle and was involved in a deadly collision one block away. Mr. King heard the accident and ran to the intersection in time to hold his son as he died. Mr. King drastically changed after that, as he got more and more depressed and disinterested in everything. One year later, he died in the house from a massive heart attack, and his whole family moved to be with his family in Estancia east of Albuquerque. I asked the lady if there was one thing, one habit he had that stood out in her mind, what would it be? Without hesitation she said, "He smoked like a fiend!"

Later that day, I told Joe about the conversation, and while he was teaching that evening, I sat alone in the darkened den and called to Mr. King. I said, "Mr. King I know you are here. I heard about how you loved this house, and I heard about the sadness in your heart holding your son as he died, and how you died right here soon after that. I know you are a kind spirit and just like living here. But, if you are looking for your family, they moved to Estancia, and you will have to go there to find them. But, if you would like to live here with us, that is fine. We only ask that you guard the house and keep it and us safe." There was no sound or reply, but I could feel him warmly in the room.

Over the next two weeks, we didn't sense him in the house at all, we didn't smell smoke, and the rocker didn't rock, either. But, gradually, he returned, and I knew he had come back to be with us. Our house was on the edge of what was called the "War Zone" where there was a lot of crime, vandalism, and violence that occasionally seeped our way. Each house in our neighborhood was broken into, mainly for petty theft, but the house across the street was broken into and the thieves started a fire by the elderly couple's back door. However, our house was the only one that was never broken into. In fact, the only vandalism we had was when someone smashed the window of Joe's truck and stole the radio while it was parked in front. We told Mr. King about it, thanked him for watching over the house, asked him to expand his influence to include the cars out front, and figured he would do his job. We never had another problem in the seventeen years we lived there.

The couple living across the street were the elderly Hernandez's – a comical pair. Twice a year, Mrs. Hernandez would bug her husband to clear out the one-car garage. We would hear her call to him, "Pedro! It's time to measure thee carpet!" Pedro would dutifully reply, "Yes, hoonee", and with much effort, he would pull the large rolled up carpet to the driveway and unroll it, and measure it, leave it in the sun for the day, then roll it up again and haul it back into the garage that evening. We couldn't figure out why she wanted him to do this, or what she expected to find, but it sure was fun to watch, and the memory has brought us many smiles over the years. Now, when we think something needs to be moved out of our house, we say, "Pedro, it's time to measure thee carpet!"

Trying to be good neighbors, we met all the homeowners and gave them our phone number in case they needed help with anything. JR's mom lived next to us to the north. She was quite elderly, and would sit in her old tattered chair in her front living room with the television on too loud, breathing with her oxygen tube hissing while she smoked cigarettes all day. I was afraid she would blow herself up and the house with her, but she would call us and ask us to go and buy more cigarettes for her, and we did. She got to be quite a pest about it, even though I knew she was probably just lonely and wanted the company of a young man. After a few ambulance runs to the hospital, one time she didn't return. We didn't know she had died until we saw JR at the house one day. He said he was going to move into the house after he cleaned it up.

JR was kind of a redneck and could get quite drunk. He wanted to make sure we knew he had served in Vietnam and had several guns in the house and wasn't afraid to use them. Late one night, the police SWAT Team swarmed his house through our backyard and arrested him for threatening his girlfriend with a gun. He was away for a while, but then moved back in. His neighbors to the north of him were from Mexico and had chickens in their yard. Every morning about five o'clock, the rooster would stand proudly on the wall separating their houses and would very annoyingly crow COCK-A DOODLE-DO continuously. We complained to the tenants there, but the rooster remained. Until, one morning, we heard the rooster crow, and then we heard BLAM from a shotgun blast. The rooster crowed his last with a

RRRrrr. JR was the hero of the neighborhood that day, and no one called the police.

And, all the other chickens went away too.

++++

A stray calico cat adopted us -- just showed up one day. We called her "Loca" – the crazy one. She was an outdoor cat and would only come a short way into the back of the house to eat and then would leave right away. I set up a plush cardboard house for her on the back patio, but she preferred to sleep on the flat part of the roof by the attic vent. She was very vocal and manipulative for attention, which she got, especially from Joey, who would play with her and throw her into the tree or up to the roof, and she would be right down begging for more. Many times, we would find dead birds and mice on the mat outside our back door with her sitting there all proud of sharing her kills with us. When people walked their dogs past the front of the house, we would often see her right there walking with them -- no doubt thinking she was also a dog. At 6:30am when we turned the light on in the bedroom, she would start meowing loudly until she got fed. We had already decided we did not want any pets when we moved into the house, but when Loca disappeared one day we genuinely cared about her welfare and missed her. After asking around with no luck, we figured she was gone for good, until suddenly one day after two months, she showed up at our backdoor again meowing loudly. We found out what had happened to her when one of the neighbors behind us came to claim her, saying she had captured her and was going to make an indoor pet out of her, and insisted on taking her away. Loca had escaped from the evil lady and needed a place to hide, coming to us, and meowing at us to please save her, and we let her down.

++++

We had many memorable parties and created many traditions at the Grove house. In October one year, Mom came to visit around the time of Joey's and Margaret's birthdays (one week apart). We decided to celebrate the occasion with a full German dinner one evening consisting of sauerbraten with gingersnap gravy, rouladen, Bavarian sauerkraut with pork, German bratwurst, red cabbage, warm potato salad, old world breads, and Schwarzwälder Kirschtorte for dessert – all made by Joe and me (except for the sauerkraut which came from cans).

I officiously announced the menu in exaggerated German to much laughter and applause. When possible, when the kids can be together at that time, the German dinner has continued to be a tradition every year to celebrate their birthdays.

Christmas is Joe's thing. He brightens up around the season and goes all out decorating, needing two trees, a white one and a colored one, and usually plans at least one party. One year (it turned out to be our last Christmas on Grove) he wanted to have a block party and invite the whole neighborhood. We went up and down the street inviting everyone, even the ones we had never met before, and most of them came along with some of our other friends.

It was probably the biggest party we ever had. All the food was eaten, all the liquor, wine and drinks were gone, and everyone had a great time. The extra bonus was that no one had to drive home.

++++

Letter from Fr. Jeremy -- April 3, 1987

What occasions my letter is that I was talking to a Capuchin provincial who told me that several of their men have received laicizations recently.

Moreover, he said that the Capuchin procurator general said that the Vatican at this time seems more open to granting them.

If you are still resolved to live as a lay person, I would urge you to apply for laicization. I think that you have good grounds for them to grant it. Please let me know.
Jeremy

Letter to Fr. Jeremy -- April 10, 1987

While I was not ready at the time to consider applying for a laicization, I am open to it now. It has taken some time, but I understand it in a different way now, and also why I was adverse to the idea earlier.

I know I am a minister who wants to minister, but without the structure, the law, or the ritual which is part of the Catholic priesthood. I am merely and most importantly appreciating myself as a minister in my own right, as one who can heal and serve the subsurface human spirit.

After counseling I was able to admit that much of my reluctance to let go of the priesthood had to do with the need for recognition that it gave me or could give me in the future. I was using it while not wanting anything to do with it. It took discovering why I felt the way I did about laicization before I could be open to it. I am ready now to begin working on it, to accept my life as it is. — Tom

++++

In accepting myself, I once again realized that I had been a "priest" my whole life even before and since ordination, and I will be forever. I was who was, I am who am, I will be who will be.
-- a mystic, a teacher, an interpreter, a prophet, born an old spirit
-- a shaman to evoke blessing and power to heal, to call forth the curse of evil and name it for what it is
-- a seer beyond this level of reality removing the mask of what is seen
-- an extremely intuitive man, a pre-cognizant
-- a gay man at peace with himself and at peace with the world
-- able to touch the solar eclipses and lunar eclipses in our lives
-- with power to heal and absolve brokenness, guilt, and fear
-- to assist in the return and restoration of harmony, unity, and peace
-- to be with and to be patient if others are willing or unwilling
-- to assist in new birth and new death and that cycle in our lives
-- to celebrate and lift up the journey of life, to sacramentalize, to be a sign
-- to hear what is not said
-- to see beyond what is seen
-- to touch the joy, and the pain, and the healing
-- to guide and to lead
-- to be a perpetual apprentice and precursor
-- knowing that we don't really want to believe in a god, we really want to believe in ourselves
-- we really don't want to be absolved or forgiven, we really want to absolve and forgive ourselves
-- like the Wizard of Oz knowing the scarecrow didn't need a brain, but he did give him a sign, a parchment diploma; the tin man didn't need a heart, but he gave him a ticking heart clock, a sign; the lion didn't need courage, but he did give him a sign, a large medal of honor. The Wizard helped them to understand they already had these things in themselves, and he taught them how to use them. He showed them they really didn't need the trinkets. What they did need was to believe in who they were. Even Dorothy needed the Good Witch to help her realize she already possessed the ruby power inside of herself to go home all along
-- things are not just what they are, never "it is what it is" (a very dismissive comment), so much individual history to what is, so much

future to come, things actually do get better as we are willing to work for and be open to the new reality
-- to see and name injustice for what it is and to stand against it
This is me and so much more.

++++

Fr. Art was still in town, and on May 30, 1987, we met and drafted the initial petition to Pope John Paul II to be freed of my vows as a religious and as an ordained priest. We also began work on June 15th on the lengthy declaration (aka deposition) as to why I was requesting laicization and dispensation. This part of the process was recorded and was the most difficult part so far, but I refused to say anything that I did not totally agree with or was not truly me. Shortly afterwards, I received the twenty-two page transcription of the interview in legal form and on official stationary. This was sent on to Rome with the petition.

Letter from Fr. Jeremy -- June 6, 1987
As you know, I did contact Fr. Art when I received your letter. He tells me that you have already met and have gotten a good start on the process.
Tom, I was touched by your letter and your insight into yourself as a minister. You are a good minister in your own right and you do reach out to others to affirm and heal and love with your own goodness and the power of the Spirit. You are a sensitive, thinking, poetic, giving person. The Lord works through you!
I know that telling your story for the laicization process probably involves pain for you, Tom. I am grateful for your willingness.
— Jeremy

Working for the Archdiocese of Santa Fe

Never in my wildest imagining or envisioning of a prospective job or career had I ever considered applying for work with the Catholic Church, but Bro. Walter, a fifteen year friend, had been appointed as the Director of the newly opened Madonna Retreat Center and needed help with the landscaping and painting around the place. The Center was previously the women's dorm of the University of Albuquerque, which had to close in 1985. The Archdiocese of Santa Fe then took over the whole campus of 52 acres and nine large university buildings so it could consolidate all of its offices and services in one place, and so it

---

could move St. Pius High School up there because they needed more room. Bro. Walter only got permission to hire someone part-time effective July 1, 1987, and that would work fine with me because I could do that during my off time from Allwoods, and I wouldn't be involved in having anything to do with even the slightest aspect of administration or Church work. The first couple of months, I worked 15 hours a week cleaning up the wild high desert landscaping around the Center since it hadn't been tended to for at least five years. The hardest part was cutting back and digging up the cactus and yucca which had become wildly overgrown, and then carrying it all to a ravine on the northside of the property. Having fallen on cactus twice on the reservation, I was extremely careful because I knew how painful those spines are and how difficult it is get them out of my skin.

After I got the outside under control, I spent my time cleaning the inside of the Center. Walter was a clean freak! Besides, the place was filthy with layers of dust and dirt, lots of bugs and mouse nests, and even some homeless vagrants living in the tunnel pipe chases between Madonna Center and the St. Pius buildings. So, I channeled all the cleaning and mechanical experience I had from my seminary years to full benefit. I can't say I enjoyed the work. It was hard scrubbing the old vinyl tile floors, using a buffer/scrubber to clean and strip off old wax and then waxing them all again. There was no carpet in any of the 50 bedrooms, on the long corridors, in the two conference rooms, or the offices. All the floor scrubbing took a long time, then Walter wanted all the woodwork, doors, closets, desks oiled heavily with lemon oil. The wood was so dry it sucked in the oil, and most of it had to be given another coat all over again.

In the Fall, Walter told me that the maintenance department of the Catholic Center was looking for a painter and would be willing to hire me part-time. In addition to the Madonna Center, I would be working full-time on the campus and helping with five university buildings. Walter also wanted to hire me separately to cook dinner for himself and another Franciscan living at Madonna. To do all this, I had to quit my job at the home improvement center, which I was glad to do since I hated doing retail by then. Basically, I was part of the maintenance crew and tried to learn everything there was to learn about large building maintenance and the mechanical systems supporting them, especially Madonna Center.

In March of 88', Bro. Walter was reassigned to the Franciscan headquarters in town and would be leaving the Center. I am sure it was with his recommendation that I was hired to manage Madonna Center full-time. When I met with his boss, the Executive Director of General

Services and the Chancellor of the Archdiocese and Archbishop Sanchez, I was very open about my past, my being a priest seeking laicization and dispensation, and my being gay. I wasn't going to hide anything and wanted to be upfront about who I was so they knew exactly who they were hiring for the position. Surprisingly to me, all that mattered was my management abilities, my maintenance skills, my people skills, and a focus on developing the place as the Archdiocesan Retreat Center for Catholic groups. The Archbishop still wanted a priest or a nun to be the director of the center (for the image and because they could be paid less), so I would only be hired as the lay manager, but with all the responsibilities of the director along with it.

++++

Letter from Fr. Jeremy -- June 16, 1988
...When I returned a letter from the Congregation of the Faith was waiting for me. The letter is addressed to the Minister General, who presented your petition to the Holy See, and is written in Italian.

The Congregation says it has considered carefully your petition for laicization and the reasons and personal history that you give. They want your good. The Congregation does not judge that it would be for the good of the whole Church to grant you a dispensation. Mention is made that you are a relatively young man.

Tom, I know that the response of the Holy See will be difficult for you. We knew that it would not be easy to get a dispensation, but I hoped they would accept your unique situation. -- Jeremy

Letter To Fr. Jeremy -- August 9, 1988
I appreciate you sending in my request for laicization, and the care you have for me which you and friars have displayed so often.

Actually, Jeremy, the response of the Holy See is not difficult for me. As you say, we knew it would not be easy to get a dispensation. I am neither surprised nor disappointed. The way I see it is that I have done my part. I have shown my good faith. I have shown my respect for the priesthood and for the legalities of the Holy See in seeking a dispensation. Their answer is no. As far as I am concerned, I wish it to end there. I do not want to re-submit my request for further scrutiny or reconsideration.

Although I accept the decision of the Holy See, Jeremy, I must also let you know that it changes nothing in regards to my life or lifestyle as it is now. I have made my peace. I am more peaceful and happy than I have ever been. --- Tom

++++

Madonna Center was in dire need of upgrading: installation of carpeting throughout, replacing all the 100 beds and linens left over from the dorm days (or the Spanish Conquistadors?), new conference room chairs, creating contracts and policies for groups using the facility, hiring a cleaning person(s) and a part-time secretary, clearing storerooms of the accumulated junk, having air-conditioning installed, painting of all 50 rooms and the corridors and conference rooms, etc., etc. Along with managing the place, I also did most of the work myself. Most of the time, I felt I was trying to create something out of nothing since the budget I had to work within was so lean. My very supportive boss understood this and went to bat for me on numerous occasions with the administration for the funding needed which was approved about half the time. After a year, I was named the Director, but still had to fight for a pay increase, and learned quickly that each improvement, each ability, each development had to be made known and seeded in the minds of the administration along every step of the way if I was going to be recognized and be paid what I was worth. Within two years, I had the retreat center paying for itself and paying its own budget in full. In effect, it didn't cost the Archdiocese anything. Yes, I made mistakes along the way, but I saw them as challenges and opportunities to learn something and do it better.

Twice the lower level was flooded with three inches of raw sewage when the two large sump pumps stopped working. Both times I had to beg the maintenance manager to bring over some large shop vacuums so I could suck up the mess. Also, twice I ruined my leather-soled dress shoes while cleaning things up in my suit. Disinfecting the areas was another arduous effort with cases of bleach, mopping floors numerous times, spraying sanitizer, and leaving the doors and windows opened for weeks. When I asked the maintenance man to show me why this was happening, he admitted that he had disconnected one of the sump pumps some time ago to save on repair, and because they were too difficult to pull out of the eight foot deep sump pit. In my fury I blew my top at him, called him many unprofessional things, which were all true in my estimation, and insisted that he reconnect the pump and have the other one pulled out and repaired. Also, I immediately went over to our common supervisor's office at the Catholic Center, explained what was happening, how his maintenance guy wasn't handling situations, and how repairing these pumps or replacing them was going to cost a lot of money. The next day both pumps were pulled, taken for repair and refurbishment, and then reinstalled the next week. Regularly I would test them both, verify that both were working as intended, and never had the problem again.

One of the best things I did to develop the retreat center was to think outside the box of "church" and convince the administration that in order for the center to be really successful and self-sustaining, I had to be allowed to market it to and open it up to groups other than Catholic groups as the "Madonna Retreat and Conference Center." The small amount of Archdiocesan groups using the place, and the small amount they paid for using it, would never be enough to keep it going. The facility was empty Monday thru Friday, and perhaps two weekends a month Catholic groups used half of it. Cautiously, the administration trusted me enough to go ahead and open it up. I learned all I could about advertising, marketing, and managing nonprofit organizations from evening classes at the University of New Mexico. I called, sent letters to, and visited many other churches and nonprofits to let them know about us and to invite them to come take a look. The Albuquerque Convention and Visitors Bureau and I had a great rapport, and they referred small low-budget conferences our way. Among my employees, I insisted on superb service and hospitality. It took about six months before the center started to get busy, and conferences, meetings, and retreats were being scheduled three years into the future.

Inside myself, I realized that I was a "fixer": someone who needed a challenge, someone who could go in, see a problem, analyze the problem, stick with it, straighten it out and make it good and make it productive. I also realized that boredom was my greatest enemy. I always needed to be doing something worthwhile, finding new ways to do something, and never be doing the same old thing over and over again while getting the same results each time. I needed to branch out and think outside the box, and above all, I needed to be creative.

++++

Letter from Fr. Jeremy -- *March 30, 1990*
 The enclosed will probably come as a surprise to you, as it did to me. Your laicization has been granted. I had heard that Rome was more likely to grant the request of someone 40 or over. I note that you had a 40th birthday in February.
 The rescript is effective immediately. The Holy See lists five restrictions: a) loss of all rights and obligations proper to clerics; b) no administration of sacraments with the exception of 976 ["Even though he lacks the faculty to hear confessions, any priest validly and licitly absolves from any kind of censures and sins any penitent who is in

danger of death, even if an approved priest is present."] and 986 ["In urgent necessity any confessor is obliged to hear the confessions of Christian faithful, and in danger of death any priest is so obliged."]; c) you are not to teach in seminaries or similar schools; d) and e) you are not to teach theology in "lesser schools." – Jeremy

<u>Letter to Fr. Jeremy</u> -- *April 16, 1990*

Having just received your letter of March 30, 1990 today, I am still in a bit of shock. The grant of laicization was the strangest birthday greeting I had received for my fortieth and the most unexpected!

On a personal note, I am relieved and yet saddened at the news. I am well into another chapter of my life. The first chapter, having been put on hold, can now be finished. Strangely, I even experience a bit of grieving, along with a thrust forward. After seven years, I can now work on putting some closure to it. – Tom

<u>Letter to Mom</u> -- *April 18, 1990*

I don't quite know how to share this with you, but I feel it is something you ought to hear from me than from someone else. Rome has granted the laicization request.

I remember you saying that you were more hurt by my leaving the priesthood and the Franciscans than by anything else. While my case was still in limbo, (i.e. still a priest, but not active, laicization denied but still pending), I know that you hoped that perhaps one day I might return. While this grant ends that possibility, even though I had not been considering returning, be assured that I will continue to serve the Church, the Lord, in ways that suit me best.

All through the years, since I was fourteen, and before, I have appreciated your help and support in the direction I wanted to go. I know that you will try to understand and support me now.

I am sure we will be talking about this in the future, and I would appreciate that. – Tom

++++

The Summer of '91 was a rough one for my boss due to many differences of opinion and his approach with the other Archdiocesan administrators. As a result, he was "asked" to leave his position in the Fall. Perhaps not too wisely, I decided to apply for that position; and perhaps not too wisely with what was going on with him, I asked him to recommend me for it. He did recommend me, and I got the job as Executive Director of General Services and Plant Operations Manager, and I became deeply involved in the administration of the Archdiocesan Catholic Center. The other person who applied for the job was the property maintenance manager, which made the choice process easy for the administration. The maintenance guy was very angry he did not get the job since he was there many years longer than I had been, and also because I would now be his boss. He did every vindictive thing he could to thwart my efforts until I told him he would do it my way, or I would find someone I could work with to get the jobs done, and he would be fired. He came around and changed his attitude slowly.

The job came with a one page job description describing my responsibilities for the Catholic Center portion of the campus. My new boss, the Chancellor, asked me to write my own job description detailing everything I would be involved in -- it came to be five pages. The new position came at the right time, as I was getting bored just directing Madonna Center. With the new position, I was still directing Madonna Center along with all my new responsibilities, and four more large university buildings and their operations. After finding out all that was involved, I began to doubt I would be able to handle it all, but they trusted me and I ran with that. I had to have confidence in myself and in my abilities.

At one of our monthly directors meetings, Archbishop Sanchez was speaking about perhaps having to close the Immaculate Heart of Mary (IHM) Seminary in Santa Fe because there were so few seminarians and most of those were from other Dioceses outside of New Mexico. Further, the Archdiocese of Santa Fe was having to subsidize it with more than $150,000.00/yr. on top of the tuition, room, and board paid by the students and their Dioceses. I saw a great opportunity. After the meeting, I met with him privately and suggested he turn the seminary, five large buildings and property over to me to manage. Give me six months, and I will turn it around. I would run it as a business and apply a lot of what I had done at Madonna Center to IHM. I would change the name to IHM Retreat and Conference Center and Seminary, open it up for other groups and businesses to use and rent the facilities, and charge the Seminary rent for the square footage it used. After discussions with his Councilors, the facilities and acreage were turned completely over to me

Some nuns from Mexico had been cooking for the seminarians for years. Food costs were out of control, and after eating lunch there a couple times – at which they served chicken soup with smashed chicken bones in it one time and lettuce soup the other time – I knew they had to go, and I would lease out the kitchen to a reputable catering company which would charge per meal to the students and contract with groups using the facility. Eventually, the mattresses and furniture for the 45 overnight rooms would have to be replaced, as would the furniture for the four conference rooms. The biggest problem I had was to find a great manager for the place who would not buck the direction and development I wanted for the place, and to confront the Santa Fean mistrust of me (or anyone) from Albuquerque only 65 miles away. Within six stressful months, it was bringing in a profit.

We Lose our Archbishop

One afternoon as I looked outside the window of my office at Madonna Center, I noticed Archbishop Sanchez slowly walking alone in the parking lot in front with his head down. I went outside and asked if he was alright. He said, "No, but I can't talk about it right now. Just walk with me." So we walked the north part of the property and all the way out the north driveway to Coors Rd. and back, all in silence. When we got back to Madonna Center, he thanked me, his handshake betrayed such heaviness, and he continued back to his office at the Catholic Center. The next day he was gone. We were told at a general employee meeting that afternoon that he had been accused by some women of improprieties at his house. He would be removed as Archbishop and would not be coming back. Since I was the one responsible for his house, my boss told me to go over to it and have all the locks changed that day, and to give no one a key. I had been there many times to visit and to address maintenance issues, sometimes not calling ahead, and I knew inside myself the accusations were totally not believable. How sad and in shock we all were, along with all the Archdiocesan parishioners. He had been the Archbishop for twenty years and was a locally born Hispanic man - one of our own.

In the weeks that followed, I went to the house many times as instructed to let in lawyers and investigators. A scan sweep for electronic devices was performed, looking for hidden mics, cameras, and surveillance devices, but nothing was found. I was told to take two weeks to pack all of the personal items the Archbishop had gathered over the twenty years of his tenure. No one was to help me. I was lonely and sad, as if the Archbishop had died suddenly and left the house empty. I was told to examine every nook and cranny, between mattresses, above ceiling tiles, crawl spaces under the house, everywhere, everything. I found nothing out of the ordinary of his life, especially nothing incriminating. I was sad for him, and knew in my heart and sharp intuition that he was innocent of any wrongdoing. As I was packing I labeled each box with what was in it and what room it had come from. When finished, I took many loads of boxes in the company truck up to the Catholic Center for storage until the Archbishop or his family could come and retrieve what they wanted to save. The experience was very burdensome for me since I could share with no one where I was, what I was doing, or anything regarding what was going on.

After the local news broadcast the story the day after Archbishop Sanchez left, of course it took no time for the national outlets to sensationalize it, along with the many accusations against certain diocesan priests of criminal contact with minors. It seemed like everything at the Catholic Center switched into slow motion; employees were in a daze, with a heavy pall hanging over everyone trying to keep offices and functions operating.

One hour before it was to happen, I was given notice that Mike Wallace and the 60 Minutes crew were on their way to interview the Chancellor, Fr. Ron. I quickly went around and locked all access to the office hallways and asked everyone to stay in their offices. I stood tall in the front lobby with our receptionist, Sharon, as ready as we could be. The front doors flung open by his staff, with cameras and lights and action, this shorter-and-older-than-I-thought-he-would-be man pushed through and took forceful control like a Napoleon puffed up with his own self-importance, demanding to be given full access at once. Sharon, like a sergeant, quietly told him, "No." Standing next to her, I tried very hard not to laugh as I watched Mr. Wallace's reaction. Clearly he was not accustomed to hearing "No" from anyone. Sharon told him to take a seat in the conference room off the lobby, and Fr. Ron the Chancellor would be down when he was ready to talk to him. I was so proud of Sharon, how she spoke, how she composed herself, letting every one of them know she was a force to be reckoned with. From then on, I called her "Sarge" when no one else was around, and we both laughed remembering the incident that name came from.

The number of accusations and lawsuits against priests in our Diocese seemed to explode here as they were just starting to throughout the country. For years and years, more lawyers and more lawyers, and one settlement after another cost millions upon millions, causing employee cutbacks and the selling of lands. There was a dark cloud of uncertainty always hanging over us as there were deep budget cuts and even a mention of bankruptcy. With the gentleness of his spirit and deep care for his people, I am sure Archbishop Sanchez could not have handled the turmoil. There were death threats, protesters marching in front of the Catholic Center offices, and parishioners stopping their donations and leaving the Church. I could empathize with them not wanting their money going to pay off the lawsuits or being a part of a Church that had covered up the crimes for too long. In fact, when people would ask me where I worked, I told them I was a facilities director for a company in town. I was ashamed to say I worked for the Catholic Church and even considered not doing that at all. With the staff and media, Fr. Ron, tough as he was, tried to be as open, compassionate, and transparent as he could be without revealing details of the cases. A lot of people criticized him for being so forthright, but I thought that was exactly what was needed: cutting open the wound and revealing the festering infection to the public. There could be no trust or healing without that approach.

A New Archbishop is Appointed

Rome named a Bishop from Texas as our new Archbishop to deal with all of this, to clean things up, to fix it, and to stabilize it. His installation was a huge affair held at the Albuquerque Convention Center September '93, thousands of invitations were sent out to the public, and many Bishops and some Cardinals attended from around the country. Since security was a deep concern because of the threats, I was designated as the one to work with the Albuquerque Police Department, the Sheriff's Office, and the FBI to coordinate our concerns for protection with them. Very few realized there were also sharpshooters up in the girders of the open ceiling during the ceremonies. In spite of all this, everything went off without a hitch, and it was a high-Church glorious occasion.

From the day I picked up the Archbishop at the airport his first day on the job, and we had our little "getting-to-know-you" talk on the way to the Catholic Center, I was open and transparent with him about who I was and about my relationship with Joe. He had already heard good things about me and my abilities, and seemed to trust that I was someone he could rely on to make things happen and get things done, someone he could confide in, and someone who wasn't afraid to tell him the way things were, not somebody who would tell him what I thought he wanted to hear. We had a good rapport from the start. He was always smiling and making little jokes when appropriate, despite the heavy load he had to carry, and gradually the depression among the Center employees slowly began to lift as they experienced him to be someone they could trust to handle the situation with skill.

He kept me busy from the start. He did away with the monthly Managers and Directors Meetings and established Executive Cabinet Meetings which included the Chancellor, Executive Directors of

Tom Schellenbach

Finance, Pastoral Ministries, General Services (me), the Director of Human Resources, and later the Director of ACA fundraising to discuss and advise on issues he or us would bring to the table. My input was usually on the Plant Operations of the Catholic Center buildings and grounds, Retreat Centers, needed improvements, the Archbishop's house, and issues I had run into while at the parishes.

After the first few years, he wanted to move closer to the Catholic Center. A small group of us toured a few homes with him in the area he wanted to live, and we settled on one within a tenth of a mile of the Center. However, it needed some renovation and construction of a chapel above the garage, as it turned out. The changes to his new home were also added to my responsibilities, as I would be the Project Manager. My multi-tasking abilities were stretched to the brink dealing with the architect, construction company and crew, choosing materials, and all the other myriad items that needed to be purchased and installed when remodelling a "new" home, along with keeping up with all my other responsibilities. The Archbishop showed himself to be very impatient, asking me every day how it was going, why it wasn't done yet, and when it was going to be done. Any explanation I gave was insufficient, and the pressure on me built even to the degree that I ended up getting a severe case of shingles on my whole right side. Having waited too late to address it, neither the shot nor the medication helped, nor did any ointment. My body just said, "Okay. That's enough. Slow down. My nerves can't take it anymore." When the pain of what seemed like hundreds of burning cigarettes put out on my skin got too unbearable, I had to take two weeks off to take pain medications and sit in a warm bath, patting the sores with oatmeal while conducting work over the phone. But, I did get it done, and he moved in not soon enough, but somewhat satisfied. He put me in charge of moving out of the old house, repainting it, getting the landscaping in order for the sale, and storing the old furniture since the new house would have very nice new furnishings

Trip with Mom to Assisi and Rome, Italy

When Mom turned 75 in 1995, I asked her that if there was any place in the world she wanted to go where would that be. She immediately said, "Rome and Assisi." So we took off on a pilgrimage to Rome and Assisi sponsored by the Franciscans. It was much like an extended spiritual retreat. We spent a whole week in Assisi visiting the birthplace of St. Francis of Assisi, his tomb and basilica, and other nearby areas significant to Francis' life. What I appreciated most was the total peace of that ancient town and the opportunity to soak in the Italian culture, scenery and way of life for a week. We then proceeded to spend a whole week in Rome to experience the crush of tourists and the dangerously congested traffic. This week was all about sightseeing places associated with the early Franciscans, Roman ruins, and the impressive seat of the Roman Catholic Church. I particularly appreciated wandering through St. Peter's Basilica on three separate occasions, the vast and gold-laden Vatican Treasury, having a tour of the catacombs underneath the Basilica and the supposed tomb of St. Peter and the other dead Popes, two full days in the Vatican museums, and the Sistine Chapel. The Renaissance architecture, the sculptures, the art cannot be described. I was in total awe of it all, and despite all of its abuses, riches and misuse of power, the Church has endured somewhat as the guardian of faith and the collector and preserver of civilization (mostly Western anyhow) through much of two thousand years.

Joe couldn't take off work from teaching French to go with Mom and me to Italy, but mostly every summer he would take a group of high school students to France to improve their skills in the language, or he would take part in additional educational opportunities for himself in Canada, the U.S., and Spain. I missed him so much while he was gone, as I would get very lonely. My outlets were getting even more involved in work, and keeping up with my tomato and flower gardening, even into the early morning one night with a bright full moon.

A trip to Germany had been calling me for many years, so in the Spring I bought airline tickets for a gay friend, Jeff, and me, and made arrangements to spend two weeks in Bavaria, renting a car and freewheeling it in early October of 2001. But in August, after a colonoscopy, Joe was diagnosed with colon cancer from a walnut-sized tumor, and needed surgery very soon.

Joe's Surgery on 9/11/01

I got him to the hospital at 5am on September 11th, 2001 for the surgery prep, then sat and watched TV with his Dad and Mom, and Joey, Margaret, and his two sisters. As everyone will never forget, about 7:45 am our time, the first plane smashed into the World Trade Center tower in New York City. The news programs were going crazy, the videos were horrific, and we were in total shock. Then the second plane plowed into the other WTC tower. Then the two towers collapsed in fire, smoke, debris, and death, taking the more than 3,000 workers with them. The stunned and heart-sinking feeling I had was akin to dealing with the tornado aftermath in Xenia, Ohio in 1974, but so much more far-reaching in knowing our country, our world, our future would never be the same. I worried how Joe would feel about it, having surgery in a normal world, under anesthesia knowing nothing, and waking up to a totally different shocked world than the one there before the surgery. The good news the surgeon gave us was that he was able to remove the tumor by taking out half of the colon, that the cancer had not metastasized to any of the surrounding area or organs, and that he would not have to be on any chemotherapy. A great relief!

After recovery and into his room, Joe found us watching the TV coverage of New York City, and now a plane crashing into the Pentagon, and another plane which heroic passengers forced to crash in a Pennsylvania field instead of heading to Washington, and Joe says, "Hey! I'm here! What about me?" We quickly changed our focus to attend to him, but left the TV on. Joe had a long and painful stay in the hospital for two weeks since they would not release him until his colon started to work again; and then after being home for a few days and being very sick, he had to go back into the hospital for an additional two weeks. I visited twice a day, feeling very bad for him and very concerned.

After the terrorist attacks, the government closed down all the airports and air traffic, and I seriously had to decide whether to go to Germany or not, or whether we actually could. Within two weeks, the air travel ban was lifted, but I still thought of cancelling the trip for safety reasons and because I wanted to stay home and care for Joe. We spoke about it a lot and tried to lay out the pros and cons. Joe said if safety was my main concern, there would probably never be a safer time to fly than now with the heightened alert and security everywhere. Regarding his welfare, his Mom and Dad, Joey and Margaret, and his sisters would be there if he needed anything, but he would really rather recuperate with no one around, and besides, he would feel really bad if I didn't go and felt I would have to stay home to care for him instead. It was a lot to think about, but in the end, he said to go.

Trip to Germany and Bavaria

Apprehensively, Jeff and I went and landed in Frankfurt to be greeted by German police and soldiers everywhere in the airport, firmly holding what seemed to be AK-47 guns and a penetrating gaze. Surely, no one was going to pull off here what happened in the US. I rented an Audi, and we took off to Cologne for two days. I had a vague idea of a schedule for the trip, made no reservations anywhere for the whole trip, but we had no problem finding a very nice hotel right in the city center three blocks from the cathedral. However, here and in every city throughout Germany we had trouble finding parking. To stop driving around and looking and looking, I decided we would just park in the not-too-convenient and very expensive ($25 a night) parking garages. We walked around the city surrounding the cathedral to work off jet lag, and to imbibe in too many beers unaware until later of the much higher alcohol content. I had learned about the medieval over-the-top Gothic cathedral in my college humanities and cultural classes, and I was not disappointed. I was in awe at the "we can do this better than anyone else" pride portrayed in the construction, which wasn't actually finished until the early 1900s after 700 years. In the museum and treasury under the church, we got introduced to what was left of the riches collected all those years and to the photographic history of the total destruction of the city during WWII. Even though the cathedral was spared a direct hit by the bombing, it sustained heavy damage. How could the allied pilots have saved such a historic landmark when everything else around it was totally leveled? We spent the second day touring the vast details of the cathedral, the golden casket containing the relics of the Three Kings of nativity stories that were its draw to fame, and climbing the 500+ steps up one of the steeples, and then staying at a neighboring beer bar too long.

The next day, we took off west following the back roads, and saw numerous fields of huge cabbages and many vineyards. We were close to the French border, on the way south past Trier to a very small farming village named "Schellenbach" where my ancestors were from. There was even a rest area named Rastplatz Schellenbach on the A-1 Autobahn. The village had only about 50 homes and nothing else, and was on the east side of a stream named Theelbach (from which Schellenbach – singing brook – got its name), across from Thalexweiler. The area reminded me so much of southern Ohio with its rolling hills, bright green fields and forests, that I felt right at home and understood why so many Germans would have settled there and then in southern Ohio.

Walking around ,we stopped at the local bar in Thalexweiler to ask if anyone in the area had the last name of Schellenbach after showing the bartender my business card. He got so excited that there was actually someone named "Schellenbach" that he called the regional historian, genealogical researcher, and archeologist to come over. Johannes Naumann and I spoke for hours in Germanglish about the history of the whole area dating back to early Roman times when a small outpost was established there. The town had recently celebrated its 2,000th anniversary. The more beer I drank, the better my German became. He said there were no records of anyone named Schellenbach, but he had no doubt that we came from there since way back people would take the name of the town they were from (e.g. Michael from Schellenbach), and there weren't any other towns or villages in Germany with that name. What a joy that, by chance, I could be there and speak in depth with Johannes and know that in the distant past my blood had roots there! A destination and goal luckily accomplished!

We continued on to Baden-Baden and spent two nights, experienced the world famous Casino, and soaked in the ancient Roman Caracalla hot springs. We then headed to Freiburg for one night and toured the university town and medieval torture museum, then east through the Black Forest to Lindau on the Bodensee. It struck me again how close these towns were to each other and how I had misjudged the short distance and time it would take to get there. I just couldn't believe that the whole country of Germany was not much larger that the states of Ohio or New Mexico in the U.S. How could such a small country in the center of Europe have so many natural resources and cause so much trouble through the ages and especially in the last 100 years?

Munich was the next itinerary stop where we spent three nights and three days visiting art museums, the Hofbrauhaus, shopping for lederhosen, the Hofbrauhaus, walking the center city, the Hofbrauhaus, and finding $1.00 t-shirts from the under-attended Oktoberfest a few weeks earlier. It was hard to believe that Munich was totally destroyed in WWII and totally rebuilt to the same city it was before, same architecture and all. I could have easily spent a whole week there and the surrounding area. Back in the car, we bypassed Nuremberg on the way north to visit a young couple whose wedding I had orchestrated when they were on vacation in Albuquerque. One day, Michael and Sigrid took us to Wurzburg, another city destroyed in the war and rebuilt by the women afterward since there were so few men around, and gave us a tour of the very imposing Wurzburg castle across the river. I wanted to visit the imposing Residenz of the Prince Archbishops, but had seen the one in Munich, and we were all getting tired.

The last three days of our journey were spent in Heidelberg, a very old university town which was never bombed in the war and had many original wood frame and plaster buildings. I enjoyed walking around the town and soaking in the learning atmosphere, walking up to Heidelberg castle for a tour, and along the river Neckar, and stopping in the pastry shops for coffee and yet another sweet delicacy or two or three. A disappointment was that the river cruises had stopped for the season about a week before we got there. The same was true for river cruises on the Rhine. But here, too, I could easily have spent a week since it was just that comfortable there.

I did not mean the above to be a travel guide. If so, I would have included many meaningful details. But, I did want to express how my spirit and heart connected with the German land and culture and people. I definitely felt that I had lived there before in one of my previous lives, and belonged there now, and I grieved when I left -- after leaving a large part of my heart behind.

A Twenty-Four Year Career

How can I compress 24 years of working for the Archdiocese of Santa Fe and the Archbishop other than speaking of my consistently doing a great job, or my many successes and few failures, and the struggle throughout? As I look back, the job fit me and my many gifts of management, organization, keen sense of remodelling, getting things done, making things happen, and dealing with problems and making them go away. Intuitively, I just somehow knew how to do this. My innate analytical mind kicked in for every project and issue. I was criticized at times for taking too long to begin projects, but I had to analyze the whole situation and potential repercussions to see the whole picture before I could make a decision on where to go with it. Never was I impulsive, and I could back up every decision with facts and reasoning while trying to set aside emotions and feelings. So, I tried to focus solely on the job to be done and how I wanted it done, and did not allow my thoughts about God and Church to enter in. If I had a problem with a particular employee I supervised, who could not change his attitude toward me or what I wanted done, we would discuss the issues with opportunities to change on both our parts to negotiate some agreement; but in the end, when necessary, I would make it very clear that I was the one in charge, and it would be done my way, or I would find someone else who would do it.

What I enjoyed most about my job was that, in all actuality, I was my own boss. Through the years my immediate supervisors, the Chancellors, told me the only times they wanted to hear from me was if there was a problem or a potential problem. I felt trusted implicitly to just take care of things in the best possible manner. I saw my job was to do whatever was possible to make the environment in the Catholic Center buildings the best so all the other employees could do their job better. I contracted to have all the lighting upgraded to give more light at the desk levels, to replace all the carpeting a couple times, to remodel all the restrooms, to have all the painting renewed about every seven years, to have roofers repair leaks and totally replace roofs, to repair and upgrade the heating and air conditioning systems, to replace conference tables and chairs, to abide with safety and fire regulations and drills, to keep the landscaping appealing, to purchase a new car for the Archbishop every two years and to have it maintained, to handle all security needs and our need for security afterhours, and on and on. It seemed that a lot of what others just didn't want to do ended up on my desk. When I asked my supervisor why I was being asked to do those things that were not my responsibility, he said it was because the administration knew I would get it done.

That was how I became the EPA certified Asbestos Inspector for the whole Archdiocese. That meant keeping up-to-date all the Asbestos Management Plans for our buildings and especially all our schools throughout the northern half of New Mexico, but also inspecting parish churches and other buildings where remodelling was going to be done. On a number of occasions I communicated closely with the Environmental Protection Agency at their district office in Dallas and with the Environmental Control office of the City of Albuquerque. I fostered some close professional friendships with both of these agencies and offices. Both of them told me that if I were ever looking for a job, to call them and they would hire me on the spot. Those offers came in handy later.

One other important aspect of my job was that I was given the freedom to be very creative. Thinking outside the box of how "we've always done it that way", and showing a new and more efficient and cost effective way to do "it", really energized me. I was always thinking of a better way of doing things. This approach led to saving many thousands of dollars each year for the Archdiocese and my budget in the General Services/Plant Operations division. In all, I could be very proud of the job I was doing, I liked doing it, and I never got bored. When I would leave there, I could justly say that everything had my fingerprints on it. Since affirmation was not too forthcoming, I could happily affirm myself.

++++

My personal life was kept private from everyone except the administration and a very few trusted employees. Still, the gossip mills' wheels would turn while searching for tidbits, perhaps because I tried to keep everything about me not gossip worthy. I was even accused of improper sexual harassment by a younger female employee. The HR Director called me to his office to convey the claim. He started off very seriously telling me in detail what I was being accused of, and then we both smiled knowing the accusation could not true. Dog barking up the wrong tree. He said he would take care of it, and after his investigation she admitted she was lying just to get me in trouble. The next day she was no longer working there. My friends would share other gossip with me, but they took it upon themselves to quash it immediately, knowing I would not have responded to it at all.

++++

About this time, the Archbishop wanted the Executive Cabinet to work on an upgrade and update of the Catholic Center organizational chart. The process would involve establishing some new positions at the top and moving some offices into other divisions to be more in line with what other other Dioceses were doing with their channels of authority, accountability, and responsibility. The effort took many meetings and months before we came up with three possible charts for the Archbishop to choose from and approve. On the side, I was told by one of the directors that I was being considered for one of the new top positions, but that the Archbishop told her, "Tom would be perfect for the job, except for that one thing."

Authenticity, Integrity, Confidence -- Round One

Certainly, I was aware of the Church's teaching regarding homosexuality: hate the sin, love the sinner; unless the homosexual lived a celibate life (i.e. no sex) he or she was living in mortal sin and was surely going to hell. They could not have access to the Sacraments except Confession, and would be restricted from receiving Communion, and they could be members of the Church and share their gifts with the Church. In other words: they could become adopted children in the family and be used to support the family; but would never really belong there. They would always be second class children, could come to the table, but would not be allowed to eat anything or be fed the same way as the other children. All of this was always there underneath, but really was not an issue until the Archbishop began to make it a public issue when the State Legislature in 2004 began debate on allowing same-sex partners to become legal Domestic Partners with many of the rights and privileges of married couples.

The Archbishop wrote articles in the Archdiocesan newspaper (Feb. 2004) and the local newspapers about the implications of these bills becoming law, citing the primacy of the family, the protection of children, the protection of the institution of marriage, the dangers of pedophelia (which some of his own priests were doing), in his own idiotic remarks of "God made Adam and Eve, not Adam and Steve", and "so will this lead to a man claiming his own donkey as his domestic partner?" He even spent many thousands of dollars hiring lobbyists to influence the Legislators to vote against the bills. During our Executive Cabinet Meetings, with me sitting there with the other five, he would tout his efforts to defeat the measures. At another meeting, when the bills were defeated, he victoriously made it clear that they were defeated because of his pressure on the Legislature, the power of the Catholic Church in New Mexico, and the effectiveness of his lobbyists. I was so sickened and enraged by his words that I sat there glaring such red hatred into his eyes, and then suddenly gathered my papers from the conference table, and walked out of the room with him watching me. Whatever happened to separation of Church and State? This was not a religion issue; it was a civil rights issue.

I knew I could no longer be a dual personality working for the Church. I could no longer focus only on my job of maintaining systems and buildings, separating myself from and blocking out all that was the church as a large corporation controlling people through guilt and fear and the promise of something good or bad after death. To hold onto whatever integrity I had left in me to maintain the wholeness of my being I had worked so hard for, and to be a truly authentic person, I had to make some serious decisions. I felt that my very person was under attack. The Archbishop never discussed his approach to any of this with me, and even though he told others that he did, he lied. That hurt me rather deeply, and I did take it personally. He said I was a friend of his, and I thought I was. Joe and I had even had him over to our house for dinner. He invited me out to dinner to discuss things, but never did he bring up the above issues.

I confronted him after one dinner. He had recently said he was meeting with women and couples who had aborted their babies. He was trying to "build bridges" with them to find out how the Church might be able to help them. After that dinner, I asked him, "Archbishop, you are meeting with people who have had an abortion, to build bridges with them, to see how the Church could help them. Why do you refuse to meet with gay groups, who have committed no crime other than being born gay, so that bridges could be built with them and to ask how the Church could help them?" He said, "Well, well, ah, I have tried to meet with them, but they would have been confrontive, and it wouldn't look good." As I drove the rest of the way to his house to drop him off, there was total silence. I never went to dinner with him again. And I was convinced about what I had perceived all along. His mode of operation was: image was everything, and don't cause any controversy.

He didn't want to hear any bad news, especially the kind that would make it into the papers.

<u>No Bridges for Homos</u>

The line is drawn, the chasm wide and deep
There was no bridge to burn
One will not, cannot be built.

The Roman Catholic hierarchy stands rigid,
Opposing rights for the homo ten percent.
Claiming the voice of God to justify their prejudice.
No more hope – for understanding why.

Instead, their bigotry perpetuates
The lies and falsehoods, the segregating discrimination,
The inequality and second-class citizenship.

In their righteous hypocrisy,
In what they have done and failed to do,
They bring shame on the house of Christ.

Despite opposition and religious wrongs,
By opposing religious meddling in civil marriages,
Homo couples <u>will</u> fight for and <u>achieve</u> their civil rights. -- Tom

++++

<u>Letter to the Archbishop</u> -- *April 14,1997*
Archbishop,

I cannot describe fully the depth of disappointment and hurt I feel as a result of your letter of February 19, 1997 to the parishes on "Same Sex Marriages: Where Does the Church Stand?" Of course, it was no surprise to read once again where the Church stands on the issue. What was hurtfully surprising was your need to publicly proclaim to all the leaders and the people of the Archdiocese the Church's teaching which places judgment on same-sex relationships and to associate them with the breakdown of family and the breakdown of opposite-sex marriages. And, you did this without discussing the issue with me – a friend - not that you had to. I cannot believe that you actually realize how some of the faithful have and will take your letter.

There are parents within earshot of your letter who have once again found fuel for rejecting their same-sex sons and daughters; who once again must question the acceptability of their children as "morally wrong"; who once again must pray that their son or daughter changes so that he or she will be acceptable to God now and later. I know parents who have been struggling with this for years. As a result of your letter some will take your teaching seriously and finally sever their relationships with their same-sex children. Others will ridicule the Church as saying nothing to their lives, and separate themselves further from it, choosing an accepting and loving relationship with their children over the teaching of the Church.

There are many same-sex persons in this Archdiocese within earshot of your proclamation who have once again found themselves feeling rejected by the Church, feeling guilty for being who they believe God made them to be and who had no choice in being; who once again doubt their own self-worth and acceptability to God now and later. I know some who have been struggling with this for years. I know some who have given up the struggle and ended their own lives because of it, because they and their families have taken the Church's teaching seriously. More will take it seriously and will live a "morally wrong" life of no hope of ever being one with God. Others will ridicule the Church judgment and use your letter as more fuel to separate themselves further from it, choosing instead an accepting relationship with their own Self.

There are some parishioners who do not believe same-sex persons who are morally evil should be working in their parish, their school, or for the Archdiocese. There are some same-sex persons whose integrity will not enable them to work for a Church which considers them "morally evil."

This is why I am disappointed and saddened and angry. I hold all of these people in my heart, and I am one with all these people. You say you did not say this or that, or mean it this or that way; but I do not feel I am incorrect in stating how many have taken what you did say in your signed column in the People of God.

More personally, the judgmental proclamation came from a friend. I look at the medallion you gave me from Assisi, realizing that I must once again tame the wolf inside and out. I look at the Good Shepherd you gave me from the Holy Land and know that the lamb is carried, and loved, and accepted no matter what by Him, but not by you.

Do you see the dilemma that the Church is in regarding this teaching? The Church has lost its heart in upholding its image and teaching. How can someone feel "welcome, compassion, and respect" from a Church which consistently considers them "morally wrong and sinful"? How can the Church be accepting of those who believe deeply in their *hearts that <u>God has made them who they are</u>, who could not change, that it would be a devaluing of who they are?*

How can the Church receive them if they are not able to accept the teaching of the Church, not able to "live a life of chastity"? Why is it that same-sex persons can feel constancy of love from Christ, but only constancy of rejection and exclusion from His Church?

The moral wrong and sinfulness is in the judgment the Church has passed on same-sex persons as an aberration of humanity. The moral wrong is in fixating on what does not last to the detriment of what does last. The moral wrong is with those who focus on sexual acts rather than relationship. The moral wrong is with those who would want to blame the breakdown of family and opposite-sex marriages on same-sex relationships. Where is the logic to that? There is moral wrong and sinfulness wherever there is broken relationship: relationship with God, relationship with Self, relationship with Others, relationship with Creation. I know I am sinful in this regard, but RELATIONSHIP must be the focus.

The focus must be a consistent moral ethic of RELATIONSHIP, not sexual acts. Same-sex couples do not stay together because of the sex. Sex does not last, it fades with age. They stay together because their union has given birth to a loving, growing relationship. (As the Spirit proceeds from the Father and the Son.) It is the same as with opposite-sex unions. Relationship is what makes all of us human, fully human, fully alive in a free, committed, faithful, loving and constant relationship.

"Have a lovingly constant relationship with God, Self, Others, and Creation." Constancy of love comes from the heart, not image, not tradition, not judgment, not exclusion, not rejection.

Sincerely,

Tom Schellenbach

++++

During my complete physical exam that year, my primary care doctor talked to me about how working where I did, and the stress it was causing me, was ruining my health. "You have to get out of there!" he said then and every year afterward. He pointed out that I had increasing depression, anxiety, and vascular problems. I knew it was true.

Tom Schellenbach

Authenticity, Integrity, Confidence -- Round Two

Letter to the Archbishop -- February 19, 2005
Archbishop,

    Our phone conversation yesterday disturbed me deeply. At issue was a letter you received claiming that gay and lesbian groups were using our retreat centers. I assured you that, to our knowledge, this has not happened. You then made it very clear that "those kind of people" and groups are not to be allowed to use the retreat centers. The explanation you gave was the general homophobia and the possibility of controversy.

    On the one hand, this is a non-existent problem and a moot point — none of "those kind of people" have asked to use the Centers. I know of no homosexual groups or persons, who are convinced of their own personal integrity and self-worth, who would want to have any association with the Catholic Church or the Archdiocesan retreat center. Even if some slipped in with another group using the Centers, there is no realistic way we could tell them apart from any of the others in that group. With the homophobia, exclusion, and discrimination shown toward them by the actions and words of the Catholic Church in so many ways, homosexuals already know that they are not included, they are not allowed, they are not welcomed.

    On the other hand, your reaction to that letter shows that you are being controlled by a fear of controversy from the homophobic religious right, some of your advisor priests among them. In your published People of God editorial, February 2004, you say: "Homosexual persons have a right to and deserve our respect, compassion, and defense against bigotry, attacks and abuse." You say: "homosexual orientation, which is not immoral." You say: "Gay people are welcomed and appreciated in the Church." At the very least, I felt this was one thing I could count on from you. However, by the action of excluding them from the retreat centers you are not showing respect, compassion, defense, welcome, or appreciation. Rather than taking a stand defending against bigotry, discrimination, attacks and abuse, you have bowed to the extremists out of fear, and you have associated yourself with the bigots, attackers and abusers. I don't know whether to distrust what you say or believe that you have changed your mind.

    If you wish, I would like to discuss this personally with you.

Tom Schellenbach

The Archbishop called my office phone, and said he wanted to see me immediately. I quickly went upstairs from my basement office to his office on the third floor and without a handshake was told to sit down. Needless to say, he was not pleased. He said I was overreacting and taking the whole thing personally. I asked, "Archbishop, I am one of 'those kind of people'. How can I not take it personally? How am I to be the Director of the Retreat Centers if I am being forbidden to enter them?" He said he didn't mean it that way. I told him I was convinced of my personal integrity and self-worth and wondered how I could continue to have any association with the Church or the Archdiocese considering what his words and actions say about those who cannot follow his teaching in this regard. He said he did not appreciate what I said in the letter, asked if there was anything else I wanted to discuss, told me to never have another letter like that handed to him, threw the letter at me, and told me to "now get out of my office."

Three days after that meeting, after talking with Joe, I resigned from my job on a Monday morning, effective immediately. Perhaps because I was at such odds with the teachings of the Catholic Church and the Archbishop's pronouncements, perhaps because I needed to hold onto what integrity and authenticity I had left, perhaps because of the struggles and anxiety inside of me and needing to hold onto my own sanity, perhaps because I was tired of trying and just didn't care anymore, and all of the above, I decided I had to get out of there. I discussed it with my boss, who told me I needed to tell the Archbishop personally. I made an appointment for that day. When I told him I was resigning, he said he would not accept my resignation. "You cannot leave. I need you here. Besides, you told me when I first arrived that you would be here as long as I was Archbishop. Take a week to think about it and then get back to me." I told him my decision was well thought out, but I would get back to him no later than Friday, and that I would use those five days to look for another job.

I got on the phone and called four contacts I had made over the years and had worked with closely. My contact at the EPA in Dallas said she would hire me on the spot. Just come in and fill out an application, and we can talk. My contact with the City of Albuquerque Environmental Division said he had an opening but needed to confirm hiring me with his supervisor. My contact with the Albuquerque Public Schools said he was very interested, and I should come in and apply for a vacant position that would perfectly fit my skills. My contact with the owner of a private environmental company wanted to meet with me that afternoon. The rest of the week, I spoke with each of the four and asked and answered questions. The main question from each of them was why I was leaving the Archdiocese after so many years. I was open and honest with my reasoning, and none of them had any problems with it.

I was beginning to look forward to working totally in the public sector, finally, totally away from the Church.

Joe and I talked a lot about the options and implications. The EPA position would involve a lot of travel throughout New Mexico, Colorado, Arizona and western Texas to periodically inspect every school's asbestos management plan and how well they were following the EPA regulations. They preferred that I move to Dallas, but I might be able to work out of Albuquerque. Moving to Dallas was not an option for me, but the salary would be excellent.

The City position would be a smooth transition into much the same work I had been doing with regards to asbestos and toxic environments. It could morph into taking over the division and would involve a lot of training and learning of their systems, operations, politics, and computer programs. My salary to start would be about two thirds of what I was making. The Schools position would be much the same as the City with about the same salary. The owner of the private company was trying to retire and get out of the business, but was looking for someone to run it for him and then buy him out. I told him that day I wasn't interested.

Almost constantly all week, I thought about my options, along with the option of staying put with the Archdiocese. Whatever direction I would choose, I knew I did not want to work past seven more years, and I wanted to retire when I was 62. My financial advisor said I could retire before that if I wanted to. Having to learn so much in a new position with a new employer was not appealing to me, but neither was continuing to work under the strain where I was working. Also, I felt it would be unfair for the new employer to invest in me for only seven years. In the end, I decided to stay with the Archdiocese, but under certain conditions.

When I met with the Archbishop on Friday morning, I shared with him what my job search turned up, explaining each of the three options and the definite interest they had in hiring me. He was fidgeting. He knew I was very serious. Then I told him my final decision was to stay with the Archdiocese, but under two conditions. 1) I would be permitted to use all of my vacation and personal leave in the year it was accrued. 2) Whenever he came out with another "pastoral" letter or pronouncement that I could not agree with, I was permitted to come to his office and confront him face to face, and to leave any meeting where it was discussed. When he had enough of that, he would have to fire me. He was visibly relieved and agreed. We shook hands, and I left for the day

Authenticity, Integrity, Confidence – Round Three

Letter to Counseling Group -- February 28, 2007
Dear ......
    ...Saddened and embarrassed are the feelings I had when asking about the possible presence of Lesbian and Gay ... Counseling groups being at Madonna. I was required to ask. Those feelings, I suppose, stopped me from being more definitively prohibitive towards those groups. Too, I was hoping that the Archbishop's approach had softened since the last discussion I had with him on the subject. After speaking directly with him today, I can assure you his approach toward and the policy regarding gays and lesbians using the Archdiocese of Santa Fe Retreat Centers has not changed, i.e. they are not welcome in our Centers and he does not want those kind of people using our Centers.
    I totally understand your need to remain firm regarding your policy to never agree with or participate in oppression in any form, to never take part in any attack or discrimination or hurt of any person, not to abandon our gay and lesbian brothers and sisters. I respect your personal integrities and the integrity of your Counseling group even more.
Sincerely, Tom Schellenbach

The following letter was not given to the Archbishop's secretary to be handed to him because he had told me to never do that again. Instead, I asked for an appointment with him and then stood tall in front of his desk and read it to him.

Letter Read to the Archbishop in his office -- March 2, 2007
Archbishop,
    By telling me to prohibit gays and lesbians from having access to our retreat centers, you are telling me to actively participate in bigotry and negative discrimination. In all of my Christian and Catholic training to this day, it is my conviction that this is not something Jesus Christ would tell me to do. On the contrary, he would have me take a stand against what is hypocritical, immoral, and unethical.
    At the risk of being insubordinate, in good conscience, effecting your policy in this regard is something I cannot do. I will not do.
Tom Schellenbach

He merely replied, "Fine. I will do it myself."

The leaders of the counseling group then wrote directly to the Archbishop on August 27th requesting a face-to-face meeting with him, which he granted. After his meeting with them, he and I met to discuss his greater understanding of the group's efforts to counsel and help those with a homosexual inclination. He decided he had no objection to that group using the Retreat Centers so long as they respected the Catholic teaching in this matter and did not promote otherwise. I thought, "Huh? Is this the same man?"

Authenticity, Integrity, Confidence -- Round Four

There were other pronouncements between 2007 and 2011, but to include my reactions, and thoughts, and statements to the Archbishop would be redundant. However, I must make reference to the "Pastoral Care of Couples Who are Cohabitating" from the Archbishop, which was read at all the churches and Masses on the weekend of April 3, 2011. Personally, I am sure he did not write it; but, rather, it was written by at least one of his conservative fundamentalist priests. The style was totally not his style, but he did sign it and promulgate it:

– .".the Church opposes cohabitation without Catholic marriage, and same sex unions."

– " ...These people are objectively living in a state of mortal sin…"

[Really? Objectively? How can anyone claim to see another's spiritual status?]

– "They are in great spiritual danger. At the best...they are ignorant...At the worst, they are contemptuous…"

– .".those who have a merely civil union with no previous marriage; and those who have a civil union who were married before...have no real excuse. They should marry in the Church or separate."

Joe and I had a pre-scheduled party that evening at which about 20 of our friends, all lawyers, doctors, and other professionals came and had a great time until the Archbishop's letter was brought up. I was amazed at their reaction to it. Some laughed at how out of touch he and his Church are. Others were very angry at his judgements on their lives. All of them, recovering prior Catholics and present Catholics, saw it as the last straw they were going to put up with. They all said they were done with Church and religion. I was done with it, too. I had had enough.

<u>Letter of Resignation to the Chancellor and the Archbishop</u>
-- April 6, 2011

After twenty-four years and much thoughtful planning, I have decided to resign and retire from my position as Executive Director of General Services effective Thursday, June 30, 2011.

In total honesty I can say I have worked the best I could, and I leave the General Services Division with the best directors and employees, the leanest budgets, and the most forward goals and direction it has ever had.

If you wish, I would be willing to assist with a smooth transition to the new Director before the end of June.

Thank you for the opportunity to work here all these years.

Tom Schellenbach

During our meeting after I read my resignation letter to him, he asked if his letter from the Sunday before had anything to do with my decision. I told him that yes, it was the most immediate impetus to my resigning; but, also, I felt he needed someone working with him in my position who could in fact support his decisions and teachings, his faith and his Church, because I could no longer do that. I also told him that I didn't feel it was good to have someone he thought was "morally evil" and "objectively living in a state of mortal sin" to be working at the Catholic Center. I offered to pack up my things and leave immediately if he wanted me to, but he said he would like for me to stay throughout the transition.

<u>My email to all the employees</u> -- April 8th

My mentor, the Great Sage of the Petroglyphs, has been mentioning to me that now is the time to retire. When I asked what the Catholic Center would do if I retired, he said: "They will either find someone better or hire four people to take your place." Last Wednesday, I took his advice and handed in my resignation for retirement effective June 30th of this year.

I am grateful for the opportunity to have worked with you and to have worked here for the last 24 years. I have learned a lot. Thank you.

I encourage each of you to feel free to "give up Tom" for Lent and Advent.

Joe's Dad Moves In With Us

It was a good thing I left that work when I did. Joe's Dad, who had been living by himself for five years since Joe's Mom died, was in need of more and more constant care. He didn't take care of himself living in the old homestead. He was in and out of the hospital, had a couple heart attacks, fell and broke his pelvis, and was in a rehab-care facility for a while before Joe and I took him into our home in July 2011. Financially and logically it was the best place for him and the only option, but initially perhaps not the best solution for us. We weren't used to having someone else live with us who needed care 24/7. Joe could not have cared for him by himself, and I was glad to be there to help. I wondered: at what time does love become mainly responsibility?

It was stressful for both of us. In the middle of the night he would call for help. We gave him a small bell, and maybe shouldn't have given it to him. "I need a piece of cheese. I need my morphine. I need to use the restroom. I need some water." It was always something. Neither of us were getting much sleep, and it really wore on us. When the bell rang, when we both woke up, we would try to take equal turns to help him.

During the day, he needed breakfast, lunch and dinner. We had to prepare that, and we weren't used to having three set meals. Previously, Joe and I would just graze the fridge or prepare what we individually wanted to eat. Now we had to set menus for the week after asking Dad what he would like. Our focus definitely shifted. His Dad and I got along very well, and we had many meaningful discussions, and I listened to many stories of "In Those Days…." When we needed rain, I would ask him to go out and cut the alfalfa so it would rain - as it would so often when he was farming - thus not allowing the alfalfa to dry properly and meaning more work for him.

I wanted to allow Joe to continue his discipline of going to the gym every day, because it allowed him a couple hours away from the house, away from having to care for his dad, so I would take the mornings, breakfast and lunch. Sometimes, Joe would go about 6am so he could take over later in the morning if I needed to do something. At the time, I was working 15 hours a week at a Church of Christ as their facility manager and maintenance man three days a week mostly in the afternoons.

The most difficult part of the arrangement for me was all the caregivers coming and going -- doctors and nurses, physical and occupational therapists, and Dad's extended family and friends. There was somebody here every day and practically every evening. We felt we had to offer refreshments – which we were also not used to doing daily.

It was all part of our caretaker experience. I was losing the silence in the house and most of my solitude time.

When Joey or Joe's nephew or niece would help out in the evening, Joe and I would go out to dinner or do something just to get away together. With Dad totally dependent and bedridden towards the end, it got more difficult to get away. He couldn't dress himself, or brush his teeth, or walk to the restroom without help. What a relief that the nurses came to give him a shower-bath twice a week. He was ready to go. He wanted to go. Towards the last two months, he was just waiting for the end. Hospice saved our lives. They would come 24/7 if we needed them. One day we did need them. We called them, and they came at midnight. They would deliver the prescriptions, but focused on making Dad comfortable rather than trying to improve him.

Somehow, the Friday before he died, he thought he was going to die that night. So he had us call his sisters and daughters and all the grandchildren to ask them all to come see him for the last time. He sure did enjoy that evening with them all around him, and everybody had a good time. He didn't die that night.

The night before he did die he was having a rough time, so I got up and sat next to his bed and held his hand,. He was in pain, restless, seeing Joe's Mom and other dead relatives. I believed he was seeing them, because dying people see things we don't. These people are either there to be with them and help them pass on, or it may be some kind of chemical imbalance or a lack of oxygen getting to the brain. But, I think it might be an expression of a person's hope that these important people will be there and are still with him. When he woke up in the morning, he asked me, "Tom is this heaven?" I answered, "Joe you know how I feel about heaven, but do you feel like this is heaven?" He said, "Yes, this is heaven," and then he fell back to sleep.

I had to work at the church early that Tuesday morning. Hospice came to give him the sponge bath which he had refused the night before. Every movement hurt him, and they laid him back down in the bed. After the bath, at 1pm, the nurses checked his pulse and couldn't find one. Joe was there at his side holding his hand when his Dad sat up with wide eyes, just looked around, laid back down, and let go of his last breath.

We were both grateful that he didn't have to die in a hospital or by himself. He died right here with people who loved him. He wasn't alone and didn't have to pass alone. I was sad to see him go, and it was like he instantly wasn't around anymore. Here was this robust man all his life, who had fought in WWII, was a prisoner of war at a Japanese camp, a farmer, a very important part of all our lives, who had lost all his strength and his ability to live. Even though his death was not unexpected, his leaving was tough on both of us, especially Joe. Joe called his sisters who then called his relatives who all came over to our house for a visitation to say goodbye to Joe Sr. before the mortuary came early into the evening. I felt I had lost my outwest-father.

Dad wanted to be cremated with no visitation, and have a funeral Mass at the church with pictures of him in the army and of his life and a few small personal items. Everything was kept to a minimum. In the newspaper we noted "private disposition" and nothing about burial. After the Mass and the luncheon the close family gathered at the cemetery around his wife's grave. Dad's wife, Joe's Mom, a Grandma and Great-Grandma, and now they were together again. The grandsons had dug a deep vertical hole next to grandma's grave, into which the container with his ashes was lowered after a few memories of them both were shared -- how they had impacted all our lives and families in such significant ways.

Both Joe and I appreciated the support, encouragement, and gratitude of the family. I suppose it is natural to have feelings of relief along with the grief and guilt for feeling that way; but there was no guilt about taking him in and caring for him, and giving him dignity and quality of life the last few months of his life. We could honestly say we did our best for him and for our family.

Last Visit With Mom

In February Joe and I decided to go to Hamilton, Ohio to visit with my Mom in March while she was still alive. On the Thursday morning we were to fly out of Albuquerque, my oldest brother Dan called and said that Mom had a heart attack and was in the hospital. We visited her in the hospital for a couple of days before she was moved back to the extended care facility where she had been staying. Then she had another heart attack and was back in the hospital. It was at that time she decided to go into a Hospice facility in Hamilton on Tuesday. Our flights back to Albuquerque were scheduled for that day, but I felt I should stay with her. Joe said he needed to go home since grieving for his Dad so recently was affecting him as he saw my Mom's health failing quickly.

Most all of her 13 children and some of the grandchildren and great-grandchildren were able to visit with Mom in her final five days. My younger brothers and I took turns spending the nights with her until her death on Saturday. It was a meaningful time spending those nights with them and being with her as she was dying and watching the slow progression of life slipping away each hour, her pulse getting lighter, her breathing more infrequent. We were losing the most constant and important person in our lives.

She would have been 92 years old, coming from strong stock. The Navajos have this belief that someone's last breath is immediately breathed in by a newborn child taking his or her first breath. I wished that those present at the moment of Mom's death could have appreciated and understood the immensity of what was happening – Mom's spirit leaving, her spirit rising and shedding the body it had used for so long, to be reborn again. Something to be witnessed and experienced in total awe and silence. What an honor! What a joy! And now, connections to our past were severed except through memories, and we were each an orphan.

The visitation and funeral were tough on me, but I was able to give the eulogy, and sing Schubert's "Ave Maria" and the Franciscan "Ultima" at the Mass for her. I still don't understand completely why I never cried for her when she died.

Letter from Mom dated 1996 and given to me the day she died 3/17/2012
"Dear Tom,

You suggested this project long ago and I'm following up with letters to all. Why do I love each of our children? There are so many different reasons and so many different qualities. I believe your sisters and brothers all feel you are and have been my favorite. Must be because we have a certain rapport. I feel we always had a closeness, a understanding and peacefulness together. When you were small you preferred doing things alone or organizing others. I proudly consented to allowing you to go to the seminary so early. I realize my mistake now. I happily saw you ordained a priest and ached for you when you felt you couldn't live that life. I admit I was saddened when you left but happy later seeing your happiness. I admired you for making such a difficult decision. I'm so proud of you now. Your faith and drive enabled you to keep striving when you could have given up. I love you for the memories – Western trips, Assisi, Rome, etc. I've learned much from you. You are a good son, friend. I never felt I had to make excuses for you. Now you know why I love you and always will."   *Mom*

I miss my Mom.

Chapter Seven
A Life in Pictures

Cowboy Tommy 1.5 yrs

Dad and Mom engaged

Great-Grandparents Philomena & Teodor Bergedick

Great-Grandfather Michael Schellenbach the Grocer

Our Gang of Eight 1955

Pater's House

High School Graduation 1968

College Graduation 1973

Master's Degree Graduation 1977

Navajo Reservation Walk 1981

The log cabin friary, which is located behind the Church and Hall, is home for Fathers Larry and Tom.

Fr. Larry, Fr. Tom, Starving Dog, Lukachukai Cabin

On Lukachukai road to visit 1982

Fr. Tom Celebrating Mass at Lukachukai

Tom & Joe 1986

Chauffeur Tom, Joey's Freshman Homecoming

Tom & Joe 50th B'day 2000

Tom & Joe 50th B'Day

Navajo Family: Tom, Aunt Sarah, Mom Eva Desbah

Tom Schellenbach

Mom Dorie & Tom

Joey, Tom, Maggie

Tender Moment

Mother & Son

Tom, Joey, Margaret, Joe, 2008 France

Mom 90th B'day with Whole Family 2010

Last Photo of Mom, Feb. 2012

Wedding Day 9/3/2013

Tom reads to Granddaughter Piper 2015

Holding Granddaughter Coral 2015

Joey & Tom, Oceanside Beach

Aunt Sarah Jones and Tom With Navajo Clan T-shirts

SECTION TWO

EXCERPTS FROM THE INTERVIEWS
WITH JOE AND TOM

OCTOBER 2017

Beginnings and Culture

J: I was born in Albuquerque, New Mexico in 1950. I'm what they call a "burqueño," anyone born here is called that. I was actually born here, but I grew up in Peralta which is about 20 miles south. Even though I lived south of Albuquerque, I had a lot of relatives here in the city. I spent most of my weekends – and, sometimes, my vacations – with my grandparents here, or with my aunts and uncles who all lived here. So, I was a country-boy who was cityfied. I didn't like the country, and got away from there every time I could. I didn't like farming, didn't like getting at up at 5:30 in the morning to feed the cows. Didn't like chopping chicken-heads off, or the whole small-town thing where everybody's got their noses in your life. I definitely couldn't be myself. But, I could be myself more in the city, because there was more anonymity. Plus, my grandparents didn't care; they just let me out to do what I wanted. I went to the movies a lot and read a lot, because we went to the libraries. I gained a real appreciation for reading and writing from my aunts, who taught me before I went to school. Even to this day, I read a lot.

I felt I was privileged to go to the school I went to in Peralta – even as a public school, it was extremely sophisticated. The student-body was very diverse with Japanese, German, Italian and Spanish kids. The Spanish were the dominant culture with everything. Everybody, at first, tried to get into cliques and speak their own languages, and the teachers laid down the law and said, "Nobody speaks anything but English here." It was really neat, because there wasn't a privileged language, and I liked that because it kept people from dividing themselves as much. Requiring English really equalized the kids.

I was kind of misbehaved. My teacher couldn't deal with me anymore and put me into a little room. "I'll give you some books, and you have to study them on your own. I'll give you a test, but you're disrupting class." It was the best thing that ever happened to me, because I was a self-learner -- except for math. I had to sit in the classroom for math. I've never been good at math. I still remember all of the teachers I had in grade-school as being really good. And they were mean, I'll tell you. They would do corporal punishment. They didn't just slap you on the hand, they'd slap you on the back. Paddles, we had paddles.

I was more of a self-learner and really had a great experience in high school. My father and I had finally reached an agreement that, if I were busy with school and kept up my grades, I didn't have to work on the farm. So I joined every single club: drama club, French club,

National Honors Society, speech club. I was a public-speaker and went to tournaments and competitions. I was feature-editor of the school paper. I made sure I stayed busy with school, so I wouldn't have to work on the farm. My teachers were all from Albuquerque and were sophisticated. I took French in high school. It was a small school, but you could get a good education – if you wanted it.

T: When I think of the culture down in Peralta – well, it was certainly different from Albuquerque. They even spoke an older form of Spanish down there. Because your Mom and Dad insisted you speak English, they wanted you to fit into the larger society. In Albuquerque there was still discrimination, everyone who spoke English seemed to get the better jobs. But, now if you are bilingual, that's a plus for being hired.

When I started going down there with you, it was like a totally different culture to me at your Mom and Dad's house – especially with your Dad having the farm right there, the cow and chicken place. It was a Spanish culture, that's what it felt like, and I enjoyed it.

J: Oh yeah, it was all Spanish culture. I'm very proud of that culture to a certain degree. Really, being proud of your heritage isn't an achievement; your parents did that for you. I'm proud of it because of what I did with it. I went to Spain. I lived in Spain. I studied Castilian Spanish and know it and taught it. A lot of people are born into it, and they don't know anything about it.

I appreciated what my relatives did for me, because it was an extended-family situation. Everybody helped each other. We used to visit our revered great-aunt Tia Lupita. She was born in 1898, and we thought she knew everything. She was a very simple lady who lived south of town. Respect for elders is definitely a Spanish tradition.

T: Growing up in Ohio, especially southwestern Ohio, it was very conservative. It was not the kind of place you could speak your mind or be yourself freely -- certainly not openly gay. I think it's still somewhat that way.

J: I don't know if anyone could speak their mind in the 50s, it was such an assimilative time. Everybody had to be the same.

T: That brings up an important point, because we were born only five years after the war. World War II had a big influence on our parents and on us. I remember stories being told of my uncles who fought in the war, and Joe's Dad fought in the war. My dad wanted to fight in the war, but what he ended up doing was shipping parts for tanks. Growing up at that time -- thirty-five years after World War I, then twenty years after the Great Depression, then World War II. I think the country was tired of disruption and turmoil. They wanted uniformity. That's what happened in the suburbs with all the houses being the same.

Education and Learning

J: I went to college for a while at Eastern New Mexico University. It was very small, in a small town, very provincial, too many Texans. I didn't like it. After two years there, I took my third year abroad in France. That's where I met my future wife, Rose -- it was kind of like destiny. I met her on the ship going over – at that point, it was easier and cheaper to take a ship than a plane. I don't know how I knew it, but I knew she was going to be the mother of my children. It was my formative years, 20 and 21, when I lived there. I couldn't believe people lived like that. They read and discussed politics. They had really good food. Just the opposite of redneck America. That was a very positive experience.

My highest degree is a Masters, plus I had to get all the credentials to teach Spanish, and public-speaking and French. I taught French the majority of my career. My French is much better than my Spanish, because it's hardwired, and I will never forget it. Spanish -- I have to reach for it. I taught French for twenty-five years, then Spanish for seven. That's the extent of my formal education. Mark Twain said, "I don't let my schooling interfere with my education."

One of the things that has kept Tom and I together is we both have the same level of education, and we value that. If you marry someone with a different level of education, it's going to come up along the way. You know so much more than that other person, and they'll resent you for it eventually. They'll say, "You think you're better than me, because you have all this education." In a way, you are. So, we really value that.

T: We've been able to talk on the same level. I think age has a lot to do with that. We are the same age. But, the way we see it is, if there's a big education or age difference in a relationship, there is so much neither will be able to appreciate or understand of the other.

Sharing and dealing with life together

T: Another thing that's kept us together: we've been very open about discussing everything.

J: So many people walk out in a huff, and never talk about it. It's hard for me to talk things through, but it's not so hard for Tom. I wasn't ever encouraged to talk about anything – just sit down, shut up, and do what you're told.

T: "If you have a problem, hide it."

J: Some tips I have to make a relationship work: Don't try to complete each other's sentence; it's okay when someone can't think of the word, but not when you're having a discussion about serious matters. When that happens, you're not listening – you're anticipating what the person will say what you're going to say.

T: The other thing is how you phrase things in a discussion. It's not, "You do this to me, you make me feel this way," and so on. It's, "When you do this, this is how I feel."

J: You can't make anyone feel a certain way; they just respond to what you said or did. The "I" statements are key, but that's hard to learn, and I still haven't learned it all the way.

T: Another thing key to our relationship is being grateful for each other, being grateful for what the other person does – even the smallest things. A lot of times, it's the small things that make all the differences. When Joe does the dishes, I make a point to thank him.

J: I appreciate that Tom goes to Costco, because I hate that place. But, I go to the Kroger's grocery store a block away, and that's my job. That's another thing: you get a feel for what the other does and doesn't want to do in the relationship. You stick to that, instead of trying to get them to do what they don't want to do. Tom knows I hate yard work, so I'll help him if he really needs it.

T: I had to learn this when we got into our relationship: you can't expect the other person to be like you, to think he should be someone he isn't. For me to accept Joe, he doesn't have to be any different. It took a while, and we both had to work on it – I think we're both out of hoping the other will change. Being able to adapt to each other and each new situation is so important.

J: We're so used to each other, now. The good thing about longer relationships is getting to know a person so well. Sometimes, we don't even have to talk – just grunt. We don't have awkward silences so much anymore. People think they have to talk the whole time they're together. Sometimes, you don't have to talk at all. We do talk. Breakfast is our big time; we sit there with coffee and read the magazines, and comment on different things happening in our life and in the world.

T: If something comes up during the day, and it's not on the calendar, we write each other a note. Today, I wrote a note about going to the mountains. Another thing is to be able to kid with each other and not take it seriously, and not take life too seriously.

The Meaning of Family

J: Our big saying was, "Family is everything." Rose and I got engaged in March while we were still in France. We completed the year in France, and when we came back, I met her family at the docks in New York. Rose's parents had this idea that I didn't speak English. Her mother spoke to me slow, but her father was more reasonable. To begin with they were kind of xenophobic.

Then, we moved here to New Mexico to finish my teaching degree and do my student-teaching. We lived with my parents. We had to go back to Philadelphia for a while so Rose could finish her degree there at West Chester. When we were in Philadelphia, that's when I hooked up with Temple University as a graduate teaching assistant. They gave me a free ride. Plus, I got a free baby out of it. Temple University Hospital took the graduate students under their wing, and gave us free health plans. My son was born for free there.

Rose and I had to kind of rush our engagement. We got married in April of 1972, and my son was born in October. You should've seen the old ladies. "That's only 6 months – well, he must be premature." He actually was premature. He wasn't supposed to be born until November.

The family situation in Philadelphia was beautiful. Being from a family of 11 children Rose knew everything about babies. Having a baby of my own was so fascinating to me – I looked at him all the time. "Look, Rose, how cute, he breathed." She was so unimpressed. Her family was so accepting. I felt like I was right in there. We came back here, and Rose wanted to live here. She had an easy transition. All my family liked her, thought she was great.

T: Joey and Maggie and I have a special bond. I think it's good for Joey to have somebody to talk to on a deeper level and think things through. When Joe and I got together, Joey was 11 and Maggie was 8. So, I like to think we had a big influence on their growing up.

Maggie's Memories of Tom 4-8-18
"I have no first memory of life before Tom and after my parents' divorce. When I think of Tom, the first word that comes to mind is comfort. He was and is always making comfort food and has been known to get creative to avoid wasting food, like the time he put leftover peas on his homemade pizza. He's a quiet, reflective person by nature so I'm sure my wild brother and I were quite a challenge for him. I remember him frequently turning the TV volume down. His love of music, mainly classical, is another comfort to me. It was always

*playing in the morning when I would wake up at their house, and now
I find myself playing it at times in the morning at my house.
I remember when he helped me to buy my dream car, an Acura
Integra. He's always so generous in so many ways. His affinity for the
elderly is an inspiration. I love hearing his stories about his childhood
and growing up in such a big family, his priesthood and all the crazy
things that happened on the Navajo reservation, and his ghost stories
about his connection with the spiritual world. He's been a pillar, a
constant in my life since I can remember, an adult and mentor that has
been there for me and has encouraged me in everything I do. He still
visits and my kids love him and call him Tompa. Can't imagine my
life without him!"*

Joey's Memories of Tom 6-6-18

*"I think when you're young, you really aren't sure why people are in
your life. You tend to accept everyone at first. Then, you either have a
positive or negative experience with that person, and that tends to mold
your relationship moving forward. I have early memories of Tom, but
it's tough to remember the first. But, I know in my heart it was a
positive experience. As I mentioned earlier, I wasn't really sure why
Tom was in my life. I think I was too young to understand. But, I
was very sure about two things: he was a good person, and he made the
people around him happy, mostly my Dad.
Tom took care of us, me and my sister. He cooked for us. Took us to
practices. Watched us. I think we frustrated him a lot, but Tom was
always very patient with us. He never yelled. But, if I heard that deep-
toned inflection in his voice, I knew I was in trouble. I saw Tom as a
father figure (still do), and I knew he cared for us deeply (still does).
As I grew older, I began to understand why Tom was in our life.
When I was 16 my Dad told me who Tom was to him, that he and
Tom were gay and that they were partners. It wasn't anything I didn't
know already, but I think my Dad felt like he had to say it out loud.
Up to then, we never really talked about it. So, we had a cigarette and
did. Nothing changed for me after that day. Tom was still Tom to me.
A guy I looked up to and respected. A guy I knew I could always talk
to. A guy who was part of our family.
Tom has had a very positive impact on my life. He has helped me to
achieve several milestones. He helped me get into my first house at the
age of 27. Tom has always been extremely supportive of my decisions. I
think he really enjoys talking about the hard stuff in my life and
encourages me to face it head on. I'm not very good at that, so it's nice
to have someone to lean on when I need that kind of thing. I love Tom*

very much and can't imagine what my life would be like if he wasn't in it. I love him for being so kind to my Dad. I love him for always helping our family. I love him for who he is. I love him for being Tom, very Tom…"

T: Because of the joint custody arrangements, they'd be with us about half the time. We'd have dinner ready for them, and take care of them, help them with homework, and do things together. Every other weekend, we had them for the whole weekend. It was great having them over because our home was their home.

J: But, it was very flexible. Rose let us have them over whenever we wanted, if a party came up or anything, as long as we let her know. Rose was kind and fair when it came to the kids, unless they were already committed to something.

I have a very close relationship with my kids. There's very little I don't know about them. The rest of it Tom knows. My daughter, I call her my jewel. Joey, he's my rock. Tom, Joey, and Margaret are the only people I can travel with. I'm a bitchy traveler, but am able to travel with them.

T: I see myself as having had four separate families. When I was at home, until I was 14, my family was Mom and Dad, and my brothers and sisters. We didn't have much of an extended family, like Joe did. Sometimes, but not often, we'd see aunts and uncles. Once a year, we had a picnic with all the cousins. I'd spend time with Dad's brother, Uncle Edgar and Aunt Blanche, up in Middletown – couple of weeks in the summertime, a nice break for me. The whole time I was up there, I'd be taking care of their yard, sprucing it up, listening to classical music, and I really enjoyed it. That was family, but family was also connected to the church.

I kept in touch with my brothers and sisters as we grew older, but the distance grew. I might see their children and grandchildren at a family gathering, if I go back to Ohio for it, but I don't really know them well or some of them at all.

When I entered the seminary, the Franciscan Order, and the Priesthood became my family. During that time, I was separated from my family – the Franciscans became my second family. When I got to the Navajo reservation, that was another sense of family. I was with the Navajos, but – different from the Franciscans – I knew I never belonged. I never tried to be one of them, but to be one with them and understand what their families were going through. I was adopted by Eva Desbah, an elderly Navajo woman who used to herd sheep in the back of the parish at Chinle where I was at. To this day, her daughter and her family are my family – they adopted me into their clan.

The fourth sense of family came when I met Joe, his family, his sisters and extended family, and Joey and Margaret became my family, and our family.

J: They adopted you. They accepted you, right away.

T: I think, initially, your parents had a hard time knowing what to make of me. Your Dad said one time, "I don't care if you're into Joe, and I don't care if you're in the closet or out of the closet, I don't want to hear about it."

J: He was just in denial. I told him before. He said, "That's okay; just don't tell your mother."

T: Joe's Dad and his Mom treated us with love and respect. When we went to his Mom and Dad's place, it felt like his Mom always tried to make something I liked. She always made red chile, because I loved her red chile. She knew I liked to get corn-chips and dip them in the chile. Gosh, she made the best red chile.

[It is to be noted that in New Mexico the vegetable "chile" is spelled with an "e", while in the Midwest the dish "chili" is spelled with an "i."]

We usually went down to Joe's parents on Good Friday. His family had a tradition of serving special foods on Good Friday. The little egg-white patties Joe's Mom would whip up, fry, and then sit them on top of the red chile which had no meat in it, were called tortas

J: That was supposed to take the place of the meat. Then, quelites, "beans and greens," like every culture has. Traditionally, it's wild spinach, but I wasn't going to pick and clean wild spinach, so we used the frozen kind. Beans, onions, and that's it. Fry the onions. Put the beans in, put the spinach in. Maybe, a few chile-flakes. It's a good vegetarian dish, and it's good for you.

T: For a while too, on Good Friday, we used to go up to Tomé Hill, which is a pilgrimage place south of Peralta. It was a pilgrimage for the people in that area to go up the hill, which was steep, and pray at the three crosses. There were always a lot people walking along the highways and roads on their way to the top of the hill where they crowded around praying and the guitarist played.

J: They would sing "Alabados", which could be referred to as "adoring hymns."

T: It must've been real old Spanish, because I couldn't understand any of it.

J: It was old Spanish, from the 1600s. During World War I and II a lot of men went to to the wars, and their families would climb the hill on their knees. "Well, if I climb the hill on my knees, would you bring my son back?" It was like a bargain.

Careers

T: Most of my career as a Franciscan and priest and working for the Archdiocese is already contained in Part One, so I will only add tidbits which weren't included there.

Thinking back, deep down, and surely not consciously, becoming a priest seemed like a way to put my homosexuality aside – that I could hide there, or hide with the Franciscans. I wanted to be someone other than I was, someone more acceptable. Being a Franciscan priest, I could be someone more acceptable – not only to myself, but also to my family and society. As a gay person in the 1960s and 70s, I would not be acceptable in general society. At that time a lot of priests were leaving the priesthood, because things were opening up. They wanted to get married and have a wife and children, or wanted a relationship with a significant-other.

The whole thing with chastity, I just wished those feelings of wanting to be with another man, in a stable relationship, not being moved from parish to parish, from one side of the country to the other, would just go away.

When I was assigned to the Navajo reservation, some of the older priests asked, "What did you do wrong? The only reason you're sent to the Navajos is if you've done something wrong and they want to get rid of you." I assumed that way back, in the minds of those guys, it was like a penal colony. If bothersome priests were sent there, it made me wonder what they had done. I felt the priests I got to know were good people and wanted to be there. Some were stuck, were not flexible at all – in their thinking and their lives. When I was leaving, some of the friars and priests told me that if they were ten years younger, they would leave also.

J: I got my master's in linguistics, and there's not much you can do with that besides teach. I also had to have a language, be able to demonstrate my knowledge of it, and have a period of literature from that language. I knew French, from being overseas and everything. I had the best professors at Temple University. But, when I needed a career, my Dad got me one here in New Mexico. He knew the superintendent of schools in Los Lunas. He had the connection. I got a job in public-speaking and English. So, I was responsible for putting on the plays and taking the kids to speech tournaments. All that enriched my life so much. I could pick out the kids who were self-conscious, like I was as a teenager, and help them along.

It was a mixed-bag to work in my hometown. Everybody knows everybody, and I was teaching at the high school I graduated from. I got a transfer as soon as I could.

One thing about my careers: I never filled out an application before getting the job. I always got the job first, then filled out the application later. So, that's how I started teaching French and public-speaking at a middle school, then got transferred to the high school. They told me I got the job, and to fill out the application.

That was fantastic, because I got a chance to teach French for 25 years. Teaching French enriched me because there were so many opportunities to travel and educate myself. Every other year, I signed up with this travel agency. If I got ten kids to go to Europe, I'd get a free trip. I chose the itinerary. Probably our best trip was just Paris, for 10 days. Other times, we'd go to Normandy, or southern France, but I always determined who would go, where we would go, and got my trip free. Every other summer, I'd apply for grants and scholarships to study wherever. I studied at Old Dominion University and William & Mary, where there were French guest-professors. I got to live in Quebec, Canada for 2 months, from a scholarship allotted by the Quebec government. Got to live in Spain for 6 weeks, thanks to a grant from the Spanish government. Of course, I had to write essays in the language. For the Spanish one, you had to prove you were Spanish and fairly fluent; that gave me a whole 6 weeks in Madrid, where I got some intense study at The Prado Art Museum. We would do Tuesday and Thursday there for 2 hours, only focusing on one artist, be it Velazquez or Goya or whoever – and I really got a lot from that. Traveling so much – for free – was an enrichment. I saw it was full of opportunity and made the best of it.

What brought my career to an end is kind of a sad thing. The school leadership really matters. The people I worked with, they always treated me with the utmost respect, because of my education and experience. The last 2 years I was presented with a really good deal. I wanted to teach half-time, and I was given all the advanced and intermediate French classes – it was so much fun, those last 2 years. Except, we got a new principal, and she was the most negative, downer person I had ever met, and she's still there. She sucked the energy right out of me. Every principal before that was so much fun. They let me fill out my own evaluations – "Just fill it out and I'll sign it." That was so professional. I was doing a good job, and wasn't someone they had to worry about – they had plenty others they had to worry about. That brought an end to my career, I finally felt it was enough. I was 60 and it was enough. I chose to retire for the third time -- after retiring at 49, then at 52, and now at 60.

T: As a priest, I was able to minister to the people I wanted to minister to. It fed me, and I felt like I was offering something. It was a give and take between me and the Navajo. I don't know if they knew they were giving me as much as I was giving them – if not them giving me more. I wanted to be with them where they were at, rather than sit at the church, or the rectory office, and expect them to come to me. My way was different from being a maintenance man – which I always thought a priest had the tendency to be – at the churches. They maintained the churches and facilities, and maintained their way of life. If I were ministering alone in a parish, I probably would have closed the office Monday through Friday and be out with the people.

Beginning Life with Joe

J: At first, Tom didn't want to trust anybody too much, and I can understand that. If I would go out to a gay bar or whatever, I wouldn't tell anyone I was a teacher. You just don't know who's out there. At that time, you protected your identity as best as you could. Tom was just trying to protect his identity. In the beginning, gradually, he told me things little by little – which was fine. I didn't need to know everything at once.

T: I felt we really had a lot in common, like, "I really like this guy."

J: We made a connection.

T: I really wanted to get to know this guy. Really, Joe was the first one I met that could actually talk about more than just surface things.

J: We talked about educated stuff. We talked about music and who our favorite composers were.

T: And books and literature.

J: We both had classical college educations.

T: We both had master's degrees.

J: It was a good match, to begin with. Rose and I had made an agreement: if the kids were in the house, I wouldn't have anybody over, which was reasonable. I had other nights I could have Tom over. The kids always liked it when we cooked for them, and I cooked for them a lot. I made a lot of Spanish food, because it was easy and the kids liked it. Our basic diet was a lot of lentils with vegetables, sometimes sausage mixed in. Salads. Caldo. Which is a meat and potato soup. I knew the kids were a lot of baggage for Tom. You had the baggage of your career with the Franciscans, which was still intense.

T: We lived together, and we shared a lot.

J: Luckily, Rose was very cool with it. She never said anything against it. Rose is just the best of friends to this day. Our break-up was more an intimacy issue, or the fact that I always wanted to be with men. She didn't know about my sexuality for a long time. I had to tell her, because it was driving me nuts.

T: Did she know you were going to bars? Do you think your acting out as a gay man caused her to ask for a divorce?

J: Yeah, she kind of knew. A lot of times, I would go to gay bars after my shifts as a bartender. She knew. I think she got sick of it, too. We lasted for 12 years, and that's pretty good.

Tom was the first long-term relationship I had after the divorce. I had my slut-period of meaningless encounters. He was the first serious one. It wasn't scary, just annoying that Tom always went to counseling for this and that. I was like, "Oh, come on. How many shrinks can you see?" That was part of the baggage from being a priest, and I tried to understand. Otherwise, we got along well. I introduced Tom to several friends of mine who found him a job.

T: Every day, for the first year and a half, my leave of absence was on my mind all the time. It was a big discernment time. It was an extremely confusing time for me. I always enjoyed being around Joe. I wouldn't have made it through those times without him. It was tough being with a man who had children, because I always hoped I'd meet a person where I'd be first in his life. It really took me a while to accept that I'd never be first in Joe's life. Joey and Margaret would always be first. I could accept it. There are times I still know Joey and Margaret are first, but now they are also my children. It was quite an adjustment.

Creating a New Life Together

T: It was a tough time making a life together anew. Having tried to return to the priesthood, and finally admitting it was not for me, I felt good about not having to think about it anymore. There was no obligation to myself to find out anything more. It was over. I could focus on our relationship.

J: I was wary when he first came back, because his leaving had hurt a lot. I was taking things easy, not rushing. It was a day-to-day kind of thing. Eventually, we did get closer. Things were going well with the kids. After buying our first house, we started our real life together, in that house, because we were both invested in it. We were joint tenants, buying it together. The responsibility was ours. I felt our relationship was pretty serious, so we took off from there. That was 1986, and we lived there for 17 years. We sold it for more than twice what we paid for it, and bought our present house. Creating our life together wasn't anything sudden. Things evolved gradually. More and more we became much closer, and I was happy with that.

T: After we moved here on Cagua NE, we rented the house on Grove for a couple years. The renters didn't take care of it , so we decided to go ahead and sell it. We took the money from that house and paid off this one.

J: That again is one of our common values -- we didn't want any debt, and have paid for everything equally.

T: We even have a ledger we write things down in, then split it up at the end of the month. It helps with our budgeting.

J: We are both rather frugal, but we do splurge on travel sometimes.

Relationship is a Journey

T: Being in a relationship with someone means allowing that person to be totally separate, with their own histories and needs. To allow them to discover what those are, and help fulfill them. I'm here to help Joe discover who he is, to support and encourage him, to be that separate person, knowing I will always be there for him, always with him, whether physical or not. There's a separateness that's needed and healthy in a relationship.

It took me a while to say I didn't want to do things. Learning to say and accept "no" happens in relationships. It happens with Joe, at times. He'll ask if I want to go to a party, and I'll say no. I know going to that party would only suck the energy out of me and suck my spirit dry. It wouldn't be a choice of mine. Sometimes I go for Joe, and not for me; even then, it's a choice, because I'm doing it for him. I think that's what's good in a relationship, to allow the other person to have a choice without the pressure. Maybe help the other understand why you don't want to do it. Be happy in yourself, if you are going to the party. Go freely and have a good time, come home happy to the person who stayed home happy.

J: Most people have a phase in their relationship where they have to be joined at the hip with each other all the time. We went through that phase, to a certain extent. But, we were such different individuals, in terms of what we liked and didn't like. Tom is mostly an introvert; he gets his energy from being alone. I'm an extrovert, and get my energy from being around people, from socializing a lot. I expected him to go to every single party with me, be presentable and nice and funny. Tom didn't want to do that. After a while, I started really respecting that.

Also, having time where we didn't have to be together. When I was in my thirties, I played a lot of racquetball, played every tournament there was. I used to go square-dancing and country-western dancing with friends, but Tom wasn't into that. Tom and I never went to the bar much together. He'd meet people at different times than I wanted to, because I wanted to dance.

Some of the things Tom had trouble understanding: I was pretty much at the prime of my career, and I wanted to use at least part of my summers to enrich my own education, to take my students to Europe, or whatever. I don't think Tom liked that I was gone for such a long time, but it was something I had to do for me. I'm glad I did it. I think Tom was glad I did it, too, giving each other space. Did you ever read The Prophet by Kahlil Gibran? Part of marriage and having a relationship is giving each other space, and realizing a building is held up by two pillars spaced apart, not two pillars next to each other. That was an influence in my philosophy, and we adopted that.

T: I never asked him not to go. I understood why he had to do it -- not only for the students, but for himself. I had the time by myself. It was the hurt and working through the hurt, to see it was a good thing in the end – because Joe always came back, enriched and full of stories.

The other thing about the beginning of our relationship was wanting to be open with others about who we were for each other. We wouldn't hide anything. Joe would ask me why I wouldn't attend the high school's plays. I was reluctant because I knew Joe didn't want to be open with the people that were there. He'd introduce me as his friend. I wanted to be recognized by other people as more than Joe's friend. Certainly we were friends, but it was more like we were "partners." I think part of it was that our being partners wouldn't have been accepted by his peers. Joe never wanted me to make reference to it amongst his peers. I felt hurt by that, until I recognized and understood the whole thing.

It brought back all these memories of the hiding I'd done my whole life. I didn't want to hide anymore. I didn't want to split myself and lead two lives anymore. However, I also felt a need to struggle with the same thing at my work: I didn't want the people at the Archdiocese to know I was in a gay relationship with Joe. The gossip mills would have churned constantly.

J: Our relationship, at that time, was still fairly looked down upon by society. As a teacher who taught a lot of boys, it would make me a suspicious character. Same with Tom, most ignorant folks he worked with weren't ready for this kind of revelation. Having that sniping and biting behind your back, it weakens your position.

T: The Archbishop would've backed me up, but may have felt pressured to get rid of me – due to what people would say, and to avoid controversy.

J: Watching the culture change has been very liberating, actually.

T: But, we still don't feel free to walk down the streets of Albuquerque holding hands. I think one of the few times we feel free to kiss in public is at the gay-pride parade. Even when we're in another city where no one knows us – except New Orleans or San Francisco – we don't feel free to be expressive of our relationship. Certainly not in France, Spain, Vienna, Austria or Florence, Italy.

J: On trips we could be a bit more free. Trips furthered our intimacy, and they gave us more stories and jokes. It's a real gift to have somebody you can travel with. It is more of a bonding experience and adventure than anything else. We get to see parts of the world through each other's eyes.

T: What has grown in our relationship and the expression of that relationship, as regards society, is that we're more free now to say we're partners and we're married. When we go to the hospital, they'll ask how we're related and we tell them we're married. It's not something we would've said before.

J: Most people have a positive reaction to us. I've been in the hospital with him, he's been in the hospital with me. The only negative reaction we got was from an African doctor, who couldn't believe we were married, and had trouble accepting that – but, he was from Nigeria.

T: Society has become more open and less fearful, and so have we. Maybe it's just our age, and not giving a shit what people think anymore. When you reach a certain point in your life, you say, "I don't care whether you like me or not."

J: I had to be completely retired before I experienced being open about our relationship. One of our intimate sayings is "je t'aime du jour", and it came about this way. One day Tom said, "Did you tell me you love me today?" I said, "Oh, no, I love you today." He asked how to say that in French, then invented that. He said, "Je t'aime du jour." He had heard of soup du jour which means soup of the day, so why wouldn't "I love you today" be "Je t'aime du jour"? It stuck that way. It also came from "Je t'aime tu jour," which is "I love you, always."

T: I don't remember when we started with light grunting to communicate. But, now, we know each other so well that we know what each grunt means depending on the emphasis and inflection – anything from *"please turn down the TV,"* to *"would you unscrew this lid for me?"*

The Grandkids and Traditions

J: The grandkids refer to me as "Papi," which is what a lot of Spanish people call their grandparents. He's "Tompa," which is a grandpa with Tom at the beginning. Lowell, Rose's husband, is "Pop Pops." Ron's father is "Grandpa." So, they have four grandpas. Tom is actually much better with our granddaughters. I'm not a good grandpa. He thinks of cool stuff they can do, like the time he scattered the glass-beads in the landscaping rock out front. They like to come to Papi and Tompa's now, because they like to search for jewels.

T: We go on a treasure-hunt for jewels and diamonds, sometimes for money. I would buy back the jewels for coins I would give them to put in a cash register piggy bank. They really didn't have much of an idea what the coins could be used for, but I was trying to teach them.

J: They love it.

T: When I drove to San Diego and was there with Maggie and the grandkids, or when we'd go together, they'd seem to bother me more in those situations. They might scream and run all over the place, and I can't take that. But, when they come here, if I think of something fun they can do here. I'm controlling them in this environment, and we can have fun.

J: They're so young at three and five. Because they aren't in childcare, they don't meet other kids as much. Margaret and Ron are both extremely sociable and polite. They have to be – they're both flight attendants. I have mixed feelings about relating to the grandkids, but – in terms of how we handle the grandkids together – we're on the same page. We're not going to let them get out of control or anything.

T: The thing I'm happy about is that they really are an extension of Joe. Joe's daughter is passing on this essence of Joe onto the kids, not just through genes. It's her history and his history, and I feel honored to take part in that. With Margaret being so young when we got together, I think we've both passed on a lot to Margaret, so it's a legacy.

J: The family traditions too, like Tom's the one who invented Oktoberfest for Joey's and Margaret's birthday parties. It became a tradition for us to do it. We even did it in San Diego, when we realized the kids weren't going to be together for their birthdays except for this particular time. We have our own personal traditions too. Traditions are such an important part of our family and with other couples.

Our anniversary dinner is of ultimate importance. We go out of our way to find a nice restaurant. We used to go to the Rancher's Club and always get the same waiter – a gay waiter, outstanding and always gave us a bottle of wine or free dessert. That was part of our tradition, and he knew when we were coming in. We still do it, just don't go to the same place.

T: I think one thing that's changed, tradition wise – you know, when Joey and Maggie were kids, we'd always have them over for Thanksgiving. We invited Joe's parents or went down to their house, because they had a big meal with their kids and grandkids. It was a big thing. Joey and Margaret were always with us for celebrations. As they got older, they went their ways. Now, we don't often have them together. Maggie and Ron and the grandkids live in San Diego with their own traditions.

J: She has another set of family, because Ron's parents live in Phoenix, so they usually go there for Thanksgiving. They usually come here for Christmas. It changes all the time.

T: Even then, they don't come here for Christmas dinner – it's up at Rose's now. We were used to making them a big dinner for Thanksgiving, Christmas and Easter. I really enjoyed cooking for them on those days, and now I rarely get the chance to cook for them together.

J: The grandkids have no concept of the tradition with us, because they're seldom with us on holidays. It's kind of an old thing now, since America's such a mobile society, those conditions don't exist, or they're modified somehow. When possible, you make the Thanksgiving dinner in mid-November if the kids can be there. With the grandkids now, it's unrealistic to expect tradition from them.

For our birthdays we take each other out for a nice dinner. We don't give presents to each other; we buy something for the house, or just skip the idea of presents altogether. We have so much stuff. In fact, we're trying to get rid of stuff. We even told our friends, if they want to give us something, don't give us objects, especially objects that have to be displayed. We don't have any room. We don't want the clutter. If he sees something he knows I'll love, he doesn't wait until my birthday to get it to me.

T: All year, we do that. For my birthday, I'll buy two dozen roses from Costco so Joe can give them to me. For his birthday, I'll buy two dozen roses for him.

J: When I saw that hummingbird mobile, I thought Tom would love that, because he loves hummingbirds. It wasn't his birthday or anything. When he saw the painting that's above the fireplace, Tom knew I would love it, because I love the Asian experience and rice-paper done with unforgiving watercolors. Tom knew I'd love it, and I did.

Relationship Challenges

J: In our relationship, it has been mostly little things. I don't think there were any big challenges, after what we went through at the beginning. Who gets the remote, and at what time? He gets it on the even hours, and I get it on the odd hours. Who gets to clean the toilet? We did figure that out. The whole issue of money is not an issue. We are both very frugal. The issue of how close a tab we want to keep on our finances, I didn't care, but Tom likes to keep a closer tab.

T: I'm much more of an accountant than Joe is. It's good to see where money is going, and helps to budget.

J: I don't even look at prices. Tom has coupons and all that. Unless it's a difference of $5 for a small thing, or $100 for a big thing, I don't look at prices.

T: There was a time I wanted to go to the gay bars in the evening to sit and talk with other gay guys over a couple beers. Joe didn't want to go. I always felt that bothered him, but he says it didn't. Joe will always be first in my life, and I wasn't looking for a lover. One thing that made me stop going was the stricter regulations in Albuquerque about drunk driving.

J: They really cracked down.

T: If they'd pull you over after you'd had one or two beers, and they smelled alcohol, you could be immediately arrested. You might lose your license and your car, which I needed for my work.

J: They targeted the gay bars. There would be cops sitting outside the gay bars, waiting for people to come out.

T: There were times I shouldn't have driven home. That was a long time ago. Now that I don't drink, it's no big deal. Something inside of me changed, and alcohol now makes me very sick. That's a good thing. When we go to parties together, Joe's got a free designated driver – me.

Sometimes it's a challenge how to make the house nicer and upgrade it little by little. There were some things to improve the house that Joe didn't necessarily want to do, or didn't think were needed. What I appreciated was that Joe was willing to go with me on it to get it done.

J: As with painting the iron security bars white, I really wanted to leave them black. We came to something of a compromise: "I'll let you do this, if..." The painting was quite a project, though we didn't do it. We hired a professional, which was the best thing we could've done.

T: Joe doesn't always see the things that I see need to be done in regards to upkeep of the house.

J: Yeah, Tom's more detail-oriented. Getting things done that way is his background.

T: It has to be the give and the take, "If you want to do that, will you let me do this?" kind of thing.

Marriage Equality Becomes the Law

T: At the beginning, same-sex marriage equality either had to go through the State Legislature to create a law with the Governor approving it, which neither would have done, or the state constitution had to be changed to allow it. These approaches would have taken years and years. There was talk of the Legislature and the Governor putting the issue up for a referendum. Rather than going that way, the lawyers took it directly to the NM Supreme Court, and they made the decision in a matter of months. If anybody wanted to undo that, they'd have to work for an amendment to the state constitution.

In Santa Fe, those in favor of same-sex marriage had to deal with the strong-hold lobby the Catholic Church had on this state. I had to deal with that in my work, the Archdiocese lobbying against domestic partnerships – years ago, before the whole marriage thing.

The real movement started with the county clerk in Sandoval County (Rio Rancho) who started issuing marriage licenses to same-sex couples, because she didn't see any reason not to issue them. She got fired and a judge declared those licenses void.

J: The Sandoval County Clerk was the most famous person in New Mexico for a while. She said, "I didn't see anything wrong with doing this." She was basically a conservative, just interpreting the law as she saw it.

Then a few years later the dominoes started to fall -- Dona Ana County (Las Cruces), and then Santa Fe County (Santa Fe) started issuing marriage licenses. Bernalillo County (Albuquerque) started issuing marriage licenses, and that's when the legality was challenged by people and lawyers. It went to the courts and judges upheld the legality of the licenses. Then it ended up at the New Mexico Supreme Court and they verified it, said we had to be treated the same as anyone else. There was nothing in the New Mexico Constitution that disallowed it, because the constitution didn't specify marriage as being between a man and a woman. I think that's the reason the NM Supreme Court allowed it, and said it must be allowed, that it would be unconstitutional not to allow it. New Mexico was the fourth state to make it legal. The Court took it out of the hands of the Legislature and Governor.

T: In regards to our getting married –

J: – It was a no-brainer.

T: It's something I wanted to do, even before Joe got onto the idea. When they started issuing marriage licenses here, I wanted to go sign up for a license right away. We decided to wait.

J: To wait and see if they'd challenge it, because we didn't want to go through the whole thing to have our license voided. But, we did it fairly soon – three weeks after the NM Supreme Court approved it.

T: Even before the U.S. Supreme Court approved it we went to city hall for our marriage license from the county clerk August 29, 2013. The best thing was, we got married in our own home, and Joey as a licensed minister married us September 3, 2013 here in our living room, with just the witnesses, Joey, Maggie, Ron, and Piper. Then we had a huge party a couple of weeks later.

J: The weather was so nice, the end of September. The whole backyard was full of people. We invited most everyone we knew, including all of the neighbors. It was a lot of fun.

T: The biggest thing about getting married was: never, in my wildest imagination, did I think or hope that law would be passed or that we would be permitted to get married in our lifetime – to have the same rights and privileges as straight couples. It was a total surprise.

J: I never thought so, either. It was a pleasant surprise. Regarding the decision to get married, there wasn't any argument. One reason we wanted to get legally married was that partners have no legal jurisdiction for any medical or death decisions. Spouses do have that right and responsibility. Direct relatives would then have no say as they would if we remained just partners.

T: No matter what our wills said, the relatives could try to step in. Even before we got married we went to a lawyer and had our wills made. A lot of people don't get their will done.

J: They think they'll die if they get their will made. My father didn't. I made my will before he did. He was like, "Oh well, I don't plan to die." You don't need to plan to die, because you'll die anyway. My younger sisters and I, we had wills, but my dad wouldn't do one, because he was so superstitious.

T: Wrap things up while you're younger, while you're lucid, and can make things happen. You never know what will happen with your health, when your life will end. Get your will done and it's settled.

J: Then your descendants don't have to deal with it. As for the house, the deed is set up so I'd get the house if Tom died before me, and the other way around. Even the bank doesn't have a claim, because we paid off the house.

Our will is ironclad, we took it to a lawyer. I have powers of attorney. If Tom gets sick, I would make the decisions – and vice versa.

My children are perfectly competent to make those decisions, but I want Tom to. He knows me better than anybody. He knows what I want.

T: I would never make any decision without Joey and Maggie being in on it.

J: I talked to my sisters about it, and introduced it by assuming I wasn't in their will. They said I wasn't, and I said, "Good, because you're not in mine either." I don't want any trouble, if I go before Tom or if Tom goes before me. We built our life ourselves. No one helped us, and no one has a right to what we have.

Retirement and Freedom

J: Retirement has been sort of liberating. I call this time "The joy of doing nothing" -- not having to spend the days going to work to make money. With age, you don't care as much about what you say or what people think. If you plan your financial future right, as we did, you don't have any fights about money – you don't have to care that much about money. When we were first together, we were pretty poor. I was paying child-support. Tom had just gotten out of the priesthood, which didn't pay him retirement. We were dirt-poor. We built up some money by working hard, and because our financial advisor is fantastic. Tom took a big hit in 2008 with the market crash, but I was more conservative with my investments. I didn't take as big a hit, but I didn't make as much money. Tom has made some incredible gains by taking bigger investment risks.

T: The other thing about retirement: we don't have to live up to anyone's expectations. We can totally be ourselves. We don't have to worry about anything. Life feels free. We make time for each other in the morning, when we first wake up. I'm always up before Joe. I wake up no later than 6, usually. I have coffee and sit out in the sunroom and meditate for an hour. Joe is up between 7 and 8. I'll cut up an apple for him, then we split the apple. We sit there and talk. He works on his journal. We share how things are going.

J: When I'm working on my journal, I'm forced to recall events of the day before, so thoughts will come, and I'll talk to him about it. We don't talk a whole lot at night. In the morning when we're fresh, we can talk about insights we've had during the previous day.

T: The other time we spend time together talking is when Joe gets back from the gym, and I get back from the gym. We get back around noon and spend some time talking to each other. In the evening he has programs he likes to watch for his hour, and I have programs I like to watch for my hour.

J: We usually switch with the computer. I'll work on the computer while he's watching TV. Not so much doing work, just answering emails, looking at pictures on Facebook. As far as movies go, we have little taste in common. We went to the movies in July, but we hadn't been to the movies together in years.

T: We are not going-out-to-eat people either. We prefer to cook. We really don't go out to lunch together very often, just Joe and me. Nor do we go separately by ourselves.

J: I do, with friends. You do too. Mine are pretty regular, once a month. If we do something together, it has to be a planned event. We did go to the performances of "Man of La Mancha" and Handel's complete "Messiah", and we both really enjoyed them. I didn't think I could sit through the whole "Messiah"; but I did, and it was so worth it to see it live and hear 100 people in the choir sing. I was so absorbed in it, and it was miraculous. Most of the things Tom chooses, I end up liking. Most of the things I choose, Tom ends up liking.

T: I used to like to go to the symphony. The last time I went there, I had such an anxiety attack I had to leave. I just couldn't be around anybody. I had to go to the lobby and wait until I settled down. I went back in, and the anxiety came back, and I had to leave and go home. I'm reluctant to go there now.

J: He likes so many classical composers, and I'm ambivalent about the whole thing. I'm real picky about who I like: Bach, Mozart, Vivaldi. I do like some Beethoven. With him, I mostly listen to classical music. He won't play any other kind. I listen to whatever I want to listen to in the car or on the computer. I did record three songs for our anniversary once. It was Art Garfunkel's "All I Know."

T: Yeah. I really appreciated those recordings. What's the one I thought of as our song?

J: The one from A Mouse Tale, "Somewhere Out There."

T: That is the song I used to listen to a lot when Joe was gone those summers. I knew that Joe was somewhere out there. My favorite composers, and there are many, are Beethoven, Wagner, and Bernstein.

Moving Forward

J: It needs to be known, and it's something I always read in the magazines, older people need to communicate to younger gay people that it gets better. You don't have to commit suicide no matter how bad life is going for you.

T: There are resources, find them and take advantage of them. Ask! Maybe talk to older gay men or women who have been there and know what it is like.

J: Yeah, both of us have had our down-in-the-dumps periods. We'd both hit bottom with depression and poverty.

T: There's still injustice against gays, if you feel inclined, fight it. Well, you can't deny the fact you are gay, because you were born that way. But, it's what you do with it, and what you contribute to the community, and how you relate to other gays and to society that help you be proud of who you are.

J: You still hear it in the locker rooms, "That's so gay" -- meaning it's stupid. "You look so gay in that" -- is that supposed to be a compliment?

T: Or when others tell disparaging jokes, that's the time to speak up and say that it is inappropriate. A lot of times, it's in the subtext.

J: No matter what is going on in your life, it does gets better. I anticipate it getting even better for us.

T: I'd say go ahead, do it, get in a relationship, find the right person to love. Take a risk. Take years to understand, take years to adjust to each other. Don't give up right away. If you need help, look for help. Our lives are witness that it's possible.

J: When you asked if I would take you back and start a life together, if I'd said, "Hell no, you bitch. You rejected me," just think of it. You have to give yourself time to adjust. A lot of young people are so used to instant gratification, they let a person go the minute they piss them off.

T: Forgive each other. There's a lot of times we've had to forgive each other. Forget, somewhat, but definitely forgive and move on. The other thing is: be grateful. Compliment and complement each other. There's a spark that pulled you together. Enrich that spark.

J: Constantly.

T: Say, "Thank you."

J: I always say it, even if you don't hear me. Every night I go to bed, and Tom's already asleep. "Oh, he's so cute. Thank you, God."

T: And thank you, Joe.

SECTION THREE

THOUGHTS, STATEMENTS, QUOTES, POEMS, DREAMS, ETC.

It is always
Very important
To be clear about
What delights me,
What impassions me,
To know exactly what
I would do if I
Didn't have to do
Everything else.
-- author unknown

++++

I Am Dracula

I purposefully and stealthily entered the candlelit crypt with a sharpened wooden stake in my left hand and a steel mallet in my right. Approaching the coffin, I see him lying there as if he had been there for centuries but looking as fresh as the day he wouldn't die. Impeccably and formally dressed, the Bella-Lugosi-like vampire rises at the same time I am poised to finally pound the stake into the middle of his chest after summoning all of my anger. I am firmly pushed back by some dark force as he sits erect and turns directly to face me with his bloodshot eyes staring too deeply into mine. He speaks softly and then so loudly his deep voice pounds into every cell of my body. "Why do you want to kill Dracula? YOU ARE DRACULA!" Dropping the stake and mallet, I am frozen stone-like by his gaze and a deeper fear inside of me than can ever be spoken. Then, I woke up. -- Tom

++++

"Curses!"
Fingernails and hair
Sought by Witches
At the city dump.   -- Tom - 2013

++++

251

Tom Schellenbach

Learned Helplessness

"Believing that nothing they do
Can produce a desired outcome."
Whether from childhood training
Or childhood neglect,
An injury to the frontal lobes of the brain,
An imbalance of epinephrine stress hormone,
He learns and teaches himself and believes
That he can influence nothing or very little
To bring about what he needs to thrive.

And so he spends an enormous amount of energy
And attention on others his whole life
Through the decisions he makes,
Subconsciously begging and pleading,
Wildly trying anything to make himself worthy
Of others' attention and love, and respect, and help.
Only to learn that any amount of subconscious or
Conscious manipulation only leaves him more alone
More helpless, more not good enough.   -- Tom

++++

From the Plane

D'ya ever see the sun
        Take 40 mins. to set?
I have.
Rays skipping Ducks and Drakes
        Off the tops and tips of clouds.

Give me strength in the
        Night.   -- Tom

++++

No Time Ago

No time ago
Or else a life
Walking in the dark
I met Christ

Jesus) my heart
Flopped over
And lay still
While He passed (as

Close as I'm to you
Yes closer
Made of nothing
Except loneliness

-- e.e. cummings --

++++

Many, many people in the world today are forced to live in extreme poverty. I want to choose to live that way, not because it has merit in itself; but in order to learn absolute trust in and dependence on the Lord. I want this in order to be one with the poor in their struggle for self-worth; to know what it is like to have no control over the outside forces of this life; to feel the pain of not just having not enough, but of having nothing (no when), (no what), (no where), (no how); to experience the disregard and condemnation they experience and to prophetize against it, to repent of anything I have thought, said or done that helped forced them to live this way; to share even more every part of me and what I have with those in need; to stand on the borderline of hope and fear and see where it takes me. -- Tom 6/29/83

++++

"Evangelism is one beggar telling another where he has found bread."
--Anonymous

++++

5:15 am

I had heard of it
    --I was afraid. What if...
Refusing to even think about it,
    the right time came and I went.
    Stripped naked,
    running in the falling snow,
    flopping in one foot of fallen snow,
    flipping and flopping,
    with such happiness and joy,
Gasping as in day one swim lessons,
    bouncing from the frozen water,
    back to the cabin wood stove heat.
Done to harden me? Toughen?
    --not really the feeling. But
More like being enfolded,
    each flake bursting on my skin,
    teasing, tickling, funning joyfully.   -- Tom 1982

++++

A Friend of the Cold

Wrestling with a friend after snowballs,
"Make a friend of the cold,
    and he will not hurt you," he said.
I could worship the snow,
    God-possibility (friendship?)
    covering my footsteps with His own,
    not controlling snow-time
    no influence on flake size or depth,
Beauty beyond beautiful, beyond creativity.
Expectant void unfilled when he leaves,
But now my friend.   -- Tom 2/5/82

++++

Racing Alone

There is a time for a few
When straining with or against
(Grade school buddies
    For a mark or prize or popularity
    Or affirmation,
Partners in adulthood
    For wealth or position or time
    Or recognition)
Is no longer of great import.
From hurt leading to introspection,
Other's pain begging compassion,
Anxiety calling forth re-evaluation,
Who I had become demanding reflection,
For whatever reason or feeling,
Stepping aside from the track
Or just slowing down,
The straining against becomes being for.
And the price of doing with less
Is paid for the freedom of
Racing alone.   -- Tom 4/23/82

++++

"To be truly free you must bind yourself to nothing
And seek harmony with all." -- Kung Fu

++++

Sister Moon

Keep me awake
Full Sister Moon
And heal me
With your French
Vanilla ice cream
Light.   -- Tom 8/1/82

++++

Early Morning

Early morning
Is the lavender
Creme brulee
Of the day.
I have always
Preferred
Desserts first!   -- Tom

++++

Rebuild My House

Now in half or no use,
Half-preserved what's left as an
          Historical monument
          Tucked in canyon beauty
          Where few will go.
"Glory of the Past."
"Work of our Fathers."
"We have done well."

Rebuild My house.
          "No longer do I go out,
                    But wait 'till they come in."
          "No longer my work,
                    But now my interruptions."
          "No longer time for,
                    But a passing thought."
Rebuild My house
          Not of stone and mortared walls
          Of settled-person's disposition,
          But of bone and flesh and heart
          Of journeyed-person's possession,
                    In the wide open
                    Where all are met.
Start anew and
Build the embodied God.   -- Tom 4/30/81

++++

Keeper of the Stream

The young man was now content at nudging
The stick-boats along thru the brush and stones
And shallow places of the stream.
Used to be he would keep the company of living people,
But it was too frustrating,
Too damn intolerable as they would get mud-stuck
Unbudging, or preferring to stay dry on shore.   -- Tom

++++

The Rock

It's odd how a rock
So hard and sharp-edged
Can either be crushed
Or enfleshed
By caressing
Tree limbs.   -- Tom

++++

Leaves

Most unwilling,
Some clawing at the pavement,
All fleeing before the wind
Fear-like from some roaring monster,
Down the driveway
Around the tree
Flying again for a moment
Over the wall, into the gulley
Back into forest refuge.

And I
Still standing on the blacktop
Bend with the dark gray wind
And watch, and understand.   -- Tom

++++

Will of God

How tell it? How live with the uncertainty of trust?
Will of God: --to wait? --to struggle within to make it my own?
                --to serve in love of others?
            --a passive waiting for revelation of it?
            --an active waiting?
            --a living of life believing this is what He wills?
"The will of God is the good of man."
But how reconcile personal authority
And responsible free will with divine will?   -- Tom

++++

Peace

Gently He comes
Slowly covering, filling, changing
All He touches
Like a first snow - quiet white.
And for a while there is no rush,
No worry -- no time.
Touching our moments
Freshening our spirits.   -- Tom 12/25/82

++++

Twilight Geese

Desperately sailing to the South,
Backdropped by red-sand mountains,
Struggling below storm clouds and wind
To keep formation, left, right, up, down,
A "V", "A", "W", a square root sign downside up.
Every man for himself,
And then all bailing out
And glide-flapping for the depths. -- Tom 8/23/82

++++

No Family

I thought this morning
I have no family to remember
Who I am,
What I've done,
Who I've tried to be...
Then the calm breeze, and birdsong,
Sun breaking the clouds,
Stars bright, cocks crow,
Moon to my back making shadows forward,
Cooled the fever of confusion.
The Earth, like all mothers will always remember,
And my Father never forgets.   -- Tom 9/4/82

++++

Thought in the Creek Wash

If I'm lucky
After all my friends
Have also died,
Some young man will find
My cliff-swallowed skeleton
And wonderingly
Try to remember
Who I was.   -- Tom 3/3/82

++++

Brother Fly

I am convinced
God created Brother Fly
To try my gentleness, patience,
And non-violent stance.   -- Tom 10/21/82

++++

Opportunity

The spider takes his own time.
His corner web woven for a month
And still no cocooned carcasses,
He waits concealed in a wall crack.
Today a large insect flew into
The silk-sticky trap
Struggling to free himself
Legs and antennae and wings flailing,
Freed, but flies right back into
The web again and again.
For half an hour this goes on
And the spider watches and waits.
The insect stills, almost resigned,
Spider takes a jab, insect flies out,
Freed, and back into the web.
Spider waits, for five minutes
No motion.
Is the meal dead and
No longer desirable?
For the last time spider checks.
Insect struggles over the side and
Falls into another web,
But instantly a different spider
Jumps, and seizes, and is satisfied. -- Tom

++++

"A faith that does not become cultural is a faith not fully accepted, not
entirely thought out, not faithfully lived." Desidero Esprimervi, 2. --
John Paul II 1/16/82

"What matters is to evangelize man's culture and cultures - not in a
purely decorative way, as it were, by applying a thin veneer, but in a
vital way, indepth and right to their very roots - always taking the
person as one's starting point and always coming back to the
relationships of people among themselves and with God." Evangelii
Nunciandi, 20. -- Paul VI

++++

Only You

Lord, give me Your peace and Your joy.
When self-hate takes over, remember Your love.
When I hide inside myself, listen to Your call.
When forgiveness seems too far, remember You are near.
When frustration hits, feel that success is Yours.
When thoughts wander off, focus on Your truth.
When anger comes, approach with Your gentleness.
When I want things done, be tied to Your patience and timing.
When death laughs at me, be convinced of Your life.
When I cannot pray, let Your Spirit speak within me.
When my body yearns, know only You can satisfy. -- Tom 12/6/82

++++

Birds on a String

Why is it that birds
Like erratic self-willed kites
Never get their strings
Caught in a tree? -- Tom

++++

"People travel to wonder
At the height of the mountains
At the huge waves of the sea
At the long courses of the rivers
At the vast compass of the ocean
At the circular motion of the stars
And they pass by themselves
Without wondering."   -- St. Augustine

++++

Fall

Heavy frost
Descends in the night
On rooftops
For all to see,
And in the day
Drips off the edge
Earthbound. -- Tom

You Meet You -- a dream

In my early twenties I wanted to take a vacation, a trip to a land I would not normally have thought of going to, someplace in southeast Asia, a journey, a discovery, no plans, just open to whatever the place, the people, the food, and the culture brings along the way. The plane landed somewhere that reminded me a lot of the pictures I had seen of Thailand. So, with a medium backpack and a staff, I took off walking and soaking in the beautiful lush landscapes and some small villages. It struck me that I had not seen any vehicles of any kind, and all the roads were dirt and dust. As if I were walking back in time, most of the villages seemed to be very ancient and mostly in ruin. About half of the homes looked livable; however, I saw no people and wondered if anyone actually did live there in recent memory.

I eventually came upon the largest town so far and walked through the large gate in the wall surrounding the town, and entered the main street and perhaps the only street. Perhaps it was market day as both sides of the street as far as I could see were lined with booths of vendors all very neat and tidy, all squeezed in next to each other, some selling spices, chiles, herbs, and flowers, while others were selling all kinds of exotic vegetables with which I was mostly unfamiliar, and still others were selling fabrics and jewelry, and this went on stall after stall.

When I looked in the distance, perhaps a half mile straight down the street, I saw a large gleaming white building which might have been a temple or a palace or both sitting on the incline at the end of the street which led right up to it.

The people were beautiful, tan-skinned, with dark hair and eyes, looking healthy, wearing an explosion of colored cloths and loose fabrics, and no shoes. I must have been quite a sight to them with my blond hair, blue eyes, light skin, sweaty and filthy khaki shirt and pants, and tan hiking boots. It was then I noticed four handsome men in light blue ankle-length tunics, two on my right and two on my left, walking slowly, companioning me as I took my time trying to see everything and take in everything. The man in front on the left leaned over and very respectfully said to me, "Come."

The four men led me through a short passageway between two booths into a small and very beautiful courtyard filled with all sorts of colorful flowers and vines, some hanging down from balconies on all four sides. Wide-eyed, I was not afraid at all, and open to anything, and unusually docile. The men took my backpack, undressed me, and began to bathe me with wonderful spice-scented soap, and then massaged me with sweet smelling oils. One of the men came forward with a bright white silk ankle-length v-neck tunic with gold thread banding along the neck and sleeves and the bottom. I was in awe and hadn't felt so good throughout the journey so far. Then, the same man said again, "Come." I asked, "But where are we going?" He said, "Come. See."

Shoeless I was accompanied back to the main street for a short distance toward the large white building which was still a way off. The men then led me down another short passageway between two booths into a very similar courtyard as the last one. One of the men came back shortly with another bright white tunic, but this one was of heavier silk with a short collar, about knee length, open in the front, and had no sleeves or gold banding. My hair was oiled and combed, and the same man said again, "Come." I asked again, "Where are we going to?" He said, "Come. See." When I asked what I would see, he said, "Come. See. Meet."

Again I was led back to the main street, but this time the large white building was closer, and we walked towards it. Now I could see white marble steps leading up and up to the building. Once again I was led down a passageway to another courtyard by my companions. This time they fitted my head with a gleaming light blue turban with a large shining jewel of some sort on the front, and fitted two gold rings on my right hand and two on my left hand, and a gold necklace for around my neck. Again I was respectfully told, "Come. Meet." When I asked, "Meet who?" I was told, "Wait. You meet. You see."

When we entered the street, we immediately began ascending the marble steps up to the building, all four of my escorts close by me on either side. At the top of the steps there was a deep marble platform which we walked across and into the palace/temple and into a spacious room . Everything was white marble with intricate geometric carvings along the walls, and a single throne on a platform in the middle of the far wall. I was led to the throne.

It was the first time I felt a little uncomfortable, and I hesitated, but my companions helped me onto the platform and to sit on the throne. When I did, there was a total sense of peace and harmony, and expansiveness not felt before. I signaled my guide to come up, and I said, "I have come. I have seen. I have waited. Now, who is it I will meet." He said with reverence, "<u>You</u>. <u>You</u> <u>Meet</u> <u>You</u>."
-Tom 6/15/18

++++

<u>Targad the Nishnad</u> -- a dream

I had a dream that three of us were by this deep underground river. A voice said he would give us each what we wanted to turn into. One wanted to turn into a deer to run free and wild. I and the other wanted to be fish to swim together and see the bottom of the river. We all got our wish. The deer leapt off to the left. When we were made into fish, my friend was divided from me when the river split, so he went off to the left, and I downstream to the right. I was not as happy as I thought I would be, because now I was alone swimming down this muddy underground river. I swam on my back one time to see the tunnel the river had cut out.

Finally the river flowed into a huge ocean, clear, blue, deep, sun shining. Now I swam to the bottom of the ocean where there were many other fish and ocean creatures. But all were afraid. A huge jellyfish lived in a cave, and they said he would catch them and put them in his prison and eat them later when no one else was around. They wanted me to kill the jellyfish they called TARGAD THE NISHNAD. So I took the trident, went to the cave where he was just lying at the opening and thrust the trident into him. I then went to the prison and tore all the bars down. Inside the jail were only a set of antlers from a deer. All the other fish came near then.

TARGAD spoke and said very gently and peacefully, "I do not put them in jail, they put themselves in jail because they are afraid of me. I have never hurt anyone." I believed him because he was so kind and gentle. I felt bad I had stabbed him with the trident, but then I realized it had not even hurt him. I sat and we talked for quite a while. Then I woke up.

-- Tom 1/27/83

++++

264

THE MARKS OF WILDNESS ARE
- A LOVE OF NATURE,
- A DELIGHT IN SILENCE,
- A VOICE FREE TO SAY SPONTANEOUS THINGS,
- AN EXUBERANT CURIOSITY IN THE FACE OF THE UNKNOWN,
- TO BE MAD AS THE MIST AND SNOW.   -- Robert Bly

++++

THE MARKS OF GENIUS ARE
- WANTING TO KNOW EVERYTHING THERE IS TO BE KNOWN ABOUT EVERYTHING THAT CAN POSSIBLY OR IMPOSSIBLY EVER BE KNOWN,
- PERSISTENT CURIOSITY,
- PROBLEMS WITH AUTHORITY,
- AN EXTREME AMOUNT OF ALONENESS.   -- Tom

++++

"Talent hits a target that no one else can. Genius hits a target that no one else can see."

-- Schopenhauer

++++

Once in line at a convenience store checkout, I noticed an elderly Navajo lady in front of me buying a pomegranate. I wondered how she would describe it. I asked, "Is that an apple?" "No," she answered, "It's a pomegrant." "Does it taste like an apple or smell like an apple," I asked. "It's a pomegrant," she said, a bit irritated at this ignorant Anglo. I pressed on, "But if it looks like an apple, and smells like an apple, and tastes like an apple, then it must be an apple." She had enough of me, pulled out a pocket knife and cut the pomegranate in two and handed the pieces to me, and said, "OK! It's an apple! Only it has corn inside!"

I thought Wow! What a perfect way to describe this fruit! Then I bought her four more "pomegrants."   -- Tom 1981

++++

AIR

Of Earth, Air, Fire, and Water
Only Air in itself is invisible
Until it isn't.   -- Tom 1/10/18

++++

And he said to me, "You have very seductive eyes. They're beautiful
and yet probing. I can't look you in the eyes for long. There's a crystal
in them. Yes, a crystal." -- Tom 5/1/85

++++

Looking For His White Horse

Whenever I see him
Bridle in hand
He waves hello
Visits briefly
And off again
Always looking for
His white horse. -- Tom 9/12/83

++++

Big Sweet Eyes

A young girl
All dressed in long pink
With a teenage boy's voice
Terror to a minister's service
Rattles off name and clans
And oh those big sweet eyes. -- Tom

++++

Desert Theology

A bit like Abraham
Having known the God and willing to follow.
Then waking up in the desert
And wondering if it was true
--no more voice, no more presence, or power,
--no more God?
Just heat, and sand, and silence, and self, and nothing. --Tom
9/15/83

++++

"Under a doctor's recommendation she carried her baby too long, the
first-born at age thirty seven. Her time had come almost too late. The
baby delivered c-section pooping, screaming, starving. You see, if we
stay in the womb too long, there is no placenta nourishment left, and
we can die in the shrivelled sack."   -- Tom 10/24/83

++++

"What you can do, or dream you can do, begin it!" -- Goethe

++++

Can I?

Can I hold onto
        My integrity
And survive
        This winter
Of my discontent?   -- Tom 12/6/83

++++

Work Continues

My LIFE
(deep inside
and its expression)
Has become
Quite a job.   -- Tom 10/3/83

++++

At one time Albert Einstein tried to prove that evil exists. It got me thinking. Here is my response to his "proof."

Both light and heat are scientifically measurable. They exist on their own. Darkness and cold are words we have created to describe the absence of either light or heat. They do not exist on their own. If one takes the stand that evil does not exist on its own, but is an absence of God, then one must also prove outside the realm of faith that God exists and is scientifically measurable - which is impossible. Einstein proved nothing.

Perhaps our word for god is merely a way to describe the absence inside ourselves, the emptiness and insecurity of our human condition. Perhaps our creation of "god" is the absence of courage while facing the nothingness and insecurity of our existence, the absence of truly believing in ourselves. Perhaps this is all we are now, and after death there is nothing. We are not mighty, or knowing, and certainly not all powerful. And so we created something beyond ourselves that is all-mighty, all-knowing, and all-powerful, holding onto false hope that there is something "more" than us which would answer all our questions, all our "whys", and give meaning to our lives. The question is not whether evil exists, but whether a god exists.

A god can only exist if people believe in it and have faith in it, and then it exists only for them.

I am not saying god does not exist. I am merely saying I don't have a need for one.

-- Tom

For Ross and Lorena Blount

If it were possible
    To gobble a book
Without everyone's
    Judgemental look,
I'd say I truly did devour
With every fleeting hour,
The one you wrote
As if you spoke
To my spirit, mind and heart
Each joyful and painful part.
The memories in the present
    Come back alive,
Your lives from the past
    Again sing and thrive.
Your family made whole and healthy
By riches more deep than just wealthy.   Tom -- 1/15/18

++++

Road Trip - Durango

Why are they here so formal?
For me it is not normal.
Here they all call me "Sir",
As if I really were.
Perhaps this place is so polite
(that or they must check their sight).
AARP says that I am old,
But still I am not totally sold.
My brain says, "No,
It is not so."
My body says, "Hmm, maybe,
But let's wait and we shall see."
I think at mere sixty-eight
I have time, and I shall wait.   Tom 5/30/2018

++++

"The Fish and the Coyote"

Some time ago, and even today, the story is told about the Big Wind that used to hit the Wheatfields area. Some say that is how the fields were made when the Big Wind blew the trees off that Land. Others say the mountains there were formed when the Big Wind blew and buckled the Land, pushing it to the Sky. But nobody saw it, and nobody knows for sure.

What we do know is that one time the Big Wind came and made the Lake very rough, just like the ocean in a storm. When it finished blowing, most of the water was gone from the Lake. The Big Wind was very thirsty that day. It also left one Fish lying on the dry Land in the Sun.

Soon, a flock of Sheep and a Sheepdog came close by. So, the Fish called out to them, "Please, throw me back in the Water. It is too hot out here, and I will surely die." But they said to him, "We are on our way home before the sunset. We have walked many miles today. We are too tired and do not have time to help you." And the Fish lost a little hope and strength as they walked away.

After about an hour, a Beaver came by pulling a long aspen log in his teeth. The Fish pleaded with him, "Please, throw me back in the Water, or I will surely die." But the Beaver could not make up his mind to help him or not. "And anyhow, there is probably something wrong with you, and I might get sick," he said as he quickly pulled the tree into the Water that was left there so he could repair his home.

Then a Wildcat came to the Lake for a drink of Water. The Fish, his eyes beginning to bulge from the heat, used all his strength to ask the Wildcat, "Please, throw me back into the Water." The Wildcat was so scared at seeing such an ugly sight and hearing a Fish talk, that he forgot his thirst and ran for the hills.

The Fish was so short of breath, his eyes mostly out of their sockets, his scales standing on end, his fins and tail crisp, all he could say was "Please" to the Coyote as he came close by. "I know," said the Coyote, "you want me to help you and throw you back in the Water or you will die. Well, you know what, I am not used to helping people. And besides, what have you been doing for yourself just sitting there all this time. I'll bet if you just think real hard, you can get back into the Water all by yourself. Then you will know you really do not need anybody's help to keep on living. Besides, did you see a Wildcat pass this way? I'm chasing after him to see what trick I can play on him. Well, anyway, think about it, and I'll check on you when I come back this way."

As the Coyote trotted away, proud of the wise advice he gave to the Fish, the Fish died. Then the Big Wind came again and filled the Lake with Rain and Waves. And the Water People came and took the Fish to the bottom of the Lake with them and buried him.

After the Coyote was finished playing a trick on the Wildcat, he trotted back to the Lake to check on the Fish. He was so full of happiness and joy when he saw that the Fish was gone, that he began to dance and sing, "I should stop hurting people and start teaching them my wisdom. See, I knew with a little encouragement, the Fish could do it all by himself."

-- Tom

++++

"He will be either a great saint or a great sinner."
And gradually I came to know that I did possess that great power
To blessedly bless and blessedly curse
To cursedly curse and cursedly bless.
I thought, "Why not both?"

But, after putting such power aside for so long, and fearing its use,
I wonder which one will naturally rise to the surface
And conquer my world.   -- Tom

++++

Memories

Somehow the mind mixes and sorts and stores them,
But the news or the heart or a passage from a book recalls them.
Sometimes they come and go as a flash of light.
Other times the mouth verbalizes them with its limitations
And then there are times it's all one can focus on.

Suppose you were walking alone in a forest.
What you see and experience is insignificant when
Compared to the dew on just one leaf.
Sometimes a dead bird is all one can really recall,
Or maybe just the chill in the morning air.
Who really knows?

What exactly is it, a memory? Does it really matter?

Or is it a part of our being, inseparable but expressive nonetheless.
It isn't re-lived -- it's remembered.
What comes from that is mostly emotions -- just emotions.
Events imprinted on our feelings and impregnated with them.

So what is shared of self with all else becomes a memory,
A creation, yes, so unbounded and so limitless, but still
Just a memory.   -- E.S. Peredo

++++